GRANTA
New American Writing

Spring, 1979

	3	Introduction
William Warner	11	Interview with Theodore Solotaroff
John Hawkes	21	The Universal Fears
William Gass	31	The First Winter of my Married Life
Joyce Carol Oates	51	from *Son of the Morning*
Tony Tanner	65	Present Imperfect: a Note on the Work of Walter Abish
Marc Granetz	73	Chuckle or Gasp: a Note on the Work of Leonard Michaels
Norman Bryson	77	Orgy, hors-je, hors-jeu: a Note on the Work of James Purdy
Leonard Michaels	87	The Men's Club
James Purdy	105	Summer Tidings
Tillie Olsen	111	Requa-I
Donald Barthelme	135	The New Music
Don Guttenplan	147	The Wor(l)ds of William Gass
Jonathan Levi	161	John Cheever in the Bourgeois Tradition
John Dugdale	164	Updike's Nabokov
Stanley Elkin	167	from *The Franchiser*
Ronald Sukenick	181	from Long Talking Bad Conditions Blues
Susan Sontag	191	Unguided Tour
Henry Davis	201	A Plug for Bukowski
	207	Notes on Contributors

Copyright © 1979 by *Granta*.

GRANTA

Editors William Buford and Pete de Bolla

Assistant Editors Donald Guttenplan and Eric Burns

Business Manager Jonathan Levi

Thanks for advice and assistance to Tony Tanner, John Dugdale, Norman Bryson.

Editorial Correspondence All manuscripts are welcome but must be accompanied by a stamped addressed envelope or they cannot be returned. Contributions should be sent to the Editor, *Granta Magazine*, King's College, Cambridge CB1 2LP.

Annual subscriptions are £3.50 or $10.

No fiction included in this issue has appeared in print in Britain; for fiction which has appeared in print in the United States and for all of the fiction in general the Editors gratefully acknowledge "The Universal Fear", copyright © 1973 by John Hawkes; "The First Winter of My Married Life", copyright © 1979 by William Gass: the selection from *Son of the Morning,* reprinted by permission of Victor Gollancz Ltd., copyright © 1978 by Joyce Carol Oates; "The Men's Club", copyright © 1978 by Leonard Michaels; "Summer Tidings", copyright © 1977 by James Purdy; "*Requa* – Part One", copyright © 1971 by Tillie Olsen; "The New Music", copyright © 1979 by Donald Barthelme; the selection from *The Franchiser,* copyright © 1976 by Stanley Elkin; the selection from *Long Talking Bad Conditions Blues,* copyright © 1979 by Ronald Sukenick; "Unguided Tour" from *I, etcetera,* copyright © 1978 by Susan Sontag.

The Editors also wish to thank the George Rylands Fund of King's College for the assistance it provided.

This edition reprinted in 2010
Printed in Great Britain by CPI Antony Rowe, Chippenham, Wiltshire

Introduction

It is increasingly a discomforting commonplace that today's British novel is neither remarkable nor remarkably interesting. Current fiction does not startle, does not surprise, is not the source of controversy or contention: what is written today, what has been written since the time of the Second World War, can hardly rival what was written in the time immediately before it. And so the complaint: British fiction of the fifties, sixties, and even most of the seventies variously appears as a monotonously protracted, realistically rendered monologue. It lacks excitement, wants drive, provides comforts not challenges. "Reviewing the history of the English novel in the twentieth century", David Lodge has pointed out, "it is difficult to avoid associating the restoration of traditional realism with a perceptible decline in artistic achievement". And Robin Rabinovitz, in a book portentously called *The Reaction Against Experiment in the English Novel, 1950-1960*, observes that "the greatest fear of the English contemporary novelist is to commit a *faux pas*; every step is taken within prescribed limits, and the result is intelligent, technically competent, but ultimately mediocre". Current British fiction seems to be characterized by a succession of efforts the accomplishments of which are insistently, critically, and aesthetically negligible.

The charge, as a few apologists have tried to demonstrate, is not entirely true. Writers stand out from the rest—David Storey, for instance, B. S. Johnson, Roald Dahl, and John Berger; John Fowles or Malcolm Bradbury could not be described as adverse to innovation; and J. G. Ballard and Alan Sillitoe come to mind as do Ian McEwan and several other young writers. But there is as well something to the critics' complaint which simply can't be dismissed. Contemporary literature *is* unsatisfying and not simply because social realism predominates or a prejudice against experiment persists—contrary to what so many American critics seem to suggest, an experimental work is no more an inevitable indication of an accomplished imagination than a realistically rendered one is a failed imaginative accomplishment. Current literature is unsatisfying simply for the sense it suggests of a steady, uninspired sameness, a predictable, even if articulate prattling of predictable predicaments. There are few new voices in British writing today, mostly just echoes: the nineteenth century persists nowhere as it does in the contemporary English novel.

Insulated. Enclosed. Consider the resistance to other influences, foreign influences. In 1961 Borges shared the International Publishers' Prize with Beckett—his importance recognized at last, *internationally*. In 1962, Borges published *Labyrinths*, easily his most influential book. Translated it appeared in the United States and in France two years later. It was eight years before a British publisher printed it—ten years after the International Publishers' Prize. The time it took a writer of the stature of Borges to reach England seems preposterous to consider; in the context of the apparent British attitude toward most new fiction on the other side of the Atlantic, and especially fiction from America, it is not preposterous but perfectly consistent.

Since the Second World War, American fiction has emerged as some of the most challenging, diversified, and adventurous writing today. To describe what is happening now in the States as a literary renaissance does not seem inappropriate. A new voice has developed, a new kind of dialogue in fiction. But has England even recognized that it exists?

Who are the current American writers current in England today? Bellow, Updike, Pynchon, or Mailer? Pop stars like Jong, Robbins, or Brautigan? The less conventional authors, Kurt Vonnegut, Joseph Heller, Philip Roth, John Hawkes, Robert Coover, Grace Paley? Less conventional and less known. Barthelme, probably the most influential American author? A name. "The critical mood in England", Rabinovitz observed eleven years ago, "has produced a climate in which novels can flourish but anything out of the ordinary is given the denigratory label 'experiment' and neglected". And the neglect persists. John Barth has barely survived the British Press. Stanley Elkin's last novel, already three years old, still does not have a British publisher; and the same applies to the last work of Leonard Michaels or Barry Hannah or Walter Abish, Tillie Olsen, or Ronald Sukenick. William Gass has only one book in print in England; Coover has only two; Gaddis, one; Percy, one; McMurty, one; Purdy, one. I think the point is clear. Despite the exemplary efforts of a few literary critics, Tony Tanner, Christopher Ricks, David Lodge, Malcolm Bradbury, American fiction is still not recognized in England; or if recognized, that recognition is not acknowledged.

Much of what is written in the States today has clear, even if only casual affinities to what is written elsewhere—in France, Germany, and recently Italy. It also has its international antecedents: some of contemporary American fiction was vaguely anticipated by the French *nouveau roman* in the early fifties, or, a little later, by the literary developments in Argentina and Mexico. The importance of Joyce is, of course, obvious; it is an importance, however, which can be exaggerated: the most noticeable feature of today's writing is its newness, its independence from not only realistically rendered expression but also the expression of the Modernists as well, Lawrence, Proust, Woolf, Stein, and even Joyce himself. And it is this feature of independence which ultimately distinguishes American literature from even the *nouveau roman*, the aesthetic for which, as asserted by Robbe-Grillet and Sarraute, is a fairly obvious, commonplace creed to anyone familiar with the Modernist tradition. In "An Essay on New Fiction", Philip Stevick makes the observation that "something very basic *has* changed in the primacy and centrality of the narrative motive and the narrative appeal in the last ten years" and that this change rests upon two assumptions, first

> that the difference between Barthelme and Katherine Mansfield, between Pynchon and Hemingway, is not [simply] a difference of historical setting, or style, or technique, or subject, or tone, or mode... The difference between the two goes to the roots of the narrative act itself, is a difference in what it means to tell.

And, second, that

> a perfectly amazing number of writers of considerable skill and utterly varied convictions about the nature of their art are flourishing at the present time, that along with some remarkably innovative fiction there are also some true and moving books being written with the technical resources of Balzac and Trollope, and that anything we say

about any segment of the enormous body of contemporary fiction is bound to look partial and unjustifiably exclusive to anyone with a modest breadth of response.

This fiction arrives, of course, with its critical baggage, its terms, called variously at various times "surfiction", "metafiction" or generally "post-modernism". "Post-modernism" is easily the most popular and the most inadequate, but is useful if only because it directs us to the awareness that this fiction is different, is, as Stevick points out, discontinuous "with the dominant figures of modernism", which discontinuity is perhaps "one of the few qualities that unites new fiction".

Stevick's suggestion that it is impossible or premature to isolate many of the qualities that "unite new fiction" is fair and fairly instructive, for what we perceive in American writing is an insistent diversity of the ways in which experience can be organized in prose. Diversity, of course, might easily stand as a comforting euphemism for unmanageable chaos—perhaps a just description of some of today's writing—but for the most part we see what could be characterized as a debate, conducted through fiction, about fiction. On the one side, we have writers working out of a realist tradition, John Cheever or (but not consistently) John Updike; or an autobiographically informed realist tradition, Saul Bellow; or a naturalist one—with antecedents in Faulkner and Dreiser—as is sometimes evident in the work of Joyce Carol Oates, Eudora Welty, or Robert Penn Warren; and on the other side, well, the other side is probably the most complex, the most difficult to define, united perhaps only by its opposition to the realistic or exclusively historical aesthetic. And its most articulate manifesto was provided twelve years ago by John Barth in "The Literature of Exhaustion", which refers to the exhausted possibilities or "the used-upness" of forms and fiction possibilities, and which celebrates Borges as the artist who can "paradoxically turn the felt ultimacies of our time into material and means for his work—*paradoxically* because by doing so he transcends what had appeared to be his refutation". The danger of a kind of writing which begins with the assumption that there is nothing to write about is immediately evident: it is vulnerable to the possibility of obliterating itself in its determination to demonstrate its own inadequacies. And a casual survey of what has been published in the sixties and is, but to a lesser extent, published today gives an idea of how close American writing has approached its own self-annihilation. As Theodore Solotaroff, former Editor of the now defunct *American Review*, observes in his Introduction to *The Best American Short Stories 1978*,

> I have watched the definition of what makes a piece of writing a short story, or even fiction, pretty much collapse before my eyes and within my own mind . . . I have published a narrative monologue in which the speaker is a story that is trying to find its identity and to say alive . . . another which is based on an imaginary story by Borges. . . and another whose narrative line is a recipe for baking bread. *American Review* also published short fiction in the form of meditations and memoirs and vice versa, as well as chronicles in which the real and the imaginary freely mingle, an interview, an unsigned letter, or the liner notes to an album of songs by a country blues singer.

Much of the new fiction of the last ten or fifteen years *is* as incomplete as Solotaroff's remarks suggest, or is at least as frustrating to read as the state of mind expressed is frustrated, cribbed, contained; but equally much of it is emancipating, achieving a quality of exhilarating freedom by having kept possibilities of writing open merely by announcing that the old ones are closed. And the search for new forms, new possibilities, new ways of expression is as varied as language itself.

One possibility which has emerged is what Robert Scholes calls "Fabulation", which, he believes, signifies the contemporary writer's

> return to a more verbal kind of fiction. It also means a return to a more fictional kind. By this I mean less realistic more artistic. . . more shapely, more evocative; more concerned with ideas and ideals, less concerned with images.

Scholes definition is only a little less vague, but infinitely more inadequate, than the phenomenon he describes, but the quality he manages to isolate—the propensity to develop the fantastic, the extraordinary, the mythic—is a quality easily characteristic of today's writing, organizing, almost as a principle, much of the work of Kurt Vonnegut, Thomas Pynchon, Robert Coover, Leonard Michaels, John Barth, or even John Updike. And it is here that Stevick's point is evident, that the whole narrative act, the task of *what it means to tell*, has radically changed. The novel is seen no longer as strictly a representation of life—no simile is more out of place than the familiar mirror and the supposed nature it reflects—but rather as a *making* of life, merely an imagined configuration, a product of the mind, a verbal fiction, analogous to all the other fictions we inevitably construct when we explain experience, organize it, define it as reality. Language is the agency by which all definition is achieved, and thus language—the ways it can be shaped, developed, applied—assumes a new importance for the American writer, and assumes an importance to such an extent that Tony Tanner can advance the argument in *City of Words* that the relation of the recent American hero to his environment is virtually indistinguishable from the relation of the recent American writer to his language. The interest in language is manifest not simply as a new self-consciousness about style or as an insistently stylistic management and manipulation of idiom—tendencies certainly evident in today's writing—but also as a fascination with the ways words structure perception, cognition, existence. Language, the stuff out of which fiction is shaped, becomes the stuff of fiction itself: the form of fiction is what fiction forms. "There are metatheorems in mathematics and logic", William Gass says in "Philosophy and the Form of Fiction",

> ethics has its linguistic oversoul, everywhere lingos to converse about lingos are being contrived, and the case is no different in the novel. I don't mean merely those drearily predictable pieces about writers who are writing about what they are writing, but those, like some of the work of Borges, Barth, and Flann O'Brien, for example, in which the forms of fiction serve as the material upon which further forms can be imposed. Indeed, many of the so-called antinovels are really metafictions.

Analogues are appropriate. We see here, as Tanner points out, a vague suggestion of the Romantic impulse "to project the shape of one's consciousness against the imprisoning shapes of the external world"; we see also a relation to the basic Structuralist recognition that all explanatory models for the fundamental states of affairs are myths or fictions: language, then, is just the means, the primary means, by which we make fictions for ourselves: to what extent, then, does the fiction that an author creates differ from the ones engendered voluntarily or involuntarily by the mind? Many writers today cease to pretend that their business is to render the world; they know that their business is to make fictions in a world of fictions. The work of Nabokov comes to mind—and his influence on the American writer cannot be underestimated—as does the work of William Gass, John Hawkes, Robert Coover, and Stanley Elkin.

To consider all explanatory models myths points to a paradox central to many American writers, the paradox of being unable to believe in the objective validity of meanings but unable to do without them; or as aptly phrased by Leonard Michaels: "it is impossible to live with or without fictions". To consider the paradox seriously is to consider implications which obliterate logic and invite a tame anarchy of the mind, in which all meaning collapses like melting plastic before the eye which tries to perceive it. The celebration of the "a-logical" informs another kind of writing, the foremost representative of which is easily Donald Barthelme, whose fictions playfully demonstrate the fallacy that a relationship of value exists between the mind and the objects which surround it. The Barthelme story is a comic container for urban trash, arbitrarily collected, arbitrarily preserved. "We like books", says one of the seven dwarfs in Barthelme's *Snow White* ,

> that have a lot of *dreck* in them, matter which presents itself as not wholly relevant (or, indeed, at all relevant) but which, carefully attended to, can supply a kind of "sense" of what is going on. This "sense" is not to be obtained by reading between the lines (for there is nothing there, in those white spaces) but by reading the lines themselves—looking at them and so arriving at a feeling not of satisfaction exactly, that is too much to expect, but of having read them, of having "completed" them.

Barthelme points us to a disintegration of distinctions and leaves us, as William Gass says, with "a single plane of truth, of relevance, of style, of value—a flatland junkyard—since anything dropped in the dreck *is* dreck, at once, as an uneaten porkchop mislaid in the garbage".

Barthelme, Pynchon, Gaddis, Barth, Coover—their work represents one kind of writing which presupposes the inadequacies of linear logic, linear relationships, linear reality: and Barthelme, Pynchon, Gaddis, Barth, Coover can project a kind of art that exists almost as pure possibility, no longer enthralled by an empirical or normative order or even necessity itself. But Barthelme, Pynchon, Gaddis, Barth, and Coover represent *only* one kind and their narrative *only* one kind of rejection of the conventional. We can also look to the non-fiction novel in which fact and fiction are deftly conflated, or in which the narrative potential available in the factual event is seen as more moving, more valuable than what is available to the imagination. The term nonfiction novel was, of course, first used to describe Truman Capote's *In Cold Blood*, a retelling of an actual crime but retold with all the command and authority of a suspenseful thriller or the engaging realistic work, but the term applies itself to the work of Mailer, to that of many of today's German writers (Böll, Grass, and Andersch), and even to New Journalism. A distrust of conventional forms, the suspicion that conventional forms are dishonest, manipulative, deceiving, also appears as the impulse for the strictly, exclusively autobiographical novel, and autobiographical here is not to suggest a work autobiographically informed as, for instance, the novels of Bellow or Roth or Sylvia Plath, but merely a work of autobiography, the author's, told in a form that suggests fiction. Frederick Exley's *A Fan Notes* is an example; Frank Conroy's *Stop Time* is another, in which Conroy, at a young age, just as he is about to re-enter the university, sits down and writes his own autobiography, without any apparent manipulation—thematic or narrative—without any apparent or overt structuring of any of the details he depicts. In all this work, the non-fiction and the autobiographical novel, there is the determination to provide what the conventional narrative no longer seems to be capable of containing—existence as it appears to us now; and the source of the determination was probably best expressed as early as 1961 by Philip Roth in his "Writing Fiction Today":

> The American writer in the middle of the twentieth century has his hands full in trying to understand, describe, and then make credible much of American reality. It stupefies, it sickens, it infuriates, and finally, it is even a kind of embarrassment to one's own meagre imagination. The actuality is continually outdoing our talents, and the culture tosses up figures almost daily that are the envy of the novelist.

Roth's article was important when it appeared, articulating the concerns evident, either casually or urgently, in most American writing at that time. Roth's article, however, is somewhat dated by now: more than eighteen years have passed since it was published. Indeed, much of the work discussed here—the non-fiction, the autobiographical, and the insistently self-referential novel—represents past discoveries more than they do immediate developments; many of these efforts, although still unfamiliar to most British readers, are emblematic of past struggles and past achievements. *In Cold Blood* was published in 1961, *A Fan Notes* a year later, and *Stop Time* in the year after that. Even Barth's "The Literature of Exhaustion" was written twelve years ago. As past ambitions and achievements, however, these works are collectively noteworthy, manifesting the first recognition of the particular difficulties, the particular indeterminancies which exist not in just the twentieth century, but in the time since the Second World War. But even as an important manifestation of an important recognition, much of this writing inevitably appears incomplete, vaguely inadequate: it hasn't gone far enough. There is a sense, suggested by much of the fiction of the sixties and early seventies, of cold, passionless study—gleeful and gratuitous experimentation as regularly insensitive as the America depicted.

Introduction

Something else is demanded, and the demand is obvious as an increasing dissatisfaction elicted by fiction which demonstrates its ultimacies and nothing more; an irritation with the non-linear story that gets nowhere and takes forever not getting there. To rush into the senselessness and then to refuse to go further, to locate the incoherent and the mutable and the predominance of its impersonal media only to refuse to rise above it, is simply not enough. The power of so much of this fiction depends upon the conventions it violates. But there comes a point when the disruption of conventional expectations becomes its own convention, when the standards against which we perceive its deviations are no longer operative. And a new recognition is necessary.

Again, it is useful to return to Theodore Solotaroff. As Editor of the *American Review* through the latter part of the sixties and the first part of the seventies, Solotaroff published again and again experimental and innovative fiction. There are few people more receptive to new ideas, new forms of expression: he has seated himself squarely in the centre of the literary scene. He no longer edits the *American Review*—it no longer exists—but this year, with the death of Martha Foley, he collected the fiction for the *Best American Short Stories 1978*. The criterion he now uses is instructive: "From a simple faith in the use of the story", Solotaroff says ,

> derives most of the standpoint from which I have selected the following stories. Though I try to remain open to innovation, I am more likely to respond to it as content—the opening up of fresh areas of common experience or the reclamation of banal ones through a strongly felt and rendered point of view—than as new ways of telling a story. The nonlinear antinarrative generally leaves me cold and impatient, since for all of its air of defiance it is usually playing society's game , refragmenting the delicate membranes that join body, mind, heart, spirit—and dining out, as it were, on the incoherent.

Solotaroff's impatience with the "antinarrative" is hardly a call to return to traditional fiction, as the very stories he selects bears out: works by authors like Stanley Elkin, Harold Brodkey, Jonathan Baumbach are hardly conventional. It is more a recognition that fiction having reached its ultimacy is now going beyond it; that writers having recognized the unsurpassable are now determined to surpass it. Even in the context of the impossible, new possibilities emerge like dreams.

The kind of development obliquely claimed by Solotaroff is, we hope, evident in what we have collected for this issue. But the kind of development Solotaroff claims is only one. There are others, other patterns: far too many patterns to be traced satisfactorily by an introduction of this sort. The work of new women writers, for instance, has not even been touched upon here. Another is the work emblematic of a new emerging regionalism—a variety of fictions expressing the concerns of not just the established literary regions, the South and the East, but the West Coast and the Mid-West as well. And there is more, but to continue listing is hardly valuable. As Stevick has indicated, it is impossible to place all that is being written today in comforting categories to comfort the mind. The generalizations made here are evidence of Stevick's assertion: push them a little and they will fold over and collapse.

There are many voices expressing American fiction and that expression is hardly harmonious. But it is the discord that is the source of the literary development, the energy, the achievement. What exists in the States, what does not exist in England, is a dialogue, which to ignore is to be irresponsible. And it is this dialogue which provides the occasion for debate and definition, the possibility of the polemic, the presence to be resisted or affirmed. A place for the imagination to practise.

No one issue of any one magazine can convey an adequate impression of all that is written in States. What we present here is hardly comprehensive: it is a kind of energetic failure, if representative, suggestively representative. The issue we have organized has developed less from a specific principle of selection than a more general one of general collection: to provide, as much as possible, a broad sense of some of today's writers whose work has been neglected or even unknown in England.

It is unlikely that all of the fiction presented here will present itself as wholly attractive to any one mind, which, of course, bears out the central assertion of this issue's occasion: that discourse, even if that discourse appears as oppositions, is not just productive but necessary to the making of literature. And we believe that the elements of that discourse are evident in this collection. No one story could ever represent the whole.

The Editors wish to express a special and especially grateful thanks to the authors who have contributed to this issue or helped in its development. The response of all the authors to our solicitings has always been enthusiastic and generous. In fact, the response has been so generous and so encouraging that we have deferred much of the American fiction promised us until the next issue, which, we hope, should include, among many other pieces, stories from Robert Coover and John Updike, a selection from John Barth's forthcoming novel, and an article on current fiction by James Snead.

This issue, aside from introducing new fiction, also introduces a new policy for *Granta*, for which this issue itself is perhaps emblematic. We are now dedicated to encouraging an exchange of fiction and discussions about it, now devoted to the idea of the dialogue in prose about prose. And while we intend to publish poetry as well—and invite contributions—it will be prose that will be our primary concern. All manuscripts are welcome.

WILLIAM WARNER

Interview with Theodore Solotaroff

Over the course of the past twenty years, Theodore Solotaroff has stood out as one of the most intelligent, committed, and idealistic supporters of serious, contemporary American literature. Encouraging both innovation and intellectual rigour, he has pressed the New York publishing establishment into accomodating diversity, experimentation and youth in fiction, and into maintaining, against the pressure of big business and bestsellers, high literary standards.

Solotaroff's career has taken him through almost every area of the American literary scene. He has taught composition and creative writing, worked as the book editor for the New York *Herald Tribune*, and is currently a senior editor at Bantam, one of the world's largest mass market paper-back publishers. He is, moreover, the author of novels, essays, and numerous articles. articles.

Most notably, in 1967 Solotaroff founded *The New American Review* (retitled *American Review* in 1971). For ten years, this paperback literary magazine asserted itself as the most vital and important literary magazine in the United States. To cite only a few examples, the *Review* first brought to American readers sections of *Portnoy's Complaint, Sexual Politics, Ragtime,* and *The Public Burning*; also Handke's *A Sorrow Beyond Dreams*, Gass's "In the Heart of the Heart of the Country", Paley's "Faith: In a Tree", Brodkey's "Innocence", Mailer's essay on Henry Miller and Alvarez's memoirs of Sylvia Plath.

The *Review* sold unusually well: the first issue passed 100,000 copies and all twenty-six issues sold at least 20,000 each. Pre-eminently a writer's magazine, it paid unusually high rates, encouraged and solicited innovation, published new writers, and accomodated lengthier work. Throughout, it strove to remain topical and socially engaged; as one critic remarked, it provided "a vital dialogue between public concern and private imagination". In his Preface to the first issue, Solotaroff said he wanted the magazine to provide "more explicit and topical connections between contemporary literature and the culture-at-large".

In 1977, with the magazine's readership and Solotaroff's sense of purpose dwindling, the decision was made to close the magazine. The following interview with Solotaroff took place not long afterwards.

William Warner: **What's going to replace *American Review*?**

Theodore Solotaroff: Well, at the moment nothing specific, though I would think that within a year or so either Bantam or another publishing house will be doing another kind of paperback magazine.

I wanted out of the *Review* for several reasons. I'd pretty much either exhausted my ideas for it or else had realized them, which, I think, comes to the same thing. And I felt *American Review* had also run a course and that to develop a real commercial credibility in the market place would require a different kind of magazine than the one I'd been doing. One more attuned to the Seventies than *American Review* had become, a magazine more aware of what's happening today and expressing more of today's tone and style.

When we started *New American Review* in '66, it was very much a magazine that was growing out of developments taking place in the Sixties. But it was meant to mediate between the radical cultural revolution we were going through—call it the Movement, the Counter-Culture, the Vietnam protest, the Civil Rights Movement, the Youth Revolution, whatever—and the continuing liberal literary tradition. We wanted to be both receptive and critical of these new developments: one of the functions of a magazine is to be very critical of the area in which it carves out its own identity. So that's what I was doing: trying to negotiate this encounter between the new and the traditional, to place the new within the tradition and at the same time to restate the tradition. So I published a lot of things, beginning with an essay by Conor Cruise O'Brien on Burke and Marx which was meant to show that the understanding of revolution was not confined to radicals, that Burke probably understood as much about revolution as any 19th Century figure except Marx. And another essay by Richard Gilman which was a very sharp and abrasive attack on *MacBird*, an ostensibly radical but in fact trivial and commercial burlesque of the Johnson administration, which attracted an inexplicably enthusiastic cult. And Gilman was saying that just because something is on your side of the issues doesn't mean it's good writing. So it was in that vein that the magazine attempted to plug into the Sixties. But now there is not that going on, and I'm not sure I know what *is* going on: a lot of people say very little. I think there's more than meets the eye. In the final issue, Theodore Roszak, probably the most astute observer of the Counter-Culture, wrote an essay on what he calls personalism versus individualism. The Movement of the Sixties, he believes, has not ended but continues in the

Seventies in a different form. What's happened, in his view, is that a strong tendency of the Sixties—a pervasive opposition to institutions of any kind—has broken up into what he calls a situational network. People did not want to identify with something called the working class or the student class. So what you see happening now is people organizing, not into some large movement, but rather into smaller groups of more local concerns: Gay Liberation here, Black Power there; you know, you see all kinds of small groups, consciousness raising groups, male consciousness raising groups, you even find drug addicts organizing.

WW: So that would fit with what you have written on the current decentralization of literature.

TS: Yeah, that would. I think that people in writing are tending to say well, you know I'm really from this particular place and I write with a sense of this place much more than I do with a sense of something called the Modern Tradition. Ten or fifteen years ago, poets would have identified with the Modern Tradition in one form or another—whether it was the tradition of Wallace Stevens or the tradition of William Carlos Williams, or possibly that of Lorca or Vallejo, what have you. Whereas now, these poets identify with the poetry that's going on around them, in Minnesota or Michigan or Washington or whatever. And I think it's very healthy, on several grounds. It's healthy in that it gives the writer who comes out of this a sense of a rootedness. I think Alan Tate once said that for something to be universal it must first be parochial. And I think the Modern Tradition has become very unrooted and rootless. People belong to literary movements which are abstractions rather than to ways of life which are concrete.

The market for writing is very decentralized too. For example, we publish a writer named Tom Robbins who, up until recently, has been almost strictly West Coast phenomenon: his appeal increased amost every hundred miles west you went once you passed Denver. Or Brautigan. Or Charles Bukowski, who's a major figure on the West Coast but in New England you don't even hear of him. On the other hand, someone like Saul Bellow is a major writer from Boston to Washington and Chicago, but among those people who read Bukowski and Brautigan, he's relatively ignored. Or you find a constituency which thinks that the most important living writer in America is John Hawkes; someone else thinks it's John Updike, someone else Erica Jong. That's a sign of this kind of decentralization.

Thirty years ago, people would say that the major American novelists were Hemingway, Faulkner, and Fitzgerald. Almost everyone would have agreed. The major poets? Frost, Stevens, Cummings, Pound, and Eliot. There would have been a real consensus as to who the major writers were. But now, there is no longer any consensus as to who are the major writers and what are the important tendencies; it depends on where you're at. There's a kind of analogue here to the political situation we just looked at: that you tend to read the writers and be influenced by them because you have a particular place in common.

WW: The problem, it would seem to me than, is isolation of the readership and the writers, distribution problems, sales problems.

TS: Well, that's it. It's not just getting your manuscript accepted that counts, it's how it's published. Three thousand copies, no advertising budget to speak of, no real interest except you see your own editors—that's not being published, that's being printed. You see? The question is how much effort goes into getting the book out. Now, most publishers are here in New York, and they do not have any stake in, say, the writing that's developing in the Pacific Northwest. They may get a collection of poems by Carolyn Kaiser or Richard Hugo or James Welch, and they'll make sure that the bookstores in the Pacific Northwest are approached. And they'll probably end up with placing 30, 40 50 per cent of the first printing in the area; but still it's not the same as a local press in Seattle doing these poems with a ready network of bookstores and readings and which would give the book a real life of its own. A mutual support system: the poet's presence, his own activity on behalf of the book, a small press which is only doing maybe four books that year, bookstore appearances; maybe the poet's part of a poetry in the schools program, he's teaching in a Seattle high school; maybe he's reading his poems at a high school assembly. In other words, the small press publishing method, at least in theory, is much more attuned to the actual conditions of these author's works.

WW: But then somehow the Tom Robbinses have to get from being LA local to being nationally known.

TS: That's right. This can very easily happen more or less of its own course. In other words, for example, Bantam acquired a book called *Rubyfruit Jungle*. [Rita Mae Brown's first novel, notorious for its outspoken lesbian protagonist.] This was first published by a small feminist press, and it began to have a certain underground reputation. I think they finally asked an agent to handle it because they couldn't hope to distribute it beyond their own local outlets. So we took it over, and distributed it. We got the book reviewed and gave it a lot of promotion, but it already had its market. There was a lot of word-of-mouth about it. This is a perfect example of how this decentralization could work. Now if we had bought this book four years ago and had put it out, and it had not caught on right away, we probably would have remaindered and pulped it within a year. Maybe even less. Because Mass Market (publishing, Bantam's speciality)means mass market. We'll do a first printing of 50,000 copies on a book. The wholesalers are not exactly astute literary or cultural observers—they know what sells and what doesn't. It's hard for them to take a lesbian novel. But assuming we can persuade them to take it, or *any* novel, unless it moves very quickly, they send it back to us. The wholesaler or bookstore orders 50 copies of *Rubyfruit Jungle*. If it doesn't move right off the bat, he's got the next month's list of paperbacks coming in. So in order to make room in his warehouse and make room in the pockets of the booksellers, he pulls them out of his warehouse and sends them back to us and the book goes out of print. So unless there is some kind of market established for it, to give it a chance to simply grow, the book will die: there has to be some kind of basis in which it can grow.

WW: So this might be a place where small presses or a thing like the Fiction Collective fit in to the larger publishing industry. (The Fiction Collective authors advance the money for the printing, promotion, and distribution of their books; any profits are recycled back into the collective for future books. Past collective writers choose the future ones.)

TS: Sure. And furthermore, the small press sold *Rubyfruit Jungle* to us for several hundred thousand dollars. I'm sure this was a big shot in the arm for their publishing program.

WW: What do you think about corporate and government financing for small presses?

TS: I think that that's a very important function. As long as there's no control. Government money is money. The question is whether there are strings attached to it. For example, one of the things they did a number of years ago was something called the American Literary Anthology. This was an anthology of the best of the little magazines; and if a story from your magazine was chosen, you got a rather substantial grant, as well as the author getting a substantial payment. I think George Plimpton was the editor of it. Each of these anthologies was to be published by a different publishing house; and that was the way it was subsidized to some extent. They got into a big hassle with a Congressman who came upon a poem written by Ed Sanders. He used to have a press called Fuck You Press, and the poem was somewhat along those lines. There was big hue and cry about taxpayers' money being used. I don't know whether they published it or not, but this threw a big bucket of cold water on the whole project.

However, so far there doesn't seem to be that much interference. The real problem is that they don't give you very much money. The problem with the National Endowment for the Arts as far as publishing goes is not that they have become another centralized, surrogate capitalist entity, but that the money they have is a pittance. They give less than 2 per cent to publishing.

Meanwhile we have 250 creative writing programs that are just turning out the writers.

WW: One of the things you talked about in one of your *American Review* essays was the relation of the Sixties' writing boom to the increase in teaching jobs.

TS: You know, curiously enough, one of the areas in which there still seem to be a few jobs around is creative writing, because creative writing has become the most popular offering an English Department has. You find people just storming the creative writing courses at registration and no one's signing up for the Milton, the Browning course, even for that matter for the American Fiction course. As a result there seems to be some chance for a job in creative writing with a Master's Degree and no chance at all with a Ph.D. from Harvard or Yale in literature.

WW: So how does that affect writing and the writer's relation to publishing?

TS: I think it affects each writer in his own way. I mean Max Apple is merrily finishing a novel and another novel is three-fourths finished. He teaches at Rice. And it's terrific. Another writer might find that teaching ties him down and makes him feel part of the establishment, and he doesn't write at all. Or a third writer might say, shit, I've been teaching at the University of Chicago for the last 20 years now, and the only thing I know about is what goes on in academia; I've lost my material. God knows there've been enough novels about restless college English teachers.

WW: But it might also affect publishing. It's a change from the Thirties or the Twenties when there were the popular magazines and that was the way the writer made his money, always writing, instead of taking time off to teach.

TS: Yeah, but look, I'm not so sure that teaching a lot of kids creative writing or teaching Herman Melville is any worse than trying to write a story the Saturday Evening Post would buy.

WW: People then may be influenced as much by what their writers teach as what their writers write.

TS: You mean students.

WW: Right.

TS: Well, what's the matter with that?

WW: I just wonder if it's changing things.

TS: I don't think so . I think that one of the first things a young writer does is to find a mentor. Unless you have that early experience of someone caring about your writing, the chances are you're going to find it very hard to go on with your career anyway. If you stay under this particular writer's thumb for the rest of your career then it's no good either, but no one ever said that because some parents are possessive we shouldn't have fathers and mothers. So I don't really think that that is much of a problem.

I do think that having writers in residence is a good thing. See, one of the things a lot of young writers come to me and say is "O.K., I'm just getting my degree from Antioch or Michigan or Harvard, and I really want to go on writing now. I've got this novel that I've done a third of, that John LaRue or Bernard Malamud or Max Apple or whoever says is really very promising. And I want to go on with it but I have to support myself now that I'm out of college, so what I really want to do right now is to get a job in publishing". And I say, "What do you want to do that for?". "Well, you know, I have to support myself and so on". And I say, "Well, you know, if you work in a publishing house the chances are you're not going to do any writing because you work evenings, weekends. If you want to get anywhere in publishing you've got to really convince people that you're diligent and hardworking and at the disposal of the house. And you know, reading a lot of other people's prose 60 hours a day is not very conducive to writing your own". And they say, "Well, you, you're able to do it". "Well, I lead a rather charmed life in publishing, and even I have precious little time to do any real writing. And in any case, I didn't start as someone with an A.B. looking for a job in publishing. I came with a magazine. What I think you should do is go to a creative writing workshop for two years". And he says, "Well, I've just had all those courses".

You know it's very hard to make that transition from the campus where you've had John Hawkes reading your stuff, or John Barth, or William Harrison, or William Gass, or Robert Coover, and then suddenly, no one's reading you. You're in New York, you send your stuff out to a magazine, they send it back. Send it out, send it back. And that transition, particular if you're 21 years old, is terribly difficult to make. Why don't you give yourself a transitional period where you're in a professional setting like the Iowa Writers' Workshop, where your peers are all writers like yourself who want to be professional. And you still have a certain amount of nurture from the teachers. And by the time you leave there you're probably in a better position to set yourself up as a writer than you would be if you came to New York straight. And I think that the function of these places is to act as a sort of transitional experience from the hothouse atmosphere of an undergraduate writing program to what you might call the cold house atmosphere of New York or wherever you are.

WW: So you think the whole teaching, student approach to writing is good.

TS: Yeah, I do. I don't know if it necessarily creates William Faulkners. I don't know what creates William Faulkners except heredity and luck and tremendous will to continue and some great talent. But as far as raising the level of literary productivity in the society as a whole, yeah, I think it's great.

The problem is that the industry is almost guaranteed, by the very way it's set up, to build frustration into the experience. As I say, we're trying to run a very different literary culture than we have ever before. We no longer have a few elite talents and then a lot of popular, commercial writers. We have a couple thousand really first rate writers, and we're trying to run this with an apparatus that's practically nineteenth century, centralized publishing in New York.

WW: You are talking, then, about a democratization of writing, bringing Sixties social values to literature.

TS: Yeah, sure. What I try to do, what I would like to see New York publishing do, is to edit and distribute not fo the literary elite but for the common reader. To get the books out to that doctor in Kansas City or that steel worker in East Chicago or Indiana: people who really like to read and will read good things if you can just give them interesting good things to read.

WW: That's your Robert Bly phrase.

TS: Yeah, right: "To do something for the hive".

is pleased to announce that in spite of
*3 Solicitors,
1 Quantity Surveyor,
1 Architect,
1 Well-Dressed Structural Engineer,
2 Well-Oiled Backers,
1 Head Lessee,
1 Superior Landlord,
1 Rosy-Cheeked Irish Builder,
1 Reluctant Bank Manager,
1 Startled Bank of England,
1 Cautious Bunch of Accountants,*
and a *Very Suspicious Planning Department*
our new restaurant at Newnham Mill, Cambridge, is only six months behind schedule, and will be opening at the end of April. In these circumstances, we would request an intelligent mature attitude to your grants, until such time as you can squander them on pizza.

Restaurants at:

8 Butchery Lane
Canterbury
(0227) 53148

15 Milsom Street
Bath
(0225) 62368

The Mill
Newnham Road
Cambridge
(0223) 67507

6/12 George Street
Oxford
(0865) 723421

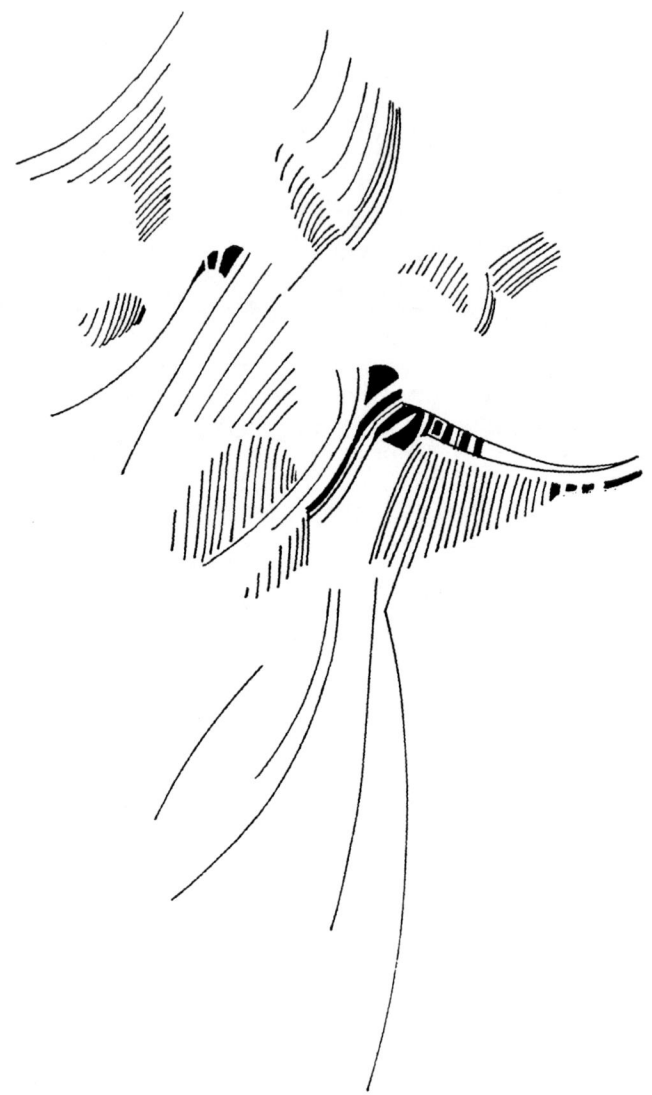

JOHN HAWKES

The Universal Fears

Monday morning, bright as the birds, and there he stood for the first time among the twenty-seven girls who, if he had only known, were already playing the silence game. He looked at them, they looked at him, he never thought of getting a good grip on the pointer laid out lengthwise on that bare desk. Twenty-seven teen-age girls – homeless, bad-off, unloved, semi-literate, and each one of their poor unattractive faces was a condemnation of him, of all such schools for delinquent girls, of the dockyards lying round them like a seacoast of iron cranes, of the sunlight knifing through the grilles on the windows. They weren't faces to make you smile. Their sexual definition was vague and bleak. Hostile. But even then, in their first institutional moment together, he knew he didn't offer them any better from their point of view – only another fat man in the mid-fifties whose maleness meant nothing more than pants and jacket and belted belly and thin hair blacked with a cheap dye and brushed flat to the skull. Nothing in the new teacher to sigh about. So it was tit for tat, for them the desolation of more of the same, for him the deflation of the first glance that destroyed the possibility of finding just one keen lovely face to make the whole dreary thing worthwhile. Or a body promising a good shape to come. Or one set of sensual lips. Or one sign of adult responsiveness in any of those small eyes. But there was nothing, except the thought that perhaps their very sullenness might actually provide the most provocative landscape for the discovery of the special chemistry of pain that belongs to girls. Still he was already sweating in the armpits and going dry in the mouth.

"Right, girls," he said, "let's come to order."

In a shabby display of friendliness, accessibility, confidence, he slid from behind the desk and stood leaning the backs of his upper thighs against the front edge of it. Through the south window came the sounds of whistles and windlasses, from closer came the sounds of unloading coal. It made him think of a prison within a prison. No doubt the docks were considered the most suitable context for a school, so-called, for girls like these. Yes, the smell of brine and tar and buckets of oil that rode faintly in on the knifing light were only complementary to the stench of the room, to the soap, the thick shellac, the breath of the girls, the smell of their hair. It was a man's world for an apparently sexless lot of girls, and there was only one exotic aroma to be caught on that tide: the flowery wash of the sweet bay rum that clung to the thick embarrassed person of their old teacher new on the job.

"Right, Girls," he said, returning warm glance for hostile stare, tic-like winks for the smoky and steady appraisal of small eyes, "right now, let's start with a few names..."

And there they sat, unmoving, silent, ranked at three wooden benches of nine girls each, and all of their faces, whether large or small, thin or broad, dark or light, were blank as paper. Apparently they had made a pact before he entered the room to breathe in unison, so that now wherever he looked – first row on the left, first on the right – he was only too aware of the deliberate and ugly harmony of flat chests or full that were rising and falling slowly, casually, but always together.

Challenging the prof? Had they really agreed among themselves to be uncooperative? To give him a few bad minutes on the first day? Poor things, he thought, and crossed his fatty ankles, rested one flat hand on the uphill side of the belly, and then once more he looked them over at random, bearing down on a pair of shoulders like broken sticks, two thin lips bruised from chewing, a head of loose brown hair and another with a thin mane snarled in elastic bands, and some eyes without lashes, the closed books, claw marks evident on a sallow cheek.

"Girl on the end, there," he said all at once, stopping and swinging his attention back to the long black hair, the boy's shirt buttoned to the throat, the slanted eyes that never moved, "what's your name? Or you," he said, nodding at one of the younger ones, "what's yours?" He smiled, he waited, he shifted his glance from girl to girl, he began to make small but comforting gestures with the hand already resting on what he called his middle mound.

And then they attacked. The nearest bench was going over and coming his way like the side of a house undergoing demolition, and then the entire room was erupting not in noise but in the massed and silent motion of girls determined to drive their teacher out of the door, out of the school, and away, away, if they did not destroy him first right there on the floor. They leaped, they swung round the ends, tightlipped they toppled against each other and rushed at him. He managed to raise his two hands to the defensive position, fingers fanned out in sheer disbelief and terror, but the cry with which he had thought to stop them merely stuck in his throat, while for an instant longer he stood there pushing air with his trembling outthrust hands. The girls tripped, charged from both sides of the room, swarmed over the fallen benches in the middle, dove with undeniable intent to seize and incapacitate this person.

The pointer, yes, the pointer, it flashed to his mind, invisibly it hovered within his reach, burned like a long thin weapon with which he might have struck them, stabbed them, beaten them, fended them off. But of course the pointer was behind him and he dared not turn, dared not drop the guard of his now frenzied hands. In an instant he saw it all — the moving girls between himself and the door, the impenetrable web of iron battened to each one of the dusty windows, and he knew there was no way out, no help. A shoe flew past his ear, a full-fifty tin of cigarettes hit the high ceiling above his head and exploded, rained down on him in his paralysis and the girls in their charge. No pointer, no handy instrument for self-defense, no assistance coming from anywhere.

And then the sound came on, adding to that turbulent pantomime the shrieks of their anger, so that what until this instant had been impending violence brimming in a blow of unnatural silence, now became imminent brutality in a conventional context of the audionics of wrath. His own cry was stifled, his head was filled with the fury of that small mob.

"Annette...!"
"Deborah...!"
"Fuck off..."
"Now...now..."
"Kill him...!"

Despite their superior numbers they were not able to smother him in the first rush, and despite his own disbelief and fear he did not go down beneath them without a fight. Quite the contrary, because the first to reach him was of medium height, about fourteen, with her ribs showing through her jersey and a cheap bracelet twirling on her ankle. And before she could strike a blow he caught her in the crook of his left arm and locked her against his trembling belly and squeezed the life from her eyes, the breath from her lungs the hate from her undersized constricted heart. He felt her warmth, her limpness, her terror. Then he relaxed the pressure of his arm and as the slight girl sank to his feet, he drove a doubled fist into the pimpled face of a young thick-lipped assailant whose auburn hair had been milked of its fire in long days and nights of dockyard rain. The nose broke, the mouth dissolved, his fist was ringed with blood and faded hair.

"You fucking old bastard," said a voice off his left shoulder, and then down he went with a knee in his ribs, arms around his neck and belly, a shod foot in the small of his back. For one more moment, while black seas washed over the deck and the clouds burst, the pit yawned, the molten light of the sun drained down as from a pink collapsing sack in the sky, he managed to keep to his all-fours. And it was exactly in this position that he opened his eyes, looked up, but only in time to receive full in the mouth the mighty downward blow of the small sharp fist of the slant-eyed girl whose name he had first requested. The black hair, the boy's gray workshirt buttoned tight around the neck, a look of steady intensity in the brown eyes, and the legs apart, the body bent slightly down, the elbow cocked, and then the aim, the frown, the little fist landing with unexpected force on the loose torn vulnerable mouth — yes, it was the same girl, no doubt of it.

Blood on the floor. Mouth full of broken china. A loud kick driven squarely between the buttocks. And still through the forests of pain he noted the little brassy zipper of someone's fly, a sock like striped candy, a flat bare stomach gouged by an old scar, bright red droplets making a random pattern on the open pages of an outmoded Form One Math. He tried to shake a straddling bony tormentor off his bruised back, bore another shock to his head, another punch in the side, and then he went soft, dropped, rolled over, tried to shield his face with his shoulder, cupped both hurt hands over the last of the male features hiding down there between his legs.

They piled on. He saw the sudden blade of a knife. They dragged each other off, they screamed. He groaned. He tried to worm his heavy beaten way toward the door. He tried to defend himself with hip, with elbow. And beneath that struggling mass of girls he began to feel his fat and wounded body slowing down, stopping, becoming only a still wet shadow on the rough and splintered wood of the classroom floor. And now and then through the shrieking he heard the distant voices.

"Cathy..."

"Eleanora..."

"Get his fucking globes..."

"Get the globes..."

They pushed, they pulled, they tugged, and then with his eyes squeezed shut he knew suddenly that they were beginning to work together in some terrible accord that depended on childish unspoken intelligence, cruel cooperation. He heard the hissing of the birds, he felt their hands. They turned him over — face up, belly up — and sat on his still-breathing carcass. One of them tore loose his necktie of cream-colored and magenta silk while simultaneously his only white shirt, fabric bleached and weakened by the innumerable Sunday washings he had given it in his small lavatory sink, split in a long clean easy tear from his neck to navel. They flung his already mangled spectacles against the blackboard. They removed one shoe, one sock, and yanked the shabby jacket off his right shoulder and bounced up and down on his sagging knees, dug fingernails into the exposed white bareness of his right breast. Momentarily his left eye came unstuck and through the film of his tears he noted that the ringleader was the girl with the auburn hair and broken nose. She was riding his thighs, her sleeves were rolled, her thick lower lip was caught between her teeth in a parody of schoolgirl concentration, despite her injury and the blood on her face. It occurred to him that her pale hair deserved the sun. But then he felt a jolt in the middle, a jolt at the hips, and of course he had known all along that it was his pants they were after, pants and underpants. Then she had them halfway down, and he smelled her cheap scent, heard their gasping laughter, and felt the point of the clasp knife pierce his groin.

"He's fucking fat, he is..."

"The old suck..."

In his welter of pain and humiliation he writhed but did not cry out, writhed but made no final effort to heave them off, to stop the knife. What was the use? And wasn't he aware at last that all his poor street girls were actually bent to an operation of love not murder? Mutilated, demeaned, room a shambles and teacher overcome, still he knew in his fluid and sinking consciousness that all his young maenads were trying only to feast on love.

"Off him! Off him!" came the loud and menacing voice from the doorway while he, who no longer wanted saving, commenced a long low moan.

"Get away from him at once, you little bitches...!"

There he was, lying precisely as the victim lies, helplessly inseparable from the sprawled and bloodied shape the victim makes in the middle of the avenue at the foot of the trembling omnibus. He was blind. He could not move, could not speak. But in customary fashion he had the distinct impression of his mangled self as noted, say, from the doorway where the director stood. Yes, it was all perfectly clear. He was quite capable of surveying what the director surveyed — the naked foot, the abandoned knife, the blood like a pattern spread beneath the body, the soft dismembered carcass fouling the torn shirt and crumpled pants. The remnants of significant male anatomy were still in hiding, dazed, anesthetized, but the pinched white hairy groin, still bleeding, was calling itself to his passive consciousness while beckoning the director to a long proud glance of disapproval, scorn, distaste.

Gongs rang, the ambulance came and went, he lay alone on the floor. Had the girls fled? Or were they simply backed against those dusty walls with legs crossed and thumbs hooked in leather belts, casually defying the man in the doorway? Or silent, sullen, knowing the worst was yet to come for them, perhaps they were simply trying to right the benches, repair the room. In any case he was too bruised to regret the hands that did not reach for him, the white ambulance that would forever pass him by.

"Sovrowsky, Coletta, Rivers, Fiume," said the director from his point of authority at the door. "Pick him up. Fix his pants. Follow me. You bitches."

In the otherwise empty room off the director's office was an old leather couch, there not merely for the girls' cramps, but, more important, for the director's rest, a fact which he knew intuitively and immediately the moment he came awake and felt beneath him the pinched and puffy leather surface of the listing couch. And now the couch was bearing him down the dirty tide and he was conscious enough of adding new blood to fading stains.

Somebody was matter-of-factly brushing the cut above his eye with the flaming tip of a long and treacherous needle. And this same person, he discovered in the next moment, was pouring a hot and humiliating syrup into the wounds in his groin.

"Look at him," murmured the thin young woman, and made another stroke, another daub at the eye, "look at him, he's coming round."

Seeing the old emergency kit opened and breathing off ammonia on the young woman's knees pressed close together, and furthermore, seeing tape and scissors in the young woman's bony hands and hearing the tape, seeing the long bite of the scissors, it was then that he did indeed came round, as his helpful young colleague had said, and rolled on gelatinous quarter-turn to the edge of the couch and vomited fully and heavily into the sluggish tide down which he still felt himself sailing, awake or not. His vomit missed the thin black-stockinged legs and narrow flat-heeled shoes of the young teacher beside him.

"I warned you," the director was saying, "I told you they were dangerous. I told you they beat your predecessor nearly to death. How do you think we had your opening? And now it's not at all clear you can handle the job. You might have been killed..."

"Next time they'll kill him, rightly enough," said the young woman, raising her brows and speaking through the cheap tin nasal funnel of her narrow mouth and laying on another foot-long strip of tape.

Slowly, lying half on his belly, sinking in the vast hurt of his depthless belly, he managed to lift his head and raise his eyes for one long dismal stare at the impassive face of the director.

"I can handle the job," he wispered, just as vomiting started up again from the pit of his life. From somewhere in the depths of the building he heard the rising screams of the girl with the thick lips, auburn hair, and broken nose.

He was most seriously injured, as it turned out, not in the groin or flanks or belly, but in the head. And the amateurish and careless ministration of the cadaverous young female teacher were insufficient, as even the director recognized. So they recovered his cream amd magenta tie, which he stuffed into his jacket pocket, helped to replace the missing shoe and sock, draped his shoulders in an old and hairy blanket, and together steadied him down to his own small ancient automobile in which the young female teacher drove him to the hospital. There he submitted himself to something under two hours of waiting and three at least of professional care, noting in the midst of fresh pain and the smells of antiseptic how the young teacher stood by to see the handiwork of her own first aid destroyed, the long strips of tape pulled off brusquely with the help of cotton swabs and a bottle of cold alcohol, and the head rather than chest or groin wrapped in endless footage of soft gauze and new strips of official tape. He felt the muffling of the ears, the thickening sensation of the gauze going round the top of his head and down his swollen cheeks, was aware of the care taken to leave stark minimal openings for the eyes, the nose, the battered mouth.

"Well," muttered the medical student entrusted with this operation of sculpting and binding the head in its helmet and face-mask of white bandages, "somebody did a job on you, all right."

No sooner had he entered the flat than his little dog Murphy, or Murph for short, glanced at the enormous white hive of antiseptic bandages and then scampered behind the conveniently open downstairs door of the china cabinet, making a thin and steady cry of uncommonly high pitch. He had frightened his own poor little dog, he with his great white head, and now he heard Murph clawing at the lower inside rear wall of the china cabinet and, leaning just inside his own doorway, became freshly nauseous, freshly weak.

"Come out, Murph," he tried to say, "It's me." But within its portable padded cell of bandage, his muffled voice was as wordless as Murphy's. From within the cabinet came the slow circular sounds of Murphy's claws, still accompanied by the steady shrill music of the little animal's panic, so that within the yet larger context of his own personal shock, he knew at once that he must devote himself to convincing the little dog that the man inside the bandages was familiar and unchanged. It could take days.

The Universal Fears

"Murphy," he meant to say, "shut your eyes, smell my hands, trust me, Murph." But even to his own steady ear the appeal sounded only like a faint wind trapped in the mouth of a mute.

It was dusk, his insulated and mummified head was floating, throbbing, while the rest of him, the masses of beaten and lacerated flesh beneath the disheveled clothes, cried out for sleep and small soft hands to press against him and slowly eliminate, by tender touch, these unfamiliar aches, these heavy pains. He wanted to lie forever on his iron bed, to sit swathed and protected in his broken-down padded chair with Murph on his lap. But the night was inimical, approaching, descending, filling space everywhere, and the flat no longer felt his own. The chair would be as hard as the bed, as unfamiliar, and even Murphy's latest hectic guilt-ridden trail of constraint and relief appeared to have been laid down by somebody else's uncontrollable household pet. Why did the window of his flat give onto the same dockyard scene, though further away and at a different angle, as the window of the schoolroom in which he had all but died? Why didn't he switch on a light, prepare his usual tea, put water in Murphy's bowl? A few minutes later, on hands and knees and with his heavy white head ready to sink to the floor, he suddenly realized that injury attacks identity, which was why, he now knew, that assault was a crime.

He did his clean-up job on hands and knees, he made no further effort to entice his dog from the china cabinet, he found himself wondering why the young teacher had allowed him to climb to the waiting and faintly kennelish-smelling flat alone. When he had dropped the last of poor little bewhiskered Murphy's fallen fruit into a paper sack now puffy with air and unavoidable waste, and in pain and darkness had sealed the sack and disposed of it in the tin pail beneath the sink, he slowly dragged himself to the side of the iron bed and then, more slowly still, hauled himself up and over. Shoes and all. Jacket and torn shirt and pants and all. Nausea and all. And lay on his side. And for the first time allowed his fingers of one hand to settle gently on the bandages that bound his head, and slowly and gently to touch, poke, caress, explore. Then at last, and with the same hand, he groped and drew to his chin the old yellow comforter that still exhaled the delicate scent of his dead mother.

> Teacher Assaulted at
> Training School for Girls
>
> Mr. Walter Jones, newly appointed to the staff at St. Dunster's Training School for Girls, received emergency treatment today at St. Dunster's Hospital for multiple bruises which, as Mr. Jones admitted and Dr. Smyth-Jones, director of the school, confirmed, were inflicted by the young female students in Mr. Jones's first class at the school. Mr. Jones's predecessor, Mr. William Smyth, was so severely injured by these same students November last that he has been forced into early and permanent retirement. Dr. Smyth-Jones expressed regret for both incidents, but indicated that Mr. Jones's place on the staff would be awaiting him upon his full and, it is to be hoped, early recovery. "The public," he commented, "little appreciates the obstacles faced by educators at a school such as St. Dunster's. After all, within the system for the rehabilitation of criminally inclined female minors, St. Dunster's

has been singled out to receive only the most intractable of girls. Occasional injury to our staff and to the girls themselves is clearly unavoidable."

With both hands on the wheel and Murph on his lap and a large soft-brimmed felt hat covering a good half of the offending white head, in this condition and full into the sun he slowly and cautiously drove the tortuous cobbled route toward Rose and Thyme, that brutally distended low-pitted slab of tenements into which his father, Old Jack, as he was known by all, had long since cut his filthy niche. The sun on the roof of the small old coffin of a car was warm, the narrow and dusty interior was filled with the hovering aroma of fresh petrol, and Murph, with his nose raised just to the level of the glass on the driver's side, was bobbing and squirming gently to the rhythm first of the footbrake and then the clutch. As for himself, and aside from the welcome heat of the little dog and the ice and glitter of the new day, it gave him special pleasure to be driving cautiously along with a lighted cigarette protruding from the mouth-slit in the bandages and, now and again, his entire head turning to give some timorous old woman the whole shock full in the face. He was only too conscious that he could move, that he could drive the car, that he filled the roaring but slowly moving vehicle with his bulk and age, that Murph's tiny pointed salt-and-pepper ears rose just above the edge of the window, and then was only too conscious, suddenly, of the forgotten girls.

Why, he asked himself, had he forgotten the girls? Why had he forced from his mind so simply, so unintentionally, the very girls whose entry into his life had been so briefly welcome, so briefly violent? Would he give up? Would he see them again? But why had he applied for that job in the first place? Surely he had not been going his own way, finally, after what his nimble old Dad called the juicy rough. All this pain and confusion for easy sex? Not a bit of it.

And then, making a difficult turn and drawing up behind a narrow flat-bedded lorry loaded down with stone and chugging, crawling, suddenly he saw it all, saw himself standing in Old Jack's doorway with Murph in his arms, saw his nimble Dad spring back, small and sallow face already contorted into the familiar look of alarm, and duck and turn, and from somewhere in the uncharted litter of that filthy room whip out his trench knife and standing there against the peeling wall with his knees knocking and weapon high and face contorted into that expression of fear and grievous pride common to most of those who lived in the ruin and desolation of Rose and Thyme. Then he heard the silent voices as the little old man threw down the trench knife and wiped his little beak and small square toothless mouth down the length of his bare arm.

It's you, is it?

Just me, Dad. Come to visit.

You might know better than to be stalking up here like some telly monster with that head of yours and that dead dog in your arms.

Murph's all right, Jack. Aren't you, Murph?

It's that school, that fucking school. My own son beaten near to death by a bunch of girls and written up in the papers. I read it, the whole sad story.

And then stalking up here like a murderous monster.
They're very strong girls. And there were a lot of them. Twenty-seven actually.
Why were you there? Tell me why, eh? Oh, the Good Samaritan...
Yes, the Good Samaritan.
Or were you really after a little juicy rough?
Mere sex? Not a bit of it. Of course I wouldn't rule out possibilities, but there's more than that.
Juicy rough. Walter, juicy rough. Don't lie.
I believe I want to know how those girls exist without romance. Or do they?
Use the glove, Walter! Let me give you the old fur glove. It does a lovely job. You can borrow it...

"Yes," he heard himself musing aloud from within the bundle of antiseptic stuffing that was his head, and pressing first the brake and then the accelerator, "yes, I want to be at the bottom where those girls are. Without romance."

At a faster pace now and passing the lorry, he headed the little dark blue car once more in the direction from which he and Murphy had started out in the first place. Occasionally it was preferable to meet Old Jack not in the flesh but in the mind, he told himself, and this very moment was a case in point.

"No," said the young female teacher in the otherwise empty corridor, "it's you! And still in bandages."

"On the stroke of eight," he heard himself saying through the mouth-slit, which he had enlarged progressively with his fingers. "I'm always punctual."

"But you're not ready to come back. Just look at you."

"Ready enough. They couldn't keep me away."

"Wait," she said then, her voice jumping at him and her face full of alarm, "don't go in there...!"

"Must," he said, and shook her off, reached out, opened the door.

The same room. The same grilled and dusty windows. The same machinery in spidery operation in the vista beyond. Yes, it might have been his first day, his first morning, except that he recognized them and picked them out one by one from the silent rows — the narrow slant-eyed face, the girl with tuberculosis of the bone, the auburn-haired ringleader who had held the knife. Yes, all the same, except that the ringleader was wearing a large piece of sticking plaster across her nose. Even a name or two came back to him and for an instant these names evoked the shadowy partial poem of the forgotten rest. But named or unnamed their eyes were on him, as before, and though they could not know it, he was smiling in the same old suit and flaming tie and dusty pointed shoes. Yes, they knew who he was, and he in turn knew all about their silence game and actually was counting on the ugliness, the surprise of the fully bandaged head to put them off, to serve as a measure of what they had done and all he had forgiven before they had struck, to serve them as the first sign of courage and trust.

"Now, girls," he said in a voice they could not hear, "If you'll take out pencils and paper and listen attentively, we'll just begin." Across the room the pointer was lying on the old familiar desk like a sword in the light.

WILLIAM GASS

The First Winter of my Married Life

The first winter of our married life, we lived in a slum near the edge of the Wabash. The university had thrown up half-a-dozen prefabricated duplexes during the war and rented them out to the faculty whom it also impoverished in other ways. The war was over. I had persuaded Martha to marry me. I carried certain glorious credentials, and we were both ready to make a start in life, as the saying was then. It proved a bitter winter in every respect. We lived side by side with a fellow from biology: his sink butted our sink; his john rubbed the rear of ours; the shower stalls were linked; and we shared laundry and storage sheds like a roll-towel in a public lavatory. Our garbage went in a common can and we parked our cars nose to tail in the street like sniffing dogs. Often the mailman got our letters mixed.

In front, the property was divided in fair-minded halves the way Solomon, in his wisdom, would surely have apportioned it (around their gum tree they planted crocus bulbs, while around our Chinese elm we put in daffs); but the backyard was enclosed by a weak wire fence which any gumptious turf would have shoved aside in a single season. There our lawn lay in pale passivity while weeds pushed through its flimsy sod like the spikes of a florist's frog. We were conscientious renters, though, and by unspoken agreement, took carefully measured turns to mow the dandelions and plantain down.

The walls were thin, and soon we were sharing our quarrels too. The sounds of love-making passed between us like cups of borrowed sugar, and cooking odors were everywhere like the same paint. When the cold water tap on our tub was first turned, a shudder went through the pipe to which it was attached, it seemed to me, all the way to the reservoir. A single furnace fired us, but somehow all our ducts were tangled, so that the moans and groans of the house would wander like lost souls, carried through them on the warm rising

---

"The First Winter of my Married Life" is a part of the novel The Tunnel, *which William Gass is presently working on.*

air, to emerge with a bright irrelevant clarity (". . . on the sofa . . ."'"Carrie called. . ." ". . . later. . .–n't the time. . .") in any odd place at all and abruptly as a belch — occasionally even returning to the room where they'd been made — echoes as battered as our cooking pans.

When we met on the walk outside, often hugging groceries or lugging books — just because we heard out toilets flush — we scarcely spoke, our heads hidden behind redly stenciled paper sacks; and in the laundry room, encounters were so brief and polite the gas man knew us better. Martha's ardor oddly came and went, and although I knew it was connected with the goings-on next door, it did not simply wax and wane with them; the correlation was more complicated, duplicitous, remote.

We were soon ashamed of our own sounds, as if every sign of life we made were a form of breaking wind. We were ashamed becuase we believed we heard the pop and creak of their floors, their stairs and settling springs, when normally we never noticed our own; because the scream of their kettle called us to our quiet kitchen; because we struggled to restore some sense to the voices which burbled and rumbled behind our common walls as one strains a pulpy juice for jelly; and we had to assume that they were curious too, had exchanged lewd grins, held fingers aside their noses like Santa Claus in that stupid poem, and had at least once listened through a wine glass to passages of passion of one kind or other. They would have been mostly about money, then, for at that time we hadn't any, nor could we hear any harmony in the loose rattle of our change; so we fought like children about whether we should spend or save.

Martha kept faith in a challenging future. I lapsed like an unpaid policy. Hence Martha conserved while I consumed. She sold. I bought. She bawled me out. She wanted me to quit smoking. It was a selfish habit, she said. She claimed we couldn't afford to buy books or pay dues in my damn clubs or fees for regular check-ups. Nothing's going to go wrong with a nice soft body like yours, she said, palping me like a roasting turkey. The university's library was large. There were lots of free lectures, and all the good movies would come round again like the famous comets. But who wants to watch a film as ancient as the family album? who cares about last year's lovers, or all those stabbings stale as buns, or auto chases on worn-out tires, I said, exasperation showing in my prose.

But we cut back. We inspected the dates on our pennies. I felt like a shabby freeloader, attending receptions just to snuffle up the cake and cookies, pocket mints. We kept magazines until they were old enough to be reread; converted boxes, cans, and jars, by means of découpage, a little sanding and shellac, into jaundiced baskets, pencil crocks, and letter bins — Christmas presents for the folks which only cost us our pride. I licked her slender virginal lips like a Roman emperor. The simple pleasures are the best, she said. I cadged returnables from our neighbor's trash; she returned the empties, saved trading stamps, suggested an extensive use of departmental stationery, the department phone for distant friends. Off and on I'd hunger for a steak, a melon, or a mound of shrimp. I think the wine we drank was trampled in Vermont.

Indiana's cold came down the river like a draft, and the deep gray sky

The First Winter of my Married Life

grew closer every day. Chimney smoke seemed simply an extension of it, as did one's steaming breath. I had suffered many a Midwest winter, but I had never been married to the snow. During an embrace, I would discover my arm clamped about my wife's waist like a frozen limb.

At first the snow helped. It kept us in. We played parchesi to calm our nerves. Martha would cook chicken livers again, and then, because they were so cheap — dear god — immediately again. She recommended peanut butter and claimed beans were a good buy. They blow balloons up your ass, I'd shout, with an embarrassed unoriginality, and then we would both look warily up and down, ducking the outcry as if I'd just hurled a tennis ball against the wall. In this toilet-tissue house, I'd hiss poisonously in her ear, we can't afford to fart. Then even when there was boot-deep snow, a cold scarf of wind, I'd leave the place to pout, closing the front door cautiously, violence in my silent face.

They'd designed our building like a pair of paper mittens, but the left mitten had been limp when we moved in, otherwise we might have been warned; and when its new tenants arrived, we found nothing amiss in the movers' tread or the gruff reality of their voices. The clear scrape of cardboard cartons did not trouble us, or the thump of heavy chests. Besides, it was warm, and windows were open. We simply had new neighbours. There was a hand now stuffed in the other glove. The noise was natural. Things would settle down. We hoped they would prove to be sympathetic types, maybe even friends. Then a headboard bumped rhythmically against what we'd thought was our most private wall. Their vacuum cleaner approached and receded like a train. Waters were released which gushed and roared and even whistled. Didn't I hear a male voice singing "Lazy Mary" one morning? Whose life could ever be the same?

After that we tiptoed, grew footpads, became stealthy. When we heard their closet hangers jangle like cattle on a hill far away, we shut our doors so silently the latches snicked like a rifle. I had heard his heavy smoker's hack (hollow, deep and wet as a well), so we took multivitamins to ward off coughs, then syrups to stifle them when colds caught us anyway, and increasingly felt like thieves and assassins.

Our ears were soon as sensitive as a skinless arm, and we spoke in whispers, registered the furtive drip of remote taps. It was like living in front of a mike as you might pose and smirk in front of a mirror. We heard ourselves as others might hear us; we read every sound the way we read the daily paper; and we came to feel as though we were being chased, caught, charged, and humiliatingly arraigned for crimes against the public silence — for making obscene sounds at the symphony or crying out loud at the circus.

In the flush of our shame, we wanted no one to know us, so we held hats in front of our voices, coats over our sinks and grains. We treated even the crudest iron cooking pot as if it were Limoges, slowing our motions as movies had shown us we should to defuse explosives. I ceased singing in the shower. We kissed only in distant corners, and as quietly as fish. We gave up our high-spirited games. Martha no longer cried out when she came, and I grew uncertain of her love. Small incidents were absurdly enlarged the way the whine of a mosquito is magnified by an enclosing darkness: a fallen spoon sounded like a broken jar, a shattered glass was a spilled tray, a dropped book a bomb. I exaggerate now, but it's true that as our neighbors sensed our presence the way we had theirs, they sent their sounds to Coventry too, and the house was shortly filled — palpably stuffed — with silence like a stomach's ache.

I began to suffer from insomnia. The dark boneless hollow of our bedroom seemed the menacing shape of my future, and I stared into it as if the energy of my eyes would act as a light. Maybe, less than a forearm away, another husband was doing the same — one whole half of his hopes discovered to be empty as a soldier's sleeve. It was not the kind of commencement I had counted on. I thought of my career (it was the commonest cliche) as one great climb — stretches of superhuman effort spelled by brief stops for rest and acclimation. People and towns would assume their true size, dwindling like the past behind me, becoming merely part of the grand patterns of history. I knew I would have to strain every nerve (as it was uncomfortably put) to realize my ambitions. A simple inspection of the past was child's play, but the composition of history was not a young man's work; it was not an arena for the display of an ill-informed or immature mind; no inept cape, however flamboyant, could turn aside the charges of time; it was not everybody's satisfying hobby or soothing Sunday scribble; for how many great ones were there in a century? when poets were as plentiful as pilchards and paintings bloomed like fields of fall weeds. I would have to climb beyond bias, become Olympian, part the clouds; and already I have resolved to work with material so racial and redvecked and cruel and costly (the extirpation of the Jews exceeded any subject), what tools or gloves or masks or prophylactic washing-up would protect me from contamination? It was not like the commitment of the poet, whose projects were likely to last as long as his latest erection — whether for elegy, ode, or little lyric — or till the clit was rubbed like an angry correction

I suddenly realized, considering this, that perhaps I spent so readily because I felt more secure in my future, while Martha conserved because she felt she hadn't any.

Home life (ho hum life, my colleague, Culp, insisted)... the home... The orphanage in my home town was called The Home. The home was supposed to be a help: a place of rest and solace you returned to at night and went forth from refreshed like a watered plant. Despite the fact thay my childhood home had been nothing like that, and although I had the satisfying cynicism of a young man who has read about more evil than he's seen, and even though I already had the deepest misgivings about every form of human relation; nevertheless, I hadn't married to be miserable, to be picked apart by fury and malice, crushed by common chores; I fully expected to inhabit such a place of peace and pleasure: a castle, a home, and Eden.

...within which the body of one's wife warmed and restored, as it had the elders of Israel from the beginning. The magic of her scented flesh made you the man you need to be "out there" where the war was (didn't the magazines and movies say so? the daily papers and the pulpit?); but already it was my work which stood steady when the world rocked. I had scarcely picked up my

The First Winter of my Married Life

pen when it began to replace my penis in everyone's affections. It wasn't fair. Culp, a man I at first found amusing, and brash as a bush on a hill of dung, claimed he went to work solely to summon the strength, simply to find the courage (he said), only to gain the time (he would insist) to close the clasp on his briefcase and go home. O to grow the guts! It's like leaving a full glass, he would say, staring like a lover at his desk. Although (the *l*'s rolled as though he were bowling). . . although I am naturally capable of living without children or chatter or contretemps for long periods, I deliberately dull the memory, he always said; I put my mind's eye out; I promise myself there'll be peace, there'll be plenty, at eleven twenty-two Liane Lane, my little mortgaged lean-to, my cottage at Lake Concrete; and by god such sanctimonious self-deceptions work until I see it sitting like a sick chicken in a mud-yard, till I hear my driveway gravel crunch like dry cereal under my wheels, till I put my key in that stiff marital lock again.

I understood Culp's attitude. The office hound was a common enough creature. But like cancer, I wasn't going to contract it. Like auto accidents, it was something which broke the legs of other people. At home (he sighs like a whistle) I sit in my easy and read the Wanteds. It's my pornography. I dream of all the jobs I might be doing which would take me off, out, up, and away; I'd be Peter Pan if they paid me peanuts; and when my hunger becomes overwhelming, I assuage it by chewing on checkbooks till the bills taste paid.

It wasn't fair. Martha slept like a plant, her senses all drawn in, at rest within her like a rug; while I marched into my sleeplessness as if it were a desert I was crossing (at the head of a column of sweaty and mutinous men); but the pain I felt was neither dry nor hot, but rather like a winter which will not release its grip — long gray rains raining coldly into May.

Our neighbors became our single subject. Their sounds composed a text we grew rabbinical about. From the slow sizzle of fat in a frying pan we inferred not the bacon but the pig, and their various treads upon the stairs drew a map of their marital emotions like those one gets from friends to find their cottage at the lake. (Deception. Lost ways. I knew that.) As for our own life: we cared only for concealment, nor could I burble at Marty's breasts as in the old days, or let an erection chase her through the house like a toy spear; and since our quietness kept our movements hidden, we would inadvertently sneak up on one another (sometimes Marty would shriek — it was hide and seek — when I came upon her suddenly). There was time when our startles seemed funny. Then we would glare at the offending wall and grin at each other; but eventually the tide of attention turned, and we could only smirk at some empty corner of the ceiling and sneer at ourselves instead.

We were two pairs of turtledoves — linked by leases not by flesh, thank god! — but they were our Siamese twin, nevertheless, the mocking shadow of our sensuality; and we had scarcely reached our car in the morning when the examination of their habits began: we were outraged, amused, we giggled like girls; we had nasty arguments on points of interpretation; we considered confusing them with a barrage of false sounds, by launching attacks of heavy breathing; I suggested some interesting scenarios, but Martha would not fall in with them. We tended to take sides, Martha preferring the trail the male left, naturally spores whose righteous quality escaped me altogether. My trust twisted to suspicion. Perhaps she was already their accomplice; perhaps she heard their passion more eagerly than she felt mine. Was the other side of the wall growing greener grass, I asked her, exasperation once more showing in my prose. Without receiving a squeak for an answer, I dropped Marty off at the local historical museum where she'd got a job minding tomahawks, propping stuffed squirrels in attitudes of life on branch-resembling sticks, and dusting flints.

The only plus was the pleasure we both took in discussing odd and often silly circumstances with the many acquaintances we were making at the university then; and we naturally lingered over the more scandalous details, describing the pressures of so public a private life on souls as newly glued by lust and law as we were. A little untoward heat (we said) might melt us down from one another like a custard from its coating; a sudden jar might shatter our fragile ties; an unexpected stress might stretch our sympathies to a point beyond elastic (so we went on, piling comparison up like fruit in a market window); we might weaken like moistened cardboard and our bottom pop. So our misery became entertainment like stories of the war, and from what had been a heap of jagged shards we shaped a graceful vase – something slightly salacious in the lush red-figured style. We guessed, and guessed again, and guessed some more, enlarging on our information like any secret service until facts were so larded with conjecture it became impossible to distinguish the marbling from the meat.

We were thought to be amusing – fresh, unique – (I *do* believe that) – and we certainly didn't hesitate to extricate whatever criticism of my powerful employer – our poor absent landlord – was implicit in our histories, but held it up for view and comment like a hair found floating in the soup, comparing the ironies of our situation to the slice of lemon which lies beside the cup of life; and these gibes provided an additional pleasure for our listeners, as it turned out, since the university was thought to be composed of three strata at that time – deans, dissidents, and dunces – with no one we met admitting to either ambition or stupidity; so we went wild; we put grotesques in every role as real as any real ones, bringing them forth as Dickens might have done – through tubas – each with traits as neatly cubed, distinct, and freshly baked, as cakes on a plate of cakes.

My student days kept step as I marched away into marriage, the military, and my profession. College had been a long and boring banquet whose food I'd somehow digested yet couldn't excrete. There were those hierarchies and ordered rows around me still like the hedges of a labyrinth; a tropical torrent of judgments, of ranks and scores, fell without fertility; the division of days into periods of improvement, hours of regulated relaxation, a few moments of pleasure paid for by pitiless stretches of melancholy which ceased only in beery sleep, went on incessantly like the little clicks of a pedometer; for what was the distance from Martha to masturbation when you put an interior tape to it? . . .yes, there was, in particular, life at close quarters.

The memory of those makeshift apartments in Urbana followed me now like a homeless animal. I could see again the room which greed had eaten out of attics like moths, coal cellars covered in oil cloth like the inside of a cheap coffin, the panelled garages smelling of grease; I reoccupied those stools under dormers which made you double-up to shit, closets where the clothes-rod was a water pipe; and I remembered a friend who had an entry straddled by a shower stall, another whose bed backed against a boiler, but I particularly could not drive away the image of those tiny preused Polish toilets which were as close to the living room as a lamp to its chair, so that we couldn't help hear the gush of the girls, always good for a giggle, and had to aim our stream against the quiet porcelain to be discreet ourselves, or pinch it painfully thin.

I saw that Martha suffered far more than I from our unaccustomed closeness. Women weren't used to long lines of nakedness as soldiers are, or the sycamores in winter. Gaunt, bleached, bony, the trees seemed a cold growth of the snow itself, a solidification of melting air the way icicles were a congealed product of the sun.

I also recalled squatting in a cold hole once on perimeter patrol, listening with the same intensity for the enemy (and since I didn't know what the enemy would sound like, I made it up out of movies: the crunch of a boot in the snow, a frightened wheeze, the unmistakable clink of metal), my ears like those dishes they tune to the stars. The world was cemetery still, and dark as the dead beneath the stones.

Now the silence was a great white field which Martha and I fled over like lines of running ink.

The trouble was, when I thought about it, that we were always the butts on the body of our anecdotes – the goats, the fall guys – the grotesques who were so amusing. And then it occurred to me to wonder whether they weren't telling tales, too, over there in biology, among faculty members we never met; and the thought was terribly sobering somehow, as if our plight were a program like Fibber Magee's that no one would want to miss; except there were two versions, two lines of listening, the right line and the left, like lobes of the brain of parties in politics; and which one was funnier, I had to speculate, which one's butts were bigger, in which did the fall guys prat more convincingly, the goats smell raunchier?

And Martha, who was always so saving, wanted to go out all the time to bars and movies, to drop in on friends where, after the customary inquiries about health and children, the rigmarole would begin again. Since we had no privacy in private, we sought it out in public. The strategy didn't succeed for either of us. Though alone in a movie with a gray screen dancing, she would throw my hand away, when it crept into hers, like a used up Kleenex, because we were married now and had, she said, no need to grope or fondle. In bars we would back ourselves in booths and speak, when we did, like conspirators. People will think we're married, all right, she said; married – but to other people. Isn't it getting to be that way (this was the general form of my reply); at home, don't you listen more to that other guy?

The cash we were conserving slipped away like our affections, literally through our fingers, as our touch became callous and mechanical. Martha grew testy about the money because she was the one who was spending it; and she grew testy about the loss of affection, because she had stopped bringing me up and never would bother again, as if her own large beauty should henceforth be enough; and though it was enough, her attitude made me resent every erection, and dislike the effect her nakedness had on me. What if all the blood became noisy, I said. What if I whistled through them like their kettle? What if, she said. What if?

In the early fall I had already begun to go down to the river to see the face of winter in the water, the slow logs and dry shoals. Crickets and hoppers were still rising ahead of my feet like miniature quail, and the weeds which had bearded the banks during the long stand of summer were high and heavily in seed; but the water returned their image to a sky which was as quiet as the river. My own face, too, fell open in the middle like the habit of a book, and by looking down, I could watch myself staring up, eyes already a bit puffy, the coming winter in my face. It was a smooth look, like an oiled door.

Here it was, our first winter, and we should have been rolled around one another like rugs. We should have been able to overcome small obstacles such as walls which were too flimsy to hold up, hide, or impede anything — which were not obstacles at all — yet here we were, our love cut judiciously in two like the front yard. How thin the skin, yet how small the poor theory that gets through, I thought, a proverb showing in my prose, a pun in my proverb like a worm. This nonsense of ours was using up my life and there was nothing I could do about it. Then I wondered whether she wasn't ashamed of me, ashamed to be heard with me in public, as though I whinnied. Would she lead a frank and noisy life with a brawny stud? Would she giggle and scream and writhe when they made love; compel that other couple to wish for pleasures they were inadequately equipt for and could not achieve even through installment dreaming?

He was tall and very thin and very dark. She was petite. She skittered, but his tread was erratic as one might imagine a scarecrow's to be — with unskillful and unfeeling feet. Mine was regular as meter (I *did* believe that), and Martha's was... Martha's was that of a thousand pound thistle. She put on bras and slips and blouses and sweaters, then added blazers and heavy wraps on top of that — overclothes to cover my eyes. Do you want to disappear entirely, to be snowed under layers of skirts, smocks and mufflers? Instead, it was I who disappeared like a magician's assistant. I knew she waited until I left the house to remove her diaphragm, a smelly elastic device that no longer went in as automatically as change in a purse or keys tossed in a drawer, and would never replace the ear as an organ. I said you're making me into a stranger. Her nose peered between the tan slats of a Venetian blind she opened with scissored fingers. Our neighbor's Plymouth, was, or was not, parked behind us. She felt grubby, she said. I received no requests to do her back. The museum, she complained. Dusty work. Scaly scalp. She washed always behind the bathroom door with washclothes moistened with mineral oil; dusted the davenport with damp rags; did the dishes at dawn; read in a dim light. She could slither from street dress to housecoat to nightgown without allowing a fellow a peek's worth, as one always imagined the bride of a Bedouin to be able, or a girl scout under a blanket — a skill I hadn't counted on. No one phoned. The brush man did not knock. She said it's late. What you couldn't see, perhaps you couldn't

The First Winter of my Married Life

hear. I could hear a fork strike an empty plate.

The first snowfall that year caught the trees with their leaves still clinging to them, and the weight of the wet snow did what the wind hadn't — pulled them free to settle on the surface of the river. There, for a few moments at least, they resembled massive, slowly moving floes. It was a vagrant similarity, but it sucked me up from Indiana the way Dorothy was inhaled out of Kansas, placing me in an airplane near the pole where I could see below me the rocking gray water and great herds of icebergs seeking their death down the roll of the globe.

This sudden switch of vision was indeed like a light, and gave me some understanding of the actual causes of our absurd situation. We were living in an image, not in a flimsy wartime throwup. There was no longer any reality to the clatter of pans and dishes, shoefall, outburst, sigh of a cushion; there was no world around our weary ears, only meaning; we were being stifled by signficance; everything was speech; and we listened as the house talked only in order to talk ourselves, to create a saving anecdote from our oppression, a Jewish character, a Jewish joke.

Walking along the edge of the river, I no longer saw those lovely pale leaves pass me like petals, as if some river flower were blooming oddly out of season (poetry appearing abruptly in my social prose) rather I took them to be elements of a threatening metaphor, because I had suddenly seen that the world was held together only be frost and by freezing, by contraction, that its bowels contained huge compressors and ice cold molds; so the place where I stood looking over a trivial Indiana landscape — snow freshly falling upon an otherwise turgid, uninteresting stream — was actually a point on the hazardous brink of Being. Consequently there appeared before me an emblem of all that was — all that was like a frozen fog — exhaust from the engines of entropy; and I saw in the whitened leaves floating by me an honesty normally missing from Nature's speech, because this adventitious coating threw open the heart of the Law: this scene of desolation — relieved only by the barren purity of the trees — this wedge was all there was; and then I understood that the soft lull of August water was but a blanket on a snow bank; the dust that a wave of wind would raise was merely the ash of a dry summer blizzard; the daffodils which would ring our Chinese elm were blooming spikes of ice, encased in green like a thug's gloves; there was just one season; and when the cottonwoods released their seeds, I would see smoke from the soul of the cold cross the river on the wind to snag in the hawthornes and perish in their grip like every love.

Uninterpreted, our neighbor's noises were harmless, and soon would have been as dim in our consciousness as the steady eeeeeen of an electric clock, or the slow glow of the nightlight; as it was, the creak of a spring signified a body on the bed; a body, a bed — that meant fornication, transports of passion as long as a line of lorries, the free use of another for the pleasure of the self, the power to produce forgetfulness, ease, peace, sleep; it meant a disturbing measure now lay alongside our own love like a meter bar — how long? how large? how full? how deep? how final and sufficient? how useful? wise? how cheap? — and in virtue of such steps our minds had moved the whole arc of the dial, from unpremeditated act to accidental sound, from accidental sound to signal, from signal to sense, from sense to system, from system to. . . the chaos implicit in any complete account.

For a month we fell toward the ice at the center of hell (grandeur finally showing in my prose), and I think it was the weather which convinced us we were bored and beaten by surveillance; we were at last embarrassed by the bloated selves our stories had made of us; close quarters had become half dollars, although, in this small pocket, we jangled together without real change. But now the wind came up the river like a steamer. The windows iced over. Would pipes freeze? I called responsible people and received assurances which didn't assure me. We told our friends of these fresh troubles, but I felt none of their former warm interest. We had worn the rug until I couldn't read it's welcome. The center was gone. Only 'we/me' remained beneath the shuffle of our feet. So we struggled into English sweaters and wore wool socks; we went to movies to replace our feelings, and sat in bars to keep warm and lose touch. With malice in my symbolism, I drank boilermakers — to lose track, I said, without a smile to greet the pun — and on placemats which displayed a map of the campus the color and shape of a spilled drink, I wrote to friends about positions in the south.

Culp was the only exception. He retold our stories for us, harboring our grudges until they seemed the flagships of his own fleet. He became another kind of auditor, his intense interest hemming us in on what we might otherwise have thought was our free and open elbow — the out side. Perhaps it was Culp who had worn our welcome thin, for he would show up at parties, picnics, and processions, to chortle and nudge, allude and remind, elaborating on our originals until they began to shrink within the convoluted enclosures he gave them the way paintings dwindle inside heavy ornate frames, or turtles hide. That predatory historian, Martha fumed, has kidnapped our life, and she was right, but not for ransom, as I still believe Culp holds whole booths of convention bars enthralled with reminiscences of those difficult early years of his marriage, when he lived in a hut on the banks of the Wabash (a double-hovel he called it), encountering everywhere in his own air the image of another, as of course he said like finding someone else's fart in your own pants.

How are you, I'd ask Martha with real worry. How are you feeling? Of course I was concerned for my own safety. I wanted to know if a storm was coming. It sometimes seemed to me I could see snow sliding out of the ceiling and melting on us as it melted on the river, though now the river was beginning to freeze, to disguise the flow of its feeling beneath a shell of ice. The sycamores were stoic, and there were deep crusted holes in the drifts where I'd walk. I found my tracks a comfort. Where I had been I would be again, returning to old holes, yet they were only the weather's memory. I wondered whether this winter's warfare would disappear in the spring, or would we be mired down in mud like the troops in Flanders?

We'll look for another place, I promised. What's in the fine print? Perhaps we can break our lease; maybe keep a big flea-barking dog.

Martha's enthusiasm was persuasively unconvincing. Perhaps she didn't want to be alone with me again. Did she sense what was surfacing? Maybe she liked the protection. Say, I said, suppose I turned vicious, you'd be safe. One peep would be as good as calling police. Martha mimed a scream, her mouth so wide it would have swallowed a fist. O no, even if you were murdering me, they wouldn't murmur, she said — would we murmur? We might shout "shut up!" like they do in the big city movies; we might bang on pipes the way you do to call the super; we might return outcries like party invitations. Martha shrugged. Her cleavage was another cunt. Well, I might do any one of those things, I suppose, she said; I think they're in my nature; but not you—oh no, not you, ever. It would be impolite and forward and beneath your blessed dignity. Then why am I staring at the floor like a schoolboy? The gods look down, don't forget, she said. Our floors were made of that hard asphalt tile which broke your feet (I had dubbed the color "abbatoir brown" when we'd first moved in), and that's what I saw when I hung my head: the frozen bleeding feet of every piece of furniture which had stood there through the war, leaving their pitiful dents, as if the scars were records of wounds in the weight which made them; and of course that was it, the world was tipping toward the north, relations were in deep reverse, blooms invading their buds, snow rising like steam from the earth, as in this doubled house, where stoves seemed warmed by their pots and compliments were a curse; for now when I entered my pale, silent, snowed-over wife, given legally to me by family, god, and social custom, it was through a cunt which lit up like an exit, and I was gone before I arrived.

The gods, I said. Marty? the gods? You speak of the gods to someone who was never a choirboy. I'm the sort of lonely little gid who looks into his shoes for a sight of the stars.

I had wanted to be put in charge of her body, not exactly as though she were a platoon, but as though my soul would wear her flesh for a change, and I would look out for her elbows as though they were my own, eat well and not take cold; but she wouldn't play. I remembered kids like that when I was a kid. They wouldn't be the baby or the pupil or the robber or the renegade; they wouldn't lie still like the sick or the wounded; they would never fetch, seek out, or serve. They were too afraid. I'm not a train, Whiffie, and I don't need a conductor. You mean you're not a plane, and you don't need a pilot. I'm not a boat and don't need a skipper. I'm not a field that needs a tractor. I hate those images. I'm a daughter, but I *have* a father.

She could have had my body in exchange, but who wants to be the boss of a barnyard, the cock for such a nervous vane? Speaking of images, Marty, how's the one you are living in presently; the one that's made you the thunder sheet in the sound-room, a roof in a heavy rain? But it was no use. She no longer cared for what I cared for. Henceforth she'd let her body burgeon like a lima bean in a Dixie cup, though there were no kids, yet, to instruct or entertain. If she had deeded it to me; if she. . . well, both of us would be as trim now as the molding of a painted window.

Surely we haven't gone so fast in these few weeks we've passed middle age in our marriage? Is it the sound barrier we've broken, and are they the boom, now, we're supposed to hear? It makes no sense. It makes at least one, she always answered, even when we were courting, because the statement was a tic like mine, like that obnoxious nasal sniff I had , she said. As a matter of fact, Marty darling, we've grown as sluggish as a pair of snakes, and if any such barrier burst, it would have to happen from the slow side of swift, like your hymen, remember? I said, letting my prose grow unshavenly toward scratch. In this house sound certainly departs for all points like the humans of Hiroshima, she said, serene and uninsulted. Sometimes I think that's all they are over there — echoes of us — that whole half of the house is an echo, a later ring of our present life, and it's me, then, I hear, going up their stairs.

On *her* feet? that scatter of pins?

Save your jokes for the next show, Whiff. She smiled with a meanness I hadn't seen. And she had begun to braid her hair again, a bad sign, and write long letters to her mother — one a day, like pills. Oh no, Koh, not on *her* pins, on *his* needles, she said. Martha stared at our barely wrappered wall for a moment so pointedly I thought there might be a gap through which she saw a table or a teapot more substantial than the shadows of our own. What are his shoes, anyway, but the sound of my steps? You'll find my feet fastened beneath those almost negligible legs and skinny trunk next time you meet.

No such luck, Marty. Clutching groceries or garbage like a pair of paper bellies, what else do we embrace? In any case, we never see a shoe.

You've heard that small black head of his, haven't you? like a photographer's box, go click? She laughed but I never understood the cause. The pleasure it implied seemed out of place. He's a thorough look-see sort of man — complete — including that long lank hair which shuts out the light; and there's his dark transparent face as well, like exposed film you can safely see the sun through at the noon of an eclipse.

Martha did nothing to erase the extravagance of her description. A luksi sort of man, I thought. Of the monkeys, that's not the one I would have picked; but I must admit to receiving a chill from this news — a chill, a chill — though in a perverse way it restored my weakened self to life like a dead drink that's suddenly got a plop of fresh ice.

The silences which came between us now were as regular as spaces on a page of type, and far more impervious to any message than our walls.

You called yourself a gid. That must be good. So what's a gid? She hated to ask. She knew how I loved an answer.

A gid is a small god, Marty, the human kind, with more features than powers — the difference, you might say, between poetry and prose. With my fingers I made a meager measure. Mayor Daily is a gid. And Franco. Fred Astaire. Lowell Thomas.

Then you're not a gid. Do they come in smaller sizes like bras?

I hated her when she was smart-assing. A gid is as small as gods get. There's no volume for a vowel deeper down or deeper in.

She wondered whether it came from 'giddyup' or 'yid' or simply 'giddy,' and then scornfully concluded it wasn't a word, that I'd merely made it up. We argued wearily about whether a made-up word could be one, and whether making up words was a form of lying, though neither of us cared. Well, in any case, you're not a gid, she said. I hated her when she was hard-boiling. I hated her when she crossed her arms across her chest like a prison matron in the movies. Her cleavage was another cunt. Hey, why don't we? why don't we invite them to dinner? Perhaps we can reach an understanding. Maybe we can work something out.

I don't want to know him any better than I do already, Martha said, carrying a summer *Vogue* into the john.

I was resolutely bent on comedy. If we could trade one-liners maybe we could continue to live. I suggested we let our little throw-rugs grow so we could comb them across our cold bald floors.

It may be, Martha said distantly.

I began to wish I had the wind's indifference to what it did. Shall I water them then? I tried to shout. Her first flush filled both houses like the bowl. There were always two. But she had begun to hide her habits from me. She kept the corners of the toast out of her coffee; she didn't twist her table napkin she no longer whistled while doing crosswords, or used toilet paper to blow her nose. She started rubbing toothpaste on her gums with her right forefinger, and thrusting pencils between her braids. She didn't get dog-ear books; she kept caps firmly on her jars of cleansing cream; she stopped slapping around the house in scuffs. I was simply at a loss. She didn't stick her lips anymore, but that might have been fashion. I waited for that second flush which didn't come. She was disguising herself. Her voice would get gruff. Soon I could expect to see a stranger's expression on her face and a mask on her muff.

With even these petty expectations taken from me, all I had left was a little inner determination, gid-greed, ambition like a stunted bud; but I silently resolved that what Ike is, and Cotton Mather was, Whiffie Koh would be.

We lit electric fires but no others. Except for them our house was a cold grate, and we were as alive as sifting ash. Peeled outside-in by Harty's transformations — bewildered, shocked — I only professed to be surprised so she would believe I always knew. But knew what? Was my blond Martha taking on that little woman's ways? The joke became our medium of exchange.

We would drive them out like demons. I made the sign of the cross — incorrectly — and muttered Latin imprecations. Let's burn sulphur, I said. For a week I tried raising my voice and being rowdy. Martha read old *Cosmos* and did puzzles ripped from the *Saturday Review*. It's like living in a waiting room, she said. And hearing you bawl about like someone calling trains.

That's it, I said. If I took a snapshot of our life right now, what would it look like? yeah, a drawing, a cartoon. We've bound our own feelings like feet. Our cheeks have porked. My eyes are two dots. Everything we say belongs in a balloon. Listen to your own sweet voice: stars, contorted ampersands, and yellow lightning bolts. Marty, these last few weeks I've felt myself emptying into outline, as if beer could become its bottle, and because we're posed here in pitchfork, arrowed tail, and red flesh, how can our misery be any more than lines? Hey, remember how we honeyed one another? Has so much changed we've gathered only ants and flies? Marty? listen —

Lis-sen, she said. That's all I do. My left ear is as long and flat as this wall I've pressed it to so amorously, and I've kept the other to the ground as well, just as hard and down and often, so the right one here is wide and tired and dirty like the floor. My nose, Koh, in case you care, gets nothing up a nostril now but doorbell buzz and blender whirr.

So we turned up the radio to stifle our whispers and smother our shouts, as torturers did in the movies, but discovered that then we couldn't hear anything they were up to either, and that wouldn't do.

The entire house seemed to have shrunk. It had become a cheerless, shabby rented room, soon to be a bureau drawer. I had been about to suggest that we stop bugging one another, but a dreary cold light fell out of the kitchen to confound me, and my voice lay down in my throat.

The other day I saw a fire alarm — long yellow streaks like slaps across the face of the street. I've three bruises on my arm. It's the vicious way he turns off taps. Notice that? They roll marbles across their kitchen floor. He leans over her like a lens.

Marty, come on. It's our closeness in the crazy place — our closeness has kept us apart — but the natural, decent, and sensible thing to do would be to complain to the university together — club up, unionize, make common cause. We *have* a common cause, you know.

She acknowledged this by gestures, each Italian and obscene. Remember how those woppy Eytie kids would gun their Vespas through the streets? The noise came at you as though they were hurling the cobbles. Well, they loved it. They loved their loud cocks. They loved their ball-like wheels. They loved to stick it up those narrow Roman ways. A vigorous finger speared the air. She failed to strip skin from her teeth. Can't you hear them next door, then? that continuous applause? the cheers? They love it — this noise we volley. They wouldn't trade for Willie Mays.

I hated her when she was hard-assing. I hated her when her plump face resembled that of some mean and pouty child, as — so often — it resembled Charles Laughton's. But, Marty, it can't really be that only our half of the house is cold. Noise isn't a trolley on a one-way *Milano* street. It can't be that moisture is collecting on our sills and not theirs, or that just our drafts are so brisk the blinds rise and the drapes wave.

It may be, Martha said. What if?

You know, Whiff, sometimes, in a marriage, only one side hears the other cough.

Yeah? Well. What of it? Are we married to them, then? Is that the situation.

One side is cold, sometimes, in a marriage, she said. One eye does all the weeping.

Yeah. Right. Sure thing. But is our nose stuck in their mouldy jam pot? And who is the cold carrot around here anyhow? which side of our bed has a marble mattress?

Shush, she said. They've just come in.

Shit, I shouted, on the run; but no sound could give me satisfaction, nor the silence after my slam.

The bitterness of it. I had hoped her flesh might warm my life; but my body isn't blubber for your burning, she had crudely said. Alas, one's dreams are always a cliche, yet I had hoped she would fill what I felt was an emptiness; but I'm not going to let you wear me like a padded bra so you can seem complete, she said.

The wind was an acid eating at my face, my anger another sort of acid searing my insides. Soon they would be near enough to greet. There was a hint of starlight, as there often was during the many clear nights of this pitiless winter, the thin moon a menacing sickle, and the dark artery of the river ran through closing ice toward a heart far out of sight, I imagined, like a lurking troll beneath a bridge. I couldn't drive her from her fantasies, however I tried. She was persistent as a bee. My boots went again where my boots had been, and I was aware, without pleasure, of the repetition. What was my passion for this ample woman but just that amplitude, that generous expanse of self? and now her hair was coiled, her thighs tense, her feelings like a tissue wadded in an anxious hand.

We went from apology to explanation to excuse like partners at a progressive dinner.

It bothers me to be an object in other people's obscenities, she said — the dirt in a dirty joke — a filthy thought you can't wash clean or even get a little soap near.

Even in my polite pornographies, I asked, with another attempt at gaiety which would burst before blowing up like a bad balloon.

In yours, especially, now I've been his leading lady. Her head wagged toward the wall in a gesture of such furious rejection I became immediately jealous. It bothers me to be all crotch. It bothers me.

And so I thoughtlessly said I wouldn't mind being all prick, dropping my left like an amateur, exposing myself; and of course I received her swift, professional retort. Replies rose in my throat, but they had the quality of yesterday's radish, so I did not return her pings with any pong of mine. I don't see even a shadow to start at, let alone a reality to run from, I said; how can you know what either of them is thinking?

I know what *I* am thinking. I know what *my* thoughts watch. I know how he drinks his morning milk. I have the measure of his moustache, and how far along his lip his tongue creeps. I know what he sees in his wife. I know how he pees, and when he shits, how many squares of paper are pulled off. I hear the rattle of the roll. I know what he wants.

My anger would never leave me. I had contracted a malarial disease. Naturally I had to hear what she imagined our neighbor saw in his wife, and Martha answered, predictably: the same things you see in me — our sentences two halves of the same dull bell. A hammer, I said, is what I see. A pliers. God damn it, Marty, don't cheat on the truth so transparently. Do you want a use? the least utility? Just what do you believe I see when I see inside you? the peep show follies?

Hair and heat and pink toes. You see a plate of steaming meat.

I wished right then there were a god I could invoke to damn her truly, but the thought of her skin cracking open in some supreme heat gave me only a jack-off's relief. Of course I shouldn't have felt as if my soul had left me, but her words — common enough, really — were like that winter wind which rushes by so fast you can't get a bit of it for breathing.

Not quite, Marty, I said. When I look at you I see a stew congealing in its grease.

The bitch didn't even weep.

The bitterness of it. I could remember her body in its beauty waiting for me with the calmness of the coverlet. I, too, had looked at her like a lens, and she had posed for me, opened as easily as eyes to my eyes; showed a boisterous bust, a frank and honest hip, a candid cunt, as one might hand round snapshots of a trip. Then it struck me. Perhaps she believed, in those handsome early days when our lust was in its clean beginnings and the politics of the penis had not yet confused and corrupted everything, that I was gazing past her smooth full cheeks and succulent lobes toward Martha the grandly scutcheoned Mulhenberg I'd married, or grazing quite beyond her meadowed chest to Marty the blond Amazonian lass, so she didn't mind my meddling senses, my nosey fingers, my tireless tongue; whereas now she knew I was admiring nothing but her beauty right along; and though it might be, like wealth, of immense use, it remained an alien and external burden if you thought of adding it to the self, because — well — she believed she possessed her looks like one night a Pekinese or poodle, and who would want to incorporate a cold-nose, pissy-nervous, yapping one of those? yes, wasn't that it? for hadn't I always wondered that very thing about women, whom I had learned could be sensuous and passionate beyond my poor capacities; who would calculate faster than Clever Hans — cook, sing, farm, run households, wag ass and empire with equal ease and often with the same moves, betray causes, author novels, and learn French — but in whom I had never seen, for instance, what a sculptor must, namely how dirty the mind gets where it feeds like a root in the earth, or the extraordinary way the concrete is composed of numbers and relationships like sand, the fugal forms of feeling which outstrip all proof, or finally the snowy mountainous elevations, the clouded unscaled peaks, the cold remote passions of the purely physical sublime?

You don't get it, do you, Martha said. You think I'm being cranky and perverse. You think I should be locked up like a dirty line in a limerick. Koh. You dear love. You runt. You dunce. She smiled to lower the line of her malice, but there was still enough to wet my hair. I went to the bathroom a moment ago, she said. First I heard my own feet, you know? I heard the click of the light switch, the snick of the latch, the rubbered settle of the seat. It shames me to think that someone else may hear what I just heard, what I just made — the splash of my pee, that lovely shush of bubbles like soda dying in its glass — because these are my sounds, almost internal to me, Koh, the minor music of my privacy, and to hear them is to put a hand on me in a very personal place.

I heard the same snick, I said. It signals your safety, doesn't it? as if I might burst in behind you to piss between your legs myself.

Oh Koh. Please. It's not simply that my noises might be embarassing — a rumbling stomach or some raucous break of wind — or even that to hear them one would have to be a sneak — although such factors weigh... they weigh... but neither is the painful one, the last cruel twist which wrings me out.

Slowly seeping down like egg white on a wall: my depression was that desperate. A kitchen table grainy with crumbs, an ashtray heaped with butts like the burned-out bodies of our voided thoughts, a faded cushion and a shredded towel — companions for this exercise — then a light that rattled away off plates like a falling fork. And so I said: have you heard your legs lock, Marty? No snick there, no click, rather a sound like the settle of the seat.

Oh —

Not O, I said. No. X. Have you seen your arms cross on your chest like a sign warning Railroad?

Koh —

And when my hands fall on your bottom, I said, not to spank, because we never enjoyed that relation, but like a corn flake, a tree seed, ever so lightly, as air though an open doorway, surely you've felt those buttock muscles tighten?

Please, Whiff. Please be serious. Please.

Seriousness, I answered has all but overcome my prose.

I remember wanting to understand, to throw my sympathy like an arm around her shoulders (at one point I thought, "gee, she's still my girl," as if we were pinned or going steady and I was selfishly rushing her responses); but I was also angry, disappointed, deeply affronted (I began to believe we wouldn't last the year out), since here she was defending her bloomers before I'd fully got her skirt up, and I was bitter as though bereft, because the cause of her present sensitivity seemed just a case of damn bad luck like getting flashed by the cops while making out in Lovers' Lane, and had nothing to do, inherently, with us as a couple. My outrage rapidly became metaphysical. I called down on all women the character of my mother like a plague, and then cursed them with her fate.

You know that passage in *Middlemarch* —

I knew no passage in *Middlemarch*, but I can recall insisting that it was every female's favorite fiction.

— where she says about marriage that there's something awful in the nearness it brings?

I was sitting in a sugar maple chair the sticky color of its syrup. I was uncomfortably near the knobs on metal cabinets, size of my eyes. Martha was wearing a large floral print which made her look like a trellis. To my well-fed Marty, I was a bed and boarding party. Wisecracks, rhymes, lay discarded like the Sunday paper. At such close quarters, our war was now down to nickels and dimes.

I've been watching us together, Koh, and I've been thinking, too, of our twins over there like animals in a neighboring cage, and I'm convinced now that we need to live in at least the illusion that a certain important portion of our life passes unobserved; that there are walks we take which leave no tracks; acts whose following sounds are not broadcast like the bark of dogs; events to which no one need or should respond; which have, in effect, no sensuous consequences.

I wished that this were one of them, but a metal kettle and a kitchen stool threatened immediate animation — to dance a la Disney to a tune by Dukas. The cute I couldn't handle. The spout would say something like "Toot!"

I don't want to hear all I do — every squeak in my works. I want a bit of oblivion, Koh. I want a little rest from awareness. You've made me so conscious of my chest, I'm counting breaths.

I was rolling like a spool. There's no coughless cold, kiddo; no blow without a little snot, no ding without its answering ling, no —

How I hate it when you try to crack wise. You can't break clean. You mash. Sure, sneer. Never mind. You can't ride away on the back of a joke. That's what I'd like to do myself, though: become deaf to what's dumb. Grin. Go ahead. How I hate it when you put that smile on like a dirty sock. Whiff, I'm sick of the shimmy, jounce, and rattle of staying alive. I want a world for a while without echoes and shadows and mirrors, without multiples of my presence. I could cut off my silhouette and not cry.

You're a sweet one to want a smooth ride. I thought you liked life a little hump-woof-and-rumpy.

Well, Willie, at least you offer me a model, a measure, something to go by when I wonder in what way you love me: exactly like a marksman loves his bull's-eye. All you want to do is score.

She spread the slats to check for their car, facing her sweatered back to my dismay.

On our own, she said softly. Left alone. . . in time. . . to some things we can go mercifully blind, as our ears will grow swiftly indifferent, thank god, and all our other senses. . . indifferent to ourselves and the cells we calendar our days in.

Above the sink the lamp sang, and the small chain leaked from its harsh fluorescent light in little links like melting ice.

Remember when my mother had her asshole out, Marty said (she knew how I hated her coarseness, but she was an *afficionado* of my shame); remember how she had to shit in a sack? She got used to it. She got used to it because she had to to survive. She got used to it because nobody dared to remind her. The subject was delicately *dropped*.

Like those A-bombs under their umbrellas. Marty, you can't cancel the fall-out on account of rain, when it's the bloody rain itself.

What I want, Whiff — if it goes off — I want a chance to ignore the noise. Yeah, cover your ears like one of those monkeys to mock me, but I'm no longer lost in our love as I once was. I keep surfacing. I feel on film.

You don't like the lead in our little blue movies? the star part? It can't be that you're bored with the graceless grunt and huffypuffy business?

You'll laugh at me alone this time, lover. I can't keep you company. You sprawl there with your little friend crawling down your trousers waiting for me to weep so you can take it out and put it in, because quarreling makes it uncaring, hence stiff and amorous like the little toy soldier it is. Go on. Take it off somewhere on vacation. Run away to the river. Amuse the ice. The two of you can take a leak, have a good laugh with the snow and the weeds.

I did as I was told, throwing on my coat as though I were throwing off everything else. The sky was hard and brilliant with stars like a run of the right hand in a piece by Liszt. The cold air rinsed my lungs and gave them definition. All those hidden inner organs took my walk and lived no differently than I did. Even our porous duplex didn't overstep its bounds. Beneath my weight, the cold snow crushed like crisp paper in a fist.

With Martha I loved what I'd always loved: an outline, a surface, a shape — yes — a nipple, a lip; yet I'd become an alien in her household, an unwanted presence, worse than roaches or the wind, because she thought she was more than a footfall, a weight, a slack wet mouth or sack of warm skin, when no one was other than their image, print, and circumcision — none of us — we were nothing but a few rips in the general stuff of things like rust on a nickel blade, and we were each running down like radium into rays.

So I was the thin dark man next door now, not the fair round pudge she'd married. I was the swiveling radar dish, the probe, the lens, the receiver of all her transmissions. Still, it would have been useless to remind her that a dog could smell the absence of her clothes, so she'd be naked to it, though they were walls away, since she was contemptuous of my philosophizing, which she'd called mental masturbation more than once; yet if we conceived the world properly we would realize the birds, ants, and insects also know us this way: as a shadow, a sound, a scent, a sudden intrusive substance, a cutting edge — never as a soul which (please god) does not exist except in a moist cold cloud like my present breath; and that, however quiet we were, however much we muffled our ears and stoppered our mouths, little could be kept from the earth and air around us, lion our lives upwind as we'd like, because it was alive as an antelope, all ear and apprehension, anticipation and alarm.

I was too much the whole of that wide world. Yes. I sniffed you out wherever you went like a hound. I would rush from another room to say; you coughed, is everything ok? but for you that was spying, not concern; so when I rubbed your rump I did so only to molest you; and when I offered to comb your hair you wondered what was up, and jeered when you saw what was. You wanted a love which would have been a lie — to lie beyond the nostril and the hip — an imaginary island like Atlantis or those happy beaches of the blessed it cost them nothing to enjoy beyond the payment of their death.

The mouth was refused first, before her back was turned like the last page. What are we, Marty, but sense and inference? and when I feel your smooth warm skin, your breasts like playful puddles; when I nuzzle your underarms or scent the ultimate *nostos* of your nest? what do I infer from what I sense? surely not the brittle stick you've thrown me. Be large, I begged. You will be less, my love, if you give me less.

The bitterness of it. But there was, as in everything, some recompense. It was true I enjoyed the way my feet distressed the snow; and I approved the sycamores who had no pretensions and wouldn't have hid their bones from me on any account, or condemned my pleasures. I did not applaud the river for its beauty because along this stretch it had none. I loved it rather for its welcoming indifference, the way the cold was cold, and kept me together. What, of this world of memories, a young gent's hopes, the pale ashes of desire, could I control, or oversee, or lie in wait for like the man next door I now would always be?

It was a winter so prolonged their crocus bloomed beneath the snow, and the sun dreamed.

Out of a frozen bottle would be forced the frozen cream; and I felt my heart expand against my chest, my coat, as though squeezed, to press against the tree trunks, push against the pointed stars, spread out upon a sterile land.

We'd remain married. I would see to that. One life would not be long enough for my revenge. The coarse baritone in which I made my vows came like an errant echo from another skull, an outcry left behind on the stage like an actor's closing lines. My voice in my fist, I promised the wind, trampling underfoot my former prints, Iago now the new friend, blade, and ancient, of my prose.

JOYCE CAROL OATES

from Son of the Morning

Whisper unto my soul, *I am thy salvation*.

You have promised that there shall be time no longer. Yet there is nothing but time in the desolation of my soul. A vast Sahara of time surrounds me, and though the frightful minutes pleat when I manage to slip into unconsciousness, the release is so brief, so teasing, that to wake once more to my life is a horror. Am I a brother to anyone in this agony, I ask myself; is it Your design that I awaken to such a brotherhood. . . ? But I don't want mankind, nor do I want the happiness of the individual without mankind: I want only You.

There shall be time no longer, yet we are deep in time, and of it; and it courses through us like the secret bright unfathomable blood through our bodies, bearing us along despite our childlike ignorance of its power.

Is this a revelation. I ask myself. Or an aspect of my punishment.

Save me, O God, by Thy name, and judge me by Thy strength and not by my weakness. If I have come to life again it is in obedience to the simple laws governing the sun, the moon, and the earth; it is not of my doing. My strength is like that of the mist-green reeds that do nothing but bend, with alacrity and cunning, as the violent winds pass over. Or do I think of the delicate young buds of peaches, or the hair-nests of the smallest of the sparrows. I think of the improbable precision of the eye: the perfection of the iris, the pupil, the mirroring brain. I think of my mother's broken body and of my father's swarth beauty and of my own soul, which drains away in time, minute after minute, even as I compose my desperate prayer to You.

It happened that Ashton Vickery one weatherless day thirty-seven years ago climbed the remains of an old windmill on his uncle's property, a .22 rifle under one arm, a shotgun under the other. He was twenty-three years old at the time: long-boned, supple, his pale blue gaze coolly Nordic, set for distances.

"Come along, come along, little bastards, come along, I got all morning,

Joyce Carol Oates

I'm not in no hurry."

Atop the partly rotted tower he stood for a while, shading his eyes. Where were they? In which direction? He unlocked the safety catch on the rifle, he unlocked the safety catch on the shotgun. Both guns were his; he had owned them for years. Very finely were they oiled. It was a pleasure for him to caress them, to draw his cheek lightly along the stock of the rifle, to raise the heavy barrels of the shotgun and take aim.

Through the scope he sighted the butchered chickens in the irrigation ditch. His finger hesitated, he felt a queer jolt of pleasure, wishing suddenly to pull the trigger: to tug it back toward him. The well-developed muscles in his shoulders and arms tensed. His mouth drew into its customary grimace—the corners downturned, the upper lip shortened, haughty and imperious. Ashton was a good-looking young man and very much aware of it. He had the Vickerys' prominent cheekbones, their thick unruly eyebrows and hard, square chin; by the age of sixteen he had been taller than his father. His eyes resembled his mother's and were as thickly lashed. Softly he crooned to himself, drawing his gaze along the uneven horizon, in no hurry. "Come along, come along and show yourselves. Come *along* now."

He laid the shotgun carefully at his feet and cradled the rifle in his arms. It was light, lithe, a marvel to hold; a beautiful instrument. Quickly it leaped to his shoulder; quickly it arranged itself to fire. His arm extended, his right arm crooked: just so! He leaned his face against it, closing one eye. Like this. Pivoting at the waist, Ashton Vickery could, by moving the barrel as slowly as possible, contain all of the landscape; all of the visible world. He sighted it along the barrel and all was well.

"Where are you hiding? It won't do no good. I can wait. I ain't half so hungry as you—I can wait."

To the north, Mt. Ayr dissolved upward in a haze of cloud; the powerful scope could bring it no closer. Closer in, farmland belonging to Prestons and Bells and Vickerys lay perfectly still, greening wheat and oats and barley, and a field of straight young corn, and a sparse woods of beech and oak. The air was fresh, a little chill. Ashton would have liked it cooler: would have liked to see his breath turn to steam. He hated being overwarm. It pleased him that the sky was overcast and that clouds moved above in sluggish layers, clotted, the color and consistency of skim milk. No sun. Only a peculiar glowering light that was like moonlight, like mist. A blank neutrality in which only a few insects sang, and very few birds. Like sleep, it was; like the dreamless sleep of the depths of the night. Perhaps he was sleeping?—dreaming? The foliage magnified in the rifle's scope and the glimmering surface of the river some distance away and the pallid, dissolving Chautauqua Mountains and the oppressive sky itself (which looked, for a moment, like a soiled concrete floor!) were mesmerizing. Ashton found himself smiling a foolish mindless smile, drawn through the scope and into the vast silence, thinking that this had happened before, many times: and would happen many times again.

But this is false: Ashton Vickery did not really think.

He was not accustomed to thinking, for what was the need? The rifle was an extension of his arms and shoulders and eyes and soul, as everything he touched was an extension of himself. He did not think, he tasted. He tasted and chewed and swallowed. He was quite content with himself. (Since it had been decided that he would enter into a partnership with his Uncle Ewell, buying a one-third interest in his uncle's general store in Marsena, since it was settled once and for all that he not only could not emulate his father—who had an M.D. degree from the state university—but *would not*, there was peace in the Vickery household. But then, Ashton had always been at peace with himself.) It did not surprise him that women found him attractive, for he found himself attractive when he paused to contemplate himself. Tall, rangy, arrogant, cavalier, he moved about Marsena and the surrounding countryside with an unflagging confidence in his own worth. Had he not, after all, the power to kill?—as he chose?—to kill with grace, with cunning, with mercy or without. The secret of his manhood (which he could not have articulated) lay ability to destroy, his willingness to kill, the zeal with which he snatched up his guns. He had first fired a rifle at the age of five, and at the age of six he had killed for the first time. The creature had been a full-grown hare. Ashton was never to forget the amazing kick of the rifle, the cracking sound, the *certainty*—he was never to forget the astonishing life—the livingness—of the rifle as the trigger was pulled and the bullet shot to its mark. The death leap of the hare had been extraordinary; it had torn from the child a gasp of startled recognition. The *livingness* of the rifle and the bullet and the death spasm and his own bright quickening blood: never would he forget.

Patient and tender with the morning, so fond of himself he stroked his own stubbly jaw, and considered: "Ashton can wait. Ashton has plenty of time." Half-mindedly he reached in his shirt pocket for a package of chewing tobacco and bit off a thumb-sized amount and began to chew it placidly, the tip of his nose moving with the pleasurable rhythm. He hoped the morning sun would not burn off the haze; his only prayer was that the still, blank neutrality of the present moment might be extended until he had accomplished what he'd set out to do.

"Come along, you little motherfuckers," he said softly.

It would have been well for them had they been able to run free about the countryside with their jaws stretched wide, like deepwater fish, gobbling up all the life they encountered. They were hungry. It was hunger, that enormous heartbeat. The throb, the palpitation, the lust was for food dampened and spiced by blood. In one barnyard they had cornered a dozen or more chickens and rushed upon them yipping with amazed delight, tearing at their throats—they ripped off the silly squawking heads even where there was no need, no time to linger and eat. A terrified Bantam rooster, all burnished-orange and red feathers, flew drunkenly on the top of a tool shed where none of them could leap; his screams penetrated the morning haze for miles. What a noise! What a commotion! Feathers, blood, flapping wings, scrawny scaly reptilian feet whose claws were as nothing against *theirs*. By the time the human inhabitants were shouting, by the time the first of the gunshots sounded, they were far away and safe, their snouts blood-darkened and curly with damp.

Joyce Carol Oates

Then again they were hungry, panting with hunger. Where did the hours go?—they trotted in one direction and then wheeled about, panicked by a certain odor; their leader was a ragged German shepherd whose tail had been chopped off close to his rump many years ago, and it was his wisdom to run half blind, his nose close to the ground.

The pack was most commonly sighted along the Alder River, though it was once seen by Carlson Bell as far away as Rockland, north of the city, that is—eight, nine, ten, possibly eleven wild dogs trotting across the paved highway, their fur wild and filthy and matted with burrs, their ears torn, scrawny tails carried low. Carlson braked his pickup truck and skidded to a noisy stop on the gravelly shoulder of the road and reached for his rifle—which was always in the truck with him, for safety's sake—and began shooting before he'd had time even, to shut off the ignition. He leaped from the truck and ran after them and it was incredible, he claimed afterwards, how *fast* they got away; and how sinister it was that they didn't bark or yelp or even appear to take special notice of him: just ran like crazy along a dried-up ditch of cattails and marsh grasses and thistle until by instinct or cunning they came to exactly the right place to jump free of the ditch, behind a screen of dwarf hazels, and then they were in that big swampy woods that goes on acres on both sides of the old Marsena Road, all mosquitoes and snakes and rot and darkness: and naturally no sane man would follow.

Carlson Bell had fired a few shots after them, not in anger so much as in exclamation. "You see! Here I am!"

But though small posses were formed from time to time, mainly of boys, and though Old Man Arkin prowled out back of his barns all hours of the early morning muttering to himself, his shotgun ready to fire (for the pack had killed not only half his hen coop but had, for the sheer pleasure of it, torn out the throats of all but the strongest of his sheep, and killed his aged half-blind collie—whose piteous yelps Arkin believed he would hear the rest of his life—and in a frenzy of high spirits even dug and threshed in his daughter-in-law's kitchen garden a few yards from the back door), still the wild dogs ran free and struck where they would.

Carlson Bell claimed there were nearly a dozen of them, Ewell Vickery claimed there were even more—and one of them he recognized. It was a mongrel retriever that had once belonged to Harley Revere but must have run off when the family moved to town, a mean vicious stupid creature that had always acted a little wolfish so it was no wonder the Reveres left it behind—but now had gone wild, now it was a killer. What if everyone drove their dogs off and let them go wild as coyotes!—no one would be safe. Thaddeus Vickery had never sighted the pack but had treated a nine-year-old Belding boy for bites on both forearms and on his right leg (a savage wound—looked like a shark bite, Thaddeus said) after the child had been surprised by the dogs on the Alder River bank—he and his brothers were fishing and when the dogs appeared they ran toward home and, unprovoked, the dogs chased them, setting up a terrific howling and yipping and barking—a horror, a nightmare—but thank God the boys weren't killed—thank God no one had been killed so far. It was a pity, Dr. Vickery said, but absolutely necessary that the boy receive rabies shots; he knew how they hurt but the risk was too great: the dogs might very well be maddened.

The German shepherd, the mongrel retriever, a cockleburr-covered speciesless hound, a rat-sized stunted creature that was probably a coyote...Surpised at their kill, they were sporty and looked like laughter; their stained mouths appeared to be stretched wide in grins, in human grins. They pranced about, howling at the moon like legendary beasts. They scrambled up the sides of ravines and caught pheasants in their jaws, and rabbits, and even flying squirrels; and of course river rats and muskrats, and groundhogs that had wandered too far from their holes. They hunted in the foothills of the mountains where there were no real roads, only overgrown trails; shrewdly they kept their distance from mankind; then suddenly and unreasonably they appeared at four in the morning in someone's barnyard or in the vacant lot behind a white frame. Church of the Nazarene where there'd been a fund raising picnic the day before and where food had been dropped in the grass—or they appeared on Sunday at dusk, out of nowhere, to frighten children playing at a smouldering refuse dump near a trailer village along the river. They were urchins, they were Apaches, they were savage, and savage-sad, their bellies permanently stiffened with mud, their ears laid back against hard mean skulls. Were they dogs, Thaddeus Vickery wondered, or merely stomachs. Hadn't they become nothing but a certain length of guts about which the animal skeleton and flesh moved, frantic with desire...? Howling, whining, whimpering, snarling, deep-bodied growling, panting, yelping, baying, cries very nearly like a flicker's, an uncanny *ostinato* of grieved rhythm, a melody of blunt pain; eyes, brains, and teeth forever in the service of guts.

When they were first sighted a year before, there had been only three or four of them, and the farmer who came upon them huddled against the side of his barn the morning after a snow-storm—thirty below zero it was, that morning— had not the heart or the wisdom to kill them, but drove them away instead, shouting at them and waving a pitchfork. At that time they hadn't killed very much—there were no tales of raids—they were garbage scroungers mainly weakened by hunger, their ribs showing, worm-ridden, brain-damaged, tongues lolling in steamy mouths. The farmer had taken pity on them and driven them away and it wasn't until the next spring when the pack had grown in size and in meanness that he realized his mistake.

Hunting for deer in the autumn with his friends, Ashton Vickery, the doctor's only son, came upon one of their number lying in a pool of dried blood, and a few yards away were the remains of doe—probably gut-shot by a local hunter and left to stagger away through the woods to die, and so the dogs had come upon it and killed it and devoured most of it, and somehow this particular dog—part shepherd, part hound—had angered the others and they had turned on him and torn out his throat and much of his belly. Seeing that ants were at work on the carcass, Ashton did not linger; but he felt at that time a curious sense of rage, almost a sense of—could it be injustice—of something gone wrong, and very ugly it was and should be righted. "I'd like to get them dogs," Ashton said to his friends. "Let's go'n get them dogs—what d'you say to that?"

But his friends didn't take him up on it: anyway, they said, how would you know where to hunt them? They're most likely far gone from here.

Then one morning in his uncle's general store in Marsena—a red brick building eighty years old that housed the only barber-shop for twenty-five miles and the Marsena post office—Ashton's uncle Ewell Vickery complained bitterly to him about some dogs that had broken into his wife's hen-house the night before and killed seventeen hens, Rhode Island reds that were especially good for laying eggs, and the worst of it was the terrible mess the dogs had made—tossing the chickens around, flinging blood everywhere, scattering feathers to the tops of the trees. No, the *worst* of it was, Ashton's uncle said passionately, that it had taken place so fast. And without much noise except for the hens' squawking.

"Why, that's a real shame," Ashton said, blinking. It was a surprise to him for some reason that the dogs had dared come so close to *him*.

Ewell complained about the fact that the dogs had been running wild now for months and the county hadn't done anything about it, wasn't there a sheriff's posse or a committee or something a while ago, why was everyone so lazy, why didn't anyone show responsibility. . . ? One of the McCord boys claimed to have winged a strange dog with his .22 but the dog was never found; must have run away on three legs. Apart from that, nobody had done anything.

Maybe the dogs were too shrewd to be cornered, Ewell said. Maybe they weren't dogs, but devils, and nobody human could kill them.

Ashton laughed loudly. "What the hell—?"

"There's got to be some explanation for why nobody's killed them yet or even chased them away," Ewell said.

Ashton shook his head in exasperation. "Shit," he said, "you leave it to me. Take my guns and set up a blind and wipe 'em all out. Leave it to me. . . Hey," he said, leaning across the counter and extending his hand to his uncle, "you want to place a bet on it? You want to bet on it? One hundred bucks, old man, how's that? One hundred bucks says I can't do it—? C'mon and shake my hand and it's a bet!"

His uncle waved him away. He seemed rather embarrassed.

"Not one *hundred* bucks," he said, frowning.

"Seventy-five, then! C'mon, you got the cash! C'mon!"

Ewell Vickery stared at the floor and his lips moved as if in a silent prayer and his nephew couldn't help but laugh, it was such a legend around Marsena that Ewell was a miser—getting to be a silly stingy old maid, in fact, with (so it was rumored: Ashton himself helped the rumor along) a fishing tackle box stuffed with bills beneath his and his wife's sagging bed, and a savings account up in Yewville of who knows how much?—thousands, maybe tens of thousands!—yet he stood there, skinny in the chest and arms and legs and paunchy in the stomach, in washed-out overalls and a flannel shirt, the blue Vickery eyes gone all milky and squinting in his face, a man no more than five years older than Ashton's father Thaddeus—which would make him about fifty-two—yet looking shriveled and faded-out and maybe ten years older. It was the miserliness, Ashton thought; he wished he could cure his uncle of it.

"C'mon, old man," Ashton fairly sang, "give me a hand on it! Seventy-five bucks. It ain't like I was asking for a bigger share of your profits, right? Now *that* I don't look to expect."

"It might maybe be dangerous for you—"

"Not *me*. Not me and a bunch of scrawny pups."

"It might maybe—"

"*Might maybe*," Ashton said in his uncle's mournful voice, irritated by the old man's language—for it often annoyed the young man that his family—well, not his family but his relatives—the Vickery and Sayer people spread out through most of the county—were so old-fashioned. Even the word *they* used ("old timey") upset and amused him. "Look: you going to shake on the bet or back down? Talkin' about them miserable little buggers like they're the Devil himself or something nobody can touch—"

"Watch your mouth, boy: what if there was a customer in here?"

"There ain't any customer in here, not that I can see," Ashton said with an impatient smile, "and what's wrong with calling them buggers if that's they are? They killed you goddam chickens, didn't they? I don't see no point to talking about them as if they were something so special that nobody could touch—I can't halfway tolerate that kind of a mentality." Ashton felt obscurely threatened and even insulted and it seemed to him that his uncle was partly to blame. But he managed to retain his smile. "If I kill them bastards I ain't gonna haul my ass around the countryside without some remuneration. Fifty bucks?"

"Fifty bucks what?"

"As a bet. Between you and me. You are saying I can't get them and I'm saying I *can*. C'mon, Uncle Ewell, you gonna shake my hand?"

"*You* don't have any fifty bucks that I know of," Ewell said sullenly.

All things must be fulfilled... consequently they shook hands, and that evening Ashton whistled cheerfully as he cleaned and oiled his guns, and when his sister Elsa asked him was he going hunting next day, and his mother's big frame filled the doorway of the shed and *she* asked him was he going to take a holiday from the store again and anger his uncle again, Ashton said only that he was taking a day off with his uncle's permission and it was none of their business what he did. "I wouldn't halfway mind, though, if one of you sweethearts packed me a nice lunch," he said.

They both snorted with laughter, but in a few minutes Elsa returned, honey-haired sweet-faced fifteen-year-old Elsa, with the breasts and hips of a full-grown woman ("I pray God she won't grow to be *my* size," Mrs. Vickery said often), leaning in the doorway to tease him. "How far are you going? Who's going with you? Them silly old friends of yours? Just a bunch of overgrown boys, Mamma says; playing around in the woods. You going after a bear maybe? A grizzly? You going after some big game?—maybe out in our woods?"

"Honey," Ashton said, "I'll bring you back the makings for a fur outfit: coat and hat and muff. Dress you up just fine for the winter."

She laughed scornfully but made for him, nevertheless, a delicious lunch of roast beef sandwiches on rye bread, and almond and orange-peel brownies, and a thermos of coffee pale with cream. "This should fuel you up for as far as you're going." she said, setting it on the kitchen table that night for him to take in the morning.

"I thank you, sister," Ashton said with mock formality.

"I surely do thank you," He said, eating the last of the brownies atop the rotted tower.

He drank half the coffee, cold, as he liked it, and saved the rest for later, and bit off another plug of tobacco, and moved a few inches so that he was in the shade, and yawned contentedly, studying the countryside. Did he see its beauty, did he take note of the birds' morning cries?— a trio of kingfishers by the river, rattling at one another; a jay singing the gentler of its songs, liquidy and breathless; a cowbird whistling in a pasture somewhere near. He smelled the wet grass, he filled his lungs with the scent of wet clover. For a half hour he was neither awake nor asleep, in a kind of alert doze, his eyelids lowered partway, the movement of his jaws slowing but never quite coming to a halt. In his mind's eye he saw the dogs. He saw them drawing nearer. Still, very still he was, not daring to move even in his dream; but he could not control the sudden leap of his blood. Ah, he saw them now, he *saw* them: deranged with hunger and therefore incautious, flea- and mite- and mosquito-bitten, worm-gnawed, eyes rolling a sick crazy yellow, tongues aslant, teeth gleaming inside black-gummed mouths...

He waited.

He waited and it seemed to him that the fresh breeze that lifted from the river would urge the dogs to him; he sniffed the breeze and half fancied he could discern their scent upon it. He had no doubt they would turn up and that he would slaughter them one by one. It would come to pass sooner or later; if not today, then surely tomorrow; if not tomorrow, another day; wasn't Ashton Vickery a peculiar young man (so people said admiringly), brash and all-in-a-hurry sometimes, possessed of the slow cold methodical cunning of a hunting owl at other times.

He had oiled his guns and laid them atop the pine bureau in his room and he'd slept a fine, full, deep eight-hours sleep, which was what he always required; he had slept with the grateful, quivering abandon of a healthy animal, or of a very young child; he had slept as he always slept. A dreamless and absolutely satisfying sleep that refreshed him utterly (as sleep didn't seem to refresh his father: but wasn't it the old man's fault that he worried so much about the patients' illnesses and deaths and debts and quarrels and silly old-maid fears?). Waking at five-thirty, he had jumped from bed and in twenty minutes was at his uncle's farm and parked back of a lane between a cornfield and a cow pasture where the family wouldn't notice his car—for the last thing he wanted was his aunt chasing him up to offer midday dinner, or one of his boy cousins coming to join him, or one of his girl cousins coming to flirt; he had to be alone the way his grandmother had to be alone to pray if he wanted to get the job done.

"Come along, little bastards, little buggers," he whispered.

His father had written a letter to the *Yewville Journal* on the subject of the wild dogs, but the newspaper had not printed it. *That* had infuriated the old man! Ashton hadn't bothered to read the letter since he not only didn't care for his father's exaggerations and the big words he used, he didn't care for reading at all; it seemed to him that if people had anything important to say they would say it out loud and eventually it would get around; what was the need to keep things tiny and secret, writing them down. . . ? He was like his grandparents that way, like his mother's people, who hadn't even gone to school much beyond fifth or sixth grade and always brought the subject up since they were proud of it. Thaddeus Vickery had gone to school for years, years and years and years, and when he got his degree he'd had to borrow money to set himself up in a practice and where had he borrowed money from if not his in-laws, old William Sayer with his immense farm in the valley—? Now that he had been a doctor for twenty-five years he still hadn't any money, it was Sayer money that kept the house from going to the bank in the thirties, and Sayer money Mrs. Vickery had inherited that allowed the family to be superior to most of the people of Marsena—not that Ashton minded being superior, he rather liked it, but he was inclined to think his superiority had to do mainly with himself, his face and body and personality. Maybe a little with being the doctor's son: that had always impressed his teachers, who'd graded him higher than he deserved. Being the doctor's son, however, was often an embarrassment, since the old man believed he knew the cure to everything if only people would listen, and naturally they were fools for not listening, for not printing his meticulously typed-out letters to the newspaper in town and granting him a public forum for his ideas. Ashton had not read the letter, but he'd had to sit through a meal while his father read the family parts of it in a preacher-like voice, jabbing the air with his forefinger (as he forbade anyone else to do, especially at the dinner table), making some long-drawn-out clever point about the dogs being victims: victims of human beings: victims turned killer in order to survive. They were all abandoned dogs, Dr. Vickery charged, some of them had been pets belonging to Yewville residents who hadn't wanted them any longer but were too kindhearted to have them put to sleep by the Humane Society, so they took them out into the country on a Sunday drive and let them go, and drove away thinking—thinking what?— thinking the dogs would find new homes, thinking farmers would take them in and feed them and give them new pet names and love them? Selfish fools! Selfish criminal insensitive fools! Pet-owners from Yewville and Derby and Rockland and as far away, even, as Port Oriskany, strangers who saw no evil in giving their pets "freedom" out in the country—they were common criminals and should be fined it not jailed and if he, Thaddeus Vickery, were and attorney instead of a medical doctor (yes, Ashton thought, exchanging a glance with his mother, the old man *must* alllude to that: what pride!) he would certainly encourage farmers to sue for damages against the dogs' owners, could the dogs' owners be tracked down; didn't these people know it wasn't just farm animals that were slaughtered by the wild dogs, but people had been bitten, a nine-year-old child had been severely bitten and had had to undergo the agony of a series of rabies shots—didn't people know how their responsibilities branched out to include not just their own families but all families?—everyone?—everywhere? Old Thaddeus's voice had rang clear and strong and outraged. Mrs Vickery murmured assent, Elsa avoided Ashton's eyes so that she wouldn't be drawn into giggling and sent from the table, and she too murmured assent; Ashton alone said nothing, his head bent over his plate, eating beef and mashed potatoes and string beans and cauliflower and glazed carrots and cornbread and butter as fast as he could, and not lingering for dessert either—though his mother and Elsa had made blueberry pie, one of his favorites. How could these "human" pet-lovers abandon their pets to the vicissitudes of the wilderness, Dr. Vickery demanded, had they no imaginations?—no intelligence? Their beloved pets became scavengers, butchers, outlaws, maddened and diseased and terrorized, not even animals any longer but simply coils of intestines about which matted fur grew. It was only a matter of time until they killed someone. A child, perhaps. Why, within Dr. Vickery's memory there was a hideous case out around Mt. Ayr, a dog had gone mad and attacked his master and killed him and had acquired a taste for blood and before he was tracked down and shot he had attacked a half-dozen people and partly eaten a young child and—

"Thaddeus, *please*," Mrs. Vickery said suddenly.

Dr. Vickery looked up from the letter, blinking. His face was ruddy, the pupils of his eyes appeared to be dilated.

"No more," Mrs. Vickery said with finality.

Elsa giggled, Ashton guffawed and slipped away from the table.

"Ashton," his mother called, "don't you want any—"

"Nope: no thanks!" Ashton said.

The dogs were trapped and he killed them one by one, agitated at first and then more methodical and then, near the end, very agitated again—shaking with excitement. Such noise! Such struggle! And the *livingness* of it—the dogs scrambling against the high walls of the ditch and falling back, yowling, wounded, crazy with terror—the kick of the rifle, and then, as he drew closer, the masterful discharge of the shotgun, which tore a partly grown hound in two and ripped off most of the skull of a shaggy coyote-looking creature with a bad leg—and on and on it went, Ashton carried with it, buoyed along by the noise, the desperation, the clawing, the howling and wailing and barking, "Oh you little buggers, take your medicine, now, filthy little flea-bitten motherfuckers, c'mon, c'mon, you there!—where you think *you're* going," and since there was no danger now he slid down into the ditch and followed a mongrel German shepherd—a pregnant bitch, in fact—that was crawling through the underbrush, crawling on two front legs, dragging herself frantically —the lower part of the spine blasted away, gushing blood; he ran after the bitch and, standing practically over her, fired the shot-gun one last time.

"Filthy little bastards," Ashton cried. "*Now* how's it feel? Now you know!"

Had any escaped? It was possible. He counted eight bodies. But had there been more than eight; had there been more than eight in the ditch? He counted them again, counting aloud. Seven, eight, nine. Ah: nine. Had miscounted the first time. But there were bodies atop bodies, and parts of bodies. He counted again, wiping his sleeve across his forehead. Six, seven. Eight. And was that a dog there or merely part of... Yes: nine. The bitch would have had pups and so he had really killed a dozen of the buggers. See how they like it now, how did their medicine taste *now*. "Motherfuckers," Ashton said scornfully.

It was quiet. It was very quiet.

No birds, even: all flown away.

Ashton walked carefully among the bodies, for it was necessary that they be dead; no hunter allowed a dying creature to drag itself away into the bush; there to suffer until it died; no hunter worthy of the name. "That didn't hurt much, did it," Ashton crooned. He poked at the head of a Labrador retriever with a bit of Doberman pinscher blood in him, sprawled dead against a rock. Vicious-looking thing, all those teeth. Stained. Broken. Could have torn a leg off if he'd had the opportunity. One of the dead hounds resembled a dog Ashton had seen somewhere recently—hound with a brown-spotted left ear, a white right ear—might have been from the same litter: whose dog? One of his friends' father's, maybe. Ashton counted the dogs again. Five, six, seven, eight, nine. Or was it ten. Up ahead there, in a tangle of dried-out willow bushes, was something—something that lay very still. Ashton scrambled up the ditch and went to peer down shading his eyes. It was midday now and the sun was quite strong. A tangle of fur, a bloody grizzly snout, eyes rolled back into its head: ah! Did that make ten now, or did it make eleven?

Ashton laid the guns carefully on the ground and took out his hunting knife, the blade of which was razor-sharp, and went to cut off the dog's ear. That was one. Flies were already alighting on the broken body, buzzing and humming about the sticky blood. Ashton worked fast. He went to each of the dogs in turn and cut off an ear, whistling, not at all revolted, though of course the flies annoyed him. One fly bit him on the back of the hand and he cursed loudly, the sting was so painful.

"*You* want swatting, you sonuvabitch!"

One by one he attended to them, taking his time. He was still excited but he forced himself to work methodically. That heart-beat, that swelling sensation—the queer expansive awareness of—of his own body, his own life—his selfness—*him*—straddling the dogs, working over them, joshing with them as he might in other circumstances; as if, now they were dead, they had become kin to him, prized possessions. They were no prizes, however. Even the coyote had been a wretched specimen. No sheen to the coats, no flesh or muscle to disguise the protruding ribs. The pregnant shepherd was very nearly obliterated—a mass of blood and guts and fur—but Ashton could see that both her ears were eaten pink and scabby by mites on the inside. He wondered casually what the mites would do now, next. Could they remain on the body for a while or must they leap off immediately and find another host? Once on a camping trip he'd been attacked by sand fleas—he believed that's what they were, horrible little things so small he couldn't see them, they'd just started rising up his legs and he'd slapped at them absent-mindedly while he and his friends were putting up the tent—and after a while of slapping it occured to him that something was wrong, something was very wrong, and he began yelping frantically and jumping about, and at that moment his friends too realized the fleas were upon them, and crawling up their legs, and—

"Hold still now, Tiger; this ain't gonna hurt," he said, and so he rose from the last of the dogs, part of its ear in his hand.

Raw appetite and fear, Dr. Vickery had charged, where once they'd been pets beloved of man. Was there no justice, was there no—

"Hush," Ashton murmured, thinking of his father. The old man would not like it when he heard the news, but everyone else in Marsena would be excited; maybe Ashton's picture would be in the paper again, as it had a few times before (once when Ashton was the first hunter of the season to bag a deer, another time when he'd been hardly more than a boy, fourteen, and had pulled another boy from the river bank of the schoolhouse where they were swimming, like fools, in freezing-cold water one autumn day).

One by one he put the ears in the paper bag that had contained his lunch, and then he gathered up his guns and stood at the edge of the ditch for a while contemplating what he had accomplished. Strange, he thought, that everything was so quiet. Alive and yelping one minute, dead and stiffening and forever silent the next. It was the same breeze flowing from the river, the same breeze blowing up from the field of sweet clover; very distant now was a hoarse rattling call, a bird's cry of caution. He realized the tobacco he was chewing had gone tasteless, so he spat it out.

"That's the last time you're gonna trespass on Vickery land and mess around with our livestock," Ashton said.

He was feeling good. He was feeling very good. Maybe just a little tired—a little sad. Drained from all the excitement. But no: mostly he felt good. As if he'd just wakened from one of his deep dreamless nights. His muscles tingled, his brain was jumpy and alert, he eyes felt almost sun-seared from having had so much to attend to; the sensation in his groin had become now almost an ache.

Flies were settling on the dogs.

"Taught you a thing or two, huh?" he said, backing away.

He drove the mile and half back into the village and parked in the shade of the old carriage house and entered his house by the back door, noisy as always to let his mother know he was home. "Jesus God, Mamma," he called out, "you got some lemonade or something fixed?—my mouth tastes like a buzzard's crotch."

He let fall the bloodstained paper bag onto the table and laughed to think how the old woman would peer into it and give a yelp, but when Mrs. Vickery came into the kitchen she frightened him by the look she gave him and said: "What's that on your forehead? What have you been up to?"

"What's what?" Ashton said.

"Paint? Blood? Did something fly into you, did you scrape yourself going through the brush?"

From Uncle Ewell he collected only thirty-five dollars, the most the old man would hand over. (He claimed the pack was much larger than Ashton said it was, at least fifteen dogs, maybe twenty: Ashton must have let most of them escape.) Ashton's photograph was indeed published in the *Yewville Journal*, in a prominent position on the third page of the Saturday edition: posed with the dog's ears arranged before him on the ground, Ashton Vickery squinted at the camera and managed a somewhat strained smile (for cameras made him nervous: he hated to just stay still and have someone do something to *him*). Ashton and his mother bought a dozen copies of the paper to hand out to all the relatives who might have missed it, and a few friends and neighbors, and in general everyone was well pleased. Dr. Vickery said very little; he spent a while examining the ears, the ragged blood-stiffened ears, but he said very little.

"The old man's jealous 'cause *I* got in the paper and *he* didn't," Ashton laughed, slapping at his thighs.

His mother told him to hush, not to make Dr. Vickery flare up; but probably it was true.

But probably it wasn't: Thaddeus Vickery was never a mean-spirited man.

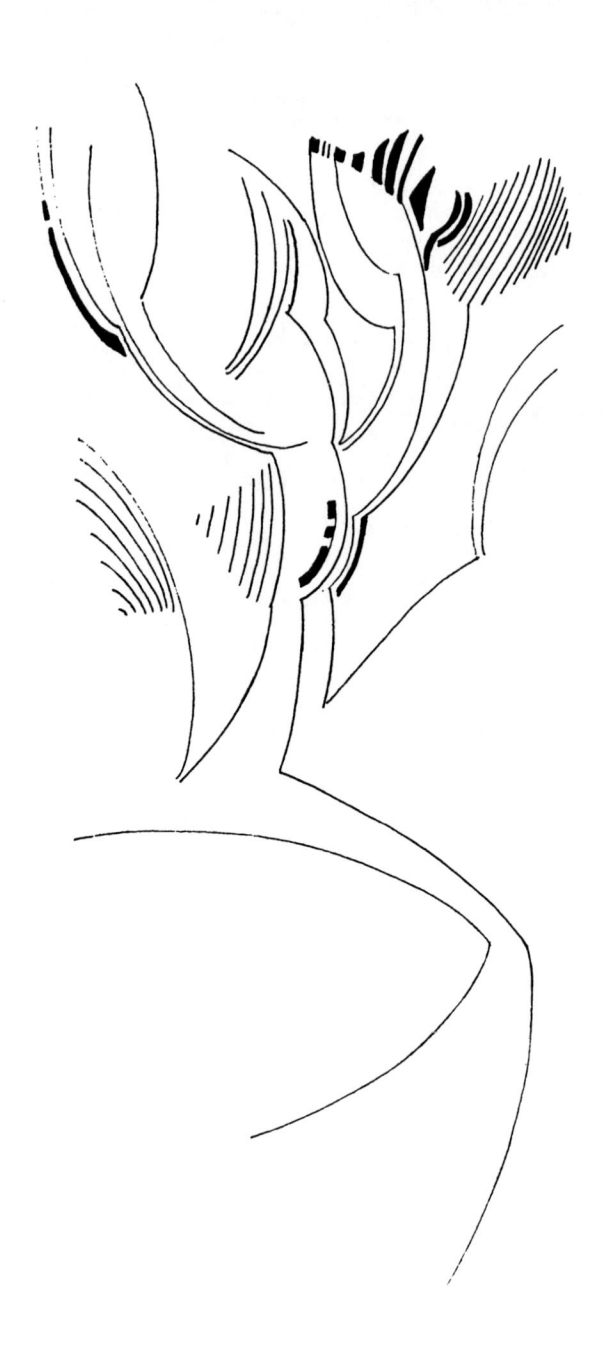

TONY TANNER

Present Imperfect:
a Note on the Work of Walter Abish

> Born in Austria, I spent my childhood in China, seeing an incredibly corrupt society slowly disintegrate. It was as if all the life processes were accentuated and crowded into the period of time I lived in Shanghai.
> I have always thought that all the life networks that enable us to proceed wherever we are going or prevent us from doing so, are predicated on a system called language. This awareness has undoubtedly influenced my approach to writing.

Thus Walter Abish in an author's note from *Statements* (Fiction Collective). Some of those slow—and not so slow—disintegrations, and those accentuated and crowded life processes have found their way into his own fiction, but it is his emphasis on that system called language which offers the main clue to his work. To be sure, there is nothing very new in the sense that the enabling or preventive life networks in which we are involved are to a large extent linguistic. To be born is to be born into a circuit of permissions and prohibitions, which constitutes the discourse (in the widest sense) of that particular culture, and I can hardly think there is a writer today who is not aware of the Lacanian contention that we are, as it were, slaves at the mercy of language (*serfs du langage*). What is somewhat more interesting, and worthy of another inquiry, is the extent to which contemporary French and American writers have tended to stress the prohibiting power of language over its permitting potentialities—for if language enslaves us it also, arguably, frees us in certain crucial ways; serfs and servants of the word we undoubtedly are, but also, even if only intermittently, we may be masters of the word as well. One aspect of a good deal of contemporary American fiction is a discernible desire among some authors to demonstrate that they can "cut the Word line" (Burroughs) in many different and unexpected places and reassemble the frag

---

In the Future Perfect *by Walter Abish is published by New Directions in New York.*

ments of received conventional discourse in singular orderings which bespeak more a mastery of the word than a servitude to it. This "mastery" may be so idiosyncratic and the cutting of the word line so wild and random, that not all the results are equally liberating—indeed, in some cases, one feels that there is a desperate attempt at "freedom" which is but another form of slavery. When Ronald Sukenick says—*a propos* of contemporary writing—"if everything is impossible, then anything becomes possible. What we have now is a fiction of the impossible that thrives on its own impossibility"—one of the things he seems to imply is that, in comtemporary fiction, anything goes. Which does not mean that everything comes off. Still, that is where a lot of the work (play) in contemporary American fiction is being carried out—in that "system called language" on which our "life networks" are predicated. (One might reverse Abish's statement to read "all language networks are predicated on a system called life"—but that too would take us off in another direction). The feeling is, I think, that by opening up new possibilities (and disrupting old clusterings) in the language system, the writer by the same token is opening up new possibilities in our life networks. It is a brave hope—though sometimes, I think, a fond one.

But to Walter Abish: his first book was called *Alphabetical Africa* which John Updike somewhat egregiously (or ironically?) called a "masterpiece" since it was "a book apt to be the only one of its kind." Rather more helpfully, John Ashbery related it to works by other writers (e.g. Roussel, Queneau) who "used constrictive forms to penetrate the space on the other side of poetry". I am not too sure about that space on the other side of poetry, but Abish's book certainly uses a constrictive form to open up some of the space on the other side of our ordinary modes of narration. Thus the book is divided into a number of sections, each starting with a new letter of the alphabet, in rigorous sequence: thus the chapters run from A to Z and then from Z back to A again. The game, or the constriction, is that in chapter A, only words beginning with the letter A can be used ("Africa again: Albert arrives, alive and arguing about African art, about African angst and also, alas, attacking Ashanti architecture, as author again attempts an agonizing alphabetical appraisal. . . asked about affection, Albert answers, Ashanti affection also aesthetically abhorrent, antagonizing all"); then in chapter B words beginning with B and A can be used; in chapter C, words beginning with C, B, A and so on, cumulatively, so that up towards Z the author is pretty free to use any old words at all. This certainly achieves some distinctly novel effects, as the text moves from constriction and gradually expands until it seems to have achieved a new kind of freedom (i.e. the freedom of choice among all available words which we tend to take for granted). We can *feel* the language network getting wider and wider, as the alphabet gradually loosens its grip, as it were, on the writer. There is a "plot" of sorts which I am not about to try to summarize: there are also all kinds of direct and indirect references to various kinds of imperialism, racism, contemporary history and politics, and so on. But the main relationship is between—happy alliteration— author, alphabet, Africa. "I haven't been here before. . . Bit by bit I have assembled Africa." Allegorical, anthropological, bibliographical, geographical and fantastical. All five groups are demonstrably dubious, because all history in Africa is hearsay, and consequently, although Africa indubitably exists, history cannot correct certain highly erroneous assumptions. But history can conceal assumptions. It can confound historians, authors, booksellers, and also doom armies. Africa is there, but we don't know what it is. We only know, or encounter, the variety of fictions called "Africa", which are inventions, projections, productions of different discourses, different delusions, different depravations, different dreams—the different alphabets of different imperialisms. In this sense "Africa" is exemplary—a paradigm.

> I am inventing another country and another "now" for my book. It is largely an African country, dark, lush, hot, green and inhabited by a multitude of giant ants. But even invented countries follow a common need, as each country heads for a common memory, a common destiny, a common materiality. But I am an unreliable reporter. I can't be depended on for exact description and details. Even Alva, to her chagrin, discovered that. I have distorted so much, concealed so much, forgotten much, but I have discovered that people are patient. They say about me: He has a longing. He is still uncovering Africa. He has a certain talent for that sort of task. . . They are understanding. They comprehend love, the shrinkage of an immense continent, and utopias, because they are familiar.

"After Z—Zanzibar is still within shouting distance of the mainland, but there doesn't seem to be anyone to whom one can shout across. The people on the other side seems to speak a different language, and as everyone knows, languages form attitudes."—there is another Z (and perhaps it is appropriate that there is at this point an account of a lesbian relationship, i.e. a relationship based on identity rather than complementarity—Z to Z, as it were). Then we are taken backwards through the alphabet, returning to A once more, which is a page of items all preceded by "another"—it is an almost entirely pointless alliterative agglomeration, tending more towards noise than, say, towards Beckett. Yet, pressed back and down to the initial, initiating letter, the writer is visibly, *lisible*-y, alive, pushing around in this very contracted semantic field as variously and vigorously as he can—"another attempt another attire another attraction another author another autography, another automat another autopsy another autumn another available average another avalanche another avenue another aversion another aviary another avoidance another avocation another avid avowal another awareness another awakening another awesome age another axis another Alva another Alex another Allen another Alfred another Africa another alphabet.' Another book.

Alphabetical Africa was strictly a one-off book. It was based on an interesting experimental idea and produced certain unusual effects—not least the sense it conveyed of a kind of vertical dictionary ordering of words gradually opening out into the horizontal flow and openness of a narrative text, and then reversing the process. But it would be dull indeed to make this idea the generating structure for another book. Walter Abish certainly has the wit to know this, and what he does is to move on to other kinds of langauge games. For instance, in his latest collection of stories (*In the Future Perfect*) there is a piece entitled, meaningfully enough, "In So Many Words". This story, hardly a story, a fragmentary depiction of a woman, her New York apartment, her environment, her routine, and her emotionless sex life, is rendered in a series of paragraphs, recounted with a dead-pan neutrality of tone which Abish often employs in his stories. But before each paragraph, we find an alphabetic recordering of most (not all) of the words to come in the following. grammatically conventional, paragraph. An example:

'40

a absolutely and at America American building certain convulsed croissant delicious eighth elongated floor four from height her intend iron is it Lee munching no of one perfection perspective quite Sara she splendor standing taking the true windows with

48

Standing at one of the elongated windows, munching a Sara Lee croissant (quite delicious) she is taking in the American perfection the American splendor—absolutely no iron intended. It is true. From a certain height and perspective, the eighth floor of her building, America is convulsed with perfection.

The alphabetization of narrative of descriptive sequence achieves effects not unlike Burrough's Cut-ups—both being extensions of the sort of games with words played by the Surrealists and Da-Daists. The new juxtapositions of words can yield unsuspected pseudo-semantic effects which can be funny, surprising, suggestive—or pointless. It is hit or miss, hit *and* miss—aleatory. The numbers in the quotation, incidentally, refer precisely to the number of words in the paragraph which follows—there are just so many words.

The other stories in the book do not indulge in so much lexical play, though there is a spareness and economy in the assembling of the stories—nearly all in short paragraphs with eloquent spaces in between—which seems to convey an almost constant vigilant irony over words, so that even the most innocent looking phrase seems to be placed with a certain pointed carefulness, making us aware that, in fact, there are no innocent phrases. "The English Garden" is a fairly straightforward account of an American writer's visit to a new-town in Germany which has been built on the site of an old concentration camp. The effects to be derived from this bit of dark archaeological irony could be all too obvious, but Abish is so in control of the tone that the easy irony is bypassed for the more oblique, more disturbing one. The writer arrives with a "coloring book", full of the outlines of things and people, but without the individuating colours of life. In the plastic-perfect German new-town there are outlines and things, but no life. It is, as it were, a city built on death, and despite the immaculate concealment of all traces of that gruesome, unspeakable (and therefore ever-to-be-gainsaid-or-disavowed) foundation, there are death and negation in all the glittering appliances and things and people-things of the new-town.

The city is named after a German philosopher, who, like so many of his predecessors, inquired into the nature of a *thing*. He started his philosophical inquiry by simply asking: *What is a thing?* For most of the inhabitants of Brumholdstein the question does not pose a great problem. They are the first to acknowledge that the hot and cold water taps in the bathroom are things, just as much as the windows in the new shopping center are things. Things pervade every encounter, every action.

It is indeed an almost totally reified self-reifying community. Even the apparently radical German writer the American author meets is basically a part of that thing-continuum. It is he who, at the end of the story, tears up a photograph of some survivors of the concentration camp which the narrator has found." I did not lift a hand to stop him from effacing the past." The only "event" in the story is the disappearance of a girl whose father had been a commander of the concentration camp. She is just found "missing" one day." I look up the German word for missing. It is *abwesend* or *fehlend* or *nicht zu finden*. I also look up the word disappear. It is *verschwinden*." The words are still in the dictionary but meanwhile people disappear. Indeed perhaps humanity has disappeared from the thing-perfect town, so that everyone, humanly speaking, has gone missing. At the end the narrator throws away his colouring book and crayons.

Abish extends his apparently neutral, actually highly subversive, account of the contemporary environment to a failing/fading relationship in a unreal/perfect New York apartment ("Parting Shot"), and the career of a girl who runs away to find success, satisfaction, and finally death in Southern California. This story, entitled "ARDOR/AWE/ATROCITY", is also alphabetized in a different way. Every section is headed by an alliterative triad of words—so we move on to "BOUYANT/BOB/BODY" through "PLEASURE/PUNISH/POSITION" and "UNBUTTONED/UNDERWEAR/UNDERTAKES", finally to "ZOO/ZODIAC/ZERO". (Words are also numbered as to when they appear—e.g. "sign^{57}" which doesn't do much for me, one way or the other). One overall effect of these lexical devices is that by making language and ordering devices unusually prominent (what used to be called "foregrounding") the contents of the story become in some way less prominent; or in current terms, as the signifier is made more visibly dominant, the signified tends to recede, to diminish in "significance": hence the somewhat unreal feeling to many of the stories, often entirely appropriate to their subject matter. Thus in "Access" the story, in conventional terms is trivial enough, a non-narrative really, grazing through restaurants, apartments, shops, and a few people in shifting relationships: it is much more a meditation on the word "barrier" so that the piece is organized in sections entitled "The Emotional Barrier", "The Physical Barrier", "The Acquisition Barrier", and so on.

> My fondness for the word barrier has nothing to do with it. Barriers are part of our everyday life. We are cheerful when we avoid the barriers placed in our path. I don't know the Japanese or Vietnamese word for barrier. I must admit that in the past my stubborn attachment to certain words, words that were no longer found to be appropriate, had cost me numerous well-paying commissions. Yes, one pays a price for clinging to words that have lost their significance. Still, it's a small price. I've been cutting down on meals for the sake of words.

Or, to rephrase it, I've been cutting down on conventional narrative for the sake of language. Thus the last section is entitled "The Language Barrier":

> Language is not a barrier. Language enables people in all circumstances to cope with a changing world; it also permits them to engage in all sorts of activities without unduly antagonizing everyone in their immediate vicinity. . . I'm not really concerned with langauge. As a writer I'm principally concerned with meaning. What, for instance, does being a writer mean in the context of this society. For one thing, in this society, it is almost taken for granted that a writer, irrespective of sex, irrespective of age, irrespective of political conviction, irrespective of wealth or geographic location, will use the language spoken by the majority of the people in this country. He will be using the words that fill their days and nights with unbearable tension and dread. In that respect, writers perform a vital task, they resuscitate words that are about to be obliterated by a kind of willful negligence and general boredom. Writers frequently are able to inject a fresh meaning into a word and thereby revitalize the brain cells of the reader by feeding the brain information it does not really require. For instance I have recently revitalized a couple of million brain cells by referring to barriers. Barriers appear in my writings more frequently than they deserve. It is now on its way to becoming a new word again. I feel there is a barrier between us, a man can once again tell a woman and be understood. The statement clearly is intended to have a slightly menacing effect. It is also intended to convey a threat. Shape up you bitch, or I'll sock you in the mouth.

This somewhat solemn, indeed ponderous, statement should not be taken as the writer's creed, awkwardly thrust or slipped into a so-called fiction. As the last few words indicate it is intended to be taken half-ironically, indeed it is made ironic by the text in which it appears. Nevertheless, if you go to Abish's work for a meal you will come away with a word. But then in his work the word is the meal.

One could make comparisons here with, say, William Gass on one side—high priest and *bon viveur* in "the sweet country of the word"—and Donald Barthelme on the other. But it should be made clear that Abish has his own way of deconstructing conventional narrative modes and, at the same time, getting something distinctly **said** about life, consciousness, and word, in contemporary America. And, through all his alphabetizing games, we can see that he is a very recognizable American writer. The last story in the book for instance—"Crossing the Great Void"—concerns a young boy who sets out to seek his lost (dead?) father in the North African Desert. He has abandoned everyone and everything, and even his deaf aid is failing him, promising or threatening to put him beyond all communication. He is a very familiar American figure underneath the circumstances of his particular quest and venture. The last paragraph:

> Now he is bound for the center of the desert, and every step he is taking is bringing him closer to the center, and every step he has taken in the past has led to his being here. Even before he was aware of the center's existence, he was traveling towards it. Everything he

has encountered so far appears familiar, as if at some time in the past his mother must have described it to him as she spoke of his father... Consequently he feels convinced that what lies ahead will also prove to be familiar. After all, the emptiness he expects to encounter at the center will be no different from the emptiness he might experience in the interior of his room after it had been denuded of all his possessions, stripped of all the things he had clung to with such persistence, such tenacity, such effort, as if his entire life depended on it.

From the thing replete German new-town, through New York apartments and stores, and Californian "paracinematic" (Pynchon's word) scenes and signs[57], on to the deaf child seeking his lost father in the African desert—everywhere there is emptiness, the emptiness of the meal, as it were, which Abish can only counter with a renewed repletion of the word. As if our entire life depended on it.

NEW YORK £59 SINGLE
LOS ANGELES £84 SINGLE

EVERY DAY

Laker Skytrain is the perfect way to New York or Los Angeles, with flights to each city every day.

You simply buy a ticket at the Skytrain ticket sales office at Victoria Station or Gatwick Airport on the day you wish to travel.

If that day's flight is full you can buy a ticket for a confirmed seat on the next available flight. There's no hanging about on standby — you know exactly when you are travelling.

And you travel in a wide-body DC10 jet with excellent meals, drinks, in-flight entertainment and duty free goods to buy if you wish.

Not only is Skytrain the convenient way to the USA — it is also the cheapest.

Ask your Student Travel Office for the Skytrain Service information referal voucher which gives full details.

For up tc the hour information on seat availability ring 01-828 7766.

For further information on Skytrain Scheduled Service to New York ring 01-828 8191, for Los Angeles ring 01-828 4300.

TICKET OFFICES OPEN 0630–1800 HRS DAILY.

Laker Skytrain
Trade mark AIR PASSENGER SERVICE

LAKER AIRWAYS · GATWICK AIRPORT · SURREY

MARC GRANETZ

Chuckle or Gasp:
a Note on the Work of Leonard Michaels

In the past two decades American fiction seems to have yielded more great short stories than great novels, and several of the best contemporary writers write primarily, or exclusively, short fiction. Experimentation has been massive, imaginative, and, as usual with experiments, mostly dismissible, but at least one experiment seems to have become a permanent addition to the short story form—the story of amalgamated parts, parts being paragraphs or prose sections related by theme, not by time or place. This type of story, essentially a remolding of the interior of the traditional story is effective and exciting both for the range and disparity of experiences it can encompass and also the ingenuity or force with which the disparate parts can be brought together, amalgamated. Different writers accomplish that amalgamation differently; mentioning in the same sentence Donald Barthelme's "Paraguay" and "Daumien", William Gass's "In the Heart of the Heart of the Country", and Robert Coover's "The Babysitter" and "The Magic Poker" give some idea of the possiblities. Several of Leonard Michael's recent stories ("I Would Have Saved Them If I Could", "Downers", "Eating Out") bring this experiment to perfection.

"I Would Have Saved Them If I Could" is the title story in the second of his two story collections. The phrase is taken from a passage in one of Byron's letters, quoted at length by Michaels. Lord Bryon, in Rome, had just witnessed the public execution by guillotine of three robbers. His letter concludes:

> The pain seems little, and yet the effect to the spectators and the preparation to the criminal, is very striking and chilling. The first turned to me quite hot and thirsty, and made me shake so that I could hardly hold the opera-glass (I was close, but was determined to see, as one should see every thing, once, with attention); the second and third (which shows how dreadfully soon things grow indifferent), I am ashamed to say, had no effect on me as a horror, though I would have saved them if I could.

The story is an assemblage of letters, vignettes, and bits of other fictions. Michaels quotes Byron's poem "The Prisoner of Chillon", in which the condemned Bonnivard, in an ecstatic state, transcends his mortality. He retells Borges's "The Secret Miracle", a story in which Jaromir Hladik, who is imprisoned by the Gestapo, rises into an ecstasy and thereby eludes his death. He describes Dostoevski before the firing squad, Jesus on the Cross, and even the dead woman in Wordsworth's lyric "A Slumber Did My Spirit Seal":

With rocks and stones, "she"—an intensified absence—is a presence. In the negation of negation, she is. So are Hladik, Bonnivard, and Jesus. My grandfather was a tailor in Brest Litovsk. He vanished.

The story is about metaphysics and reality, about those who could sublimate at the point of death into a different state, and about those—six million Jews—who couldn't. An anecdote opens the story; a Jewish boy has decided at the last minute to call off his bar-mitzvah because he realizes he doesn't believe in God. Closing the story are the lines, "stories, myths, ideologies, flowers, rivers, heavenly constellations are the phonemes of a mysterious logos; and the lights of our cultural memory, as upon the surface of black primeval water, flicker and slide into innumerable qualifications. But Jaromir Hladik, among substantial millions, is dead. From a certain point of view, none of this shit matters anymore". This seventeen-part story, which counterpoints the easy escapes of literature with real death inflicted by real bullets and real gas, is one of modern Jewish consciousness, though much different than Saul Bellow's Yiddish background or Philip Roth's guilt and craziness. The technique allows Michaels his academic intelligence, his cool humour, and still a valid and tremendous sense of loss.

Michaels has published book reviews, occasional pieces, and recently selections from a novel he's working on, but his reputation rests firmly on his two collections of short stories. Like Grace Paley, another wonderful writer whose reputation has been made on two story collections (and who also has had difficulty trying to write a novel), Michaels frequently employs a fictional alter-ego as narrator or protagonist; Paley's is named Faith, Michael's Phillip Liebowitz. Like Paley's, his first collection of stories is desperate, violent, stuck on the problems of love, and the second collection is funnier, more comfortable, more controlled and more powerful. After a dozen or so published stories Michaels seems to have mastered the story-telling art.

His voice is urban, lustful, intellectual, schizophrenic. City living is explored in "The Deal", a story in which Abbe Carlyle has to bargain with a neighborhood gang for the return of a glove she's dropped, and also in short pieces like "Getting Lucky", in which Liebowitz receives an anonymous hand-job on a packed subway. Nostalgia is given unusual and lively treatment in a piece called "In the Fifties". Early stories, especially "City Boy", display what Michaels believes to be the violent and fragile relationship between love and sex. "Storytellers, Liars, and Bores" is about writing stories:

I'd work at a story until it was imperative to quit and go read it aloud. My friend would listen, then say, "I feel so embarrassed for you." I'd tear up the story. I'd work at a new one until it was imperative to quit and read aloud. My new friend would listen, but wouldn't say good, no good, or not bad. I'd tear up the story.

Meanwhile, I turned to relatives and friends for help. My uncle Zev told me about his years in a concentration camp. "Write it," he said. "You'll make a million bucks." My friend Tony Icona gave me lessons in breaking and entering. Zev's stories I couldn't use. Tony's lessons were good as gold. Criminal life was intermittent and quick. It left me time to work at stories and learn about tearing them up.

The overall impression of Michaels's style is one of sophistication and polish, but often the sentences stab like splinters. Some are fragments. In others, parts of speech are scrambled for freshness. Commas replace most conjunctions; words are squeezed close: "Twenty were jammed together on the stoop; tiers of heads made one central head, and the wings rested along the banisters: a raggedy monster of boys studying her approach." Sentences pivot on a central, metaphorical comma: "The room was full of light, difficult as a headache." His style can be breathless, filled with quick jokes, and still realistic:

> My mother was taking me to the movies. We were walking fast. I didn't know what movie it would be. Neither did my mother. She couldn't read. We were defenseless people. I was ten years old. My mother was five foot nothing. We walked with fast little steps, hands in our pockets, faces down. The school week had ended. I was five days closer to the M.D. My reward for good grades was a movie—black, brilliant pleasure.

But often—and the following passage is taken from the same story—the style achieves something more, something quite important:

> During actual basketball games I also played basketball. I played games within games. When I lost my virginity I eluded my opponent and sank a running hook. Masses saw it happen. I lost my virginity and my girl lost hers. The game had been won. I pulled up my trousers She snapped her garter belt. I took a jump shot from the corner and and another game was underway. I scored in a blind drive from the foul line. We kissed good night. The effect was epileptic. Masses thrashed in their seats, loud holes in their faces. I acknowledged with an automatic nod and hurried down the street, dribbling.

The final *double entendre* testifies to the wholeness of these two visions yoked together. Through the use of puns, witty transitions and linkage by free association the precise, staccato style becomes electrified with meanings, almost phantasmagoric. It is too early to venture any assessment of the body of Michaels's work, but his style, which captures and intensifies all the force and colour of an identifiable personal experience, is a unique and significant contribution to the art. The best writers are known by their voices; Michaels's voice is perfectly worked. Soon we will be treated to a novel; it will be interesting to see what adjustments will be made to a style whose intensity and febricity suit it so well—possibly exclusively?—to short fiction. One thing we don't have to worry will change is the humour—ironic, childish, wild, worldly—which is capable of making us chuckle or gasp, and capable also of giving us wisdom about contemporary life and art: "it is impossible to live with or without fiction".

NORMAN BRYSON

Orgy, hors-je, hors-jeu:

a Note on the Work of James Purdy

Reviews can be a little like antibodies. There appears, somewhere in the language-organism, an entity of unfamiliar contour and unknown purpose: it may be hostile. At once a cluster of lesser language-particles rush to the site of intrusion, to surround, cordon off, and probe the mysterious molestation of the discourse. After deliberation they agree to disperse and to circulate their findings to the awaiting organism, but what they got up to in their secret huddle, and what they saw, no-one ever discovers, since the news they distribute is always the same and always good: no danger. And by the time they have finished their work most invaders are harmless enough, indeed rather familiar-looking creatures.

I think that Purdy's novel *is* hostile and to convey my sense of its threat I am going to lay aside the usual tools of containment as inadequate: tools that include " Where *In a Shallow Grave* fits the pattern of Purdy's *Malcolm* (1959) and *Cabot Wright Begins* (1965)", "Where its interests coincide with those of the class, contemporary American fiction", and the special kit of sharp-edged probes that begins with the words *deconstruction, entropy, literarity, paranoia.* The particular menace of this novel is that it knows about the emergency kit, as the sophisticated virus knows about penicillin. The forms familiar to the antibody—like the Pynchon-strain, deadly to critics—are the very ones it mimics. Rudimentary example: every novel knows that its plot is likely to be summarised, not only by the review, but by the reader using plot as a basic instrument of containment. Where Pynchon blocks summary by impossible excess (*V, Gravity's Rainbow*), Purdy actively solicits readerly focus on a plot in which he simulates a diegetic orderliness, classically familiar as a variant on a known figure: the ambiguous and irresistible outsider who suddenly appears in a stable community, obsesses and transforms it, and as suddenly disappears (Evangelists, *Wuthering Heights*, Pasolini's *Tearama*). Daventry, a young boy who seems to embody some sort of rare beauty, a "spring zephyr", almost literally materialises outside a homestead in Virginia. He claims to be on the run for murder, though this information—all he supplies about his past—may be unreliable. He is taken in by one Garnet Montrose, veteran of the American war in Indo-China, and sole survivor of a massacre which has left him hideously disfigured. Garnet is looking for someone to watch over him and attend in particular to two tasks the text establishes as interrelated: when Garnet is seized by the strange rigor or fit of coldness which periodically strikes him, to rub his feet and "the area above his heart"; and to deliver love-letters to a woman known as the Widow Rance, centre of Garnet's erotic and necessarily hopeless imaginings (the first reaction of most people who clap eyes on Garnet is to vomit). Daventry, whose glance is angelically mild, tolerates Garnet's monstrosity ("all my veins and arteries have moved from the inside where they belong to the outside"): at the onset of rigor he rubs and warms Garnet back to life, and he acts as messenger. By another classically familiar narrative figure (*The Mayor of Casterbridge*, Maugham/Losey's *The Servant*, Bergman's *Persona*), the roles of dependence/power invert, and Daventry comes gradually to possess everything that is Garnet's: first his sexual self-expression, by taking over the task of writing the lover-letters to the Widow Rance, dictating them aloud while Garnet transcribes his words; then Garnet's "secret" the one thing Garnet believes no one knows about him, namely that on certain nights he steals or lopes away from the house to a deserted, tumble-down dance hall, where until dawn he dances alone to imaginary music; and then Garnet's beloved, the Widow herself, who, overcome by Daventry's beauty forces him to make love to her, after an elaborate foreplay in which Daventry must submit to having his skin kissed all over (skin, and the cognate ideas of integument and boundary, come to be crucial in the book's lyrical structure). Garnet is about to lose indeed everything when, by a deliberately improbable and virtually disowned plot-motive, he is threatened with dispossession of his property. Daventry, who has by this time announced that Garnet is the one thing in this world he loves, offers to save the estate, but warns that "he may never be the same again". A hurricane strikes the house, and at the height of the storm Daventry calls for a knife and removes his shirt; and slashes himself and catches the blood in a receptacle from which he forces Garnet to drink; the hurricane subsequently dies down, the estate is mysteriously saved from confiscation, and Daventry disappears. In the aftermath of the storm Garnet's disfigurements begin to heal. Daventry is found to be living with the Widow Rance, until a second hurricane strikes, carries him off, and dashes him against a tree.

Besides this bare account of the book's violent and mysterious plot, I want to mention certain details which, as the novel develops, come to establish a synchronic lyrical order that at times all but displaces the diachronic narrative order just outlined. Garnet frequently describes his disfigurement as a condition where his "insides" have become "outsides", where private and inward spaces have become public and exterior surfaces. Within this context, the long and painful act of self-revelation which constitutes his diary, that is this novel, is an attempt to overcome that inversion by establishing a place, the place of the text, where the display of inwardness is no longer an unwilled mutilation but a willed expression and creation. If the destructive tearings of the world have turned him inside out, like a glove, the restorations of the word promise a return to a normal alignment of outer and inner zones. Now, Garnet's condition is symmetrically balanced by that of Daventry: where Garnet has "no skin", Daventry is "all skin", a creature who seems to exist exclusively as integument. After his blank and beautiful eyes, it is the unusual clarity of his complexion that is remarkable, not only to the avid Widow Rance, but to Garnet himself, who enters his homoerotic love for Daventry through contact by friction (where the healing rubbing of feet and "the area above his heart" function, by transposition, as erotic metaphor). Garnet has only the bones left from his old, pre-massacre body, from the time before the "explosion" (or implosion, from Garnet's point of view): one of his sadder rituals is to examine his bone-structure in a mirror by candlelight. Though his appearance is hideous, the intactness of bone gives Garnet a gravity and groundedness that Daventry lacks. A fairly stressed lyrical pattern connects "Garnet" via "semi-precious stone" to "granite", and Daventry makes Garnet's chthonic status clear by calling him "the underground river of life ". By contrast with this rock-like stability, Daventry himself is weightless: he may be a "spring zephyr", but he is also terrified by the sound of the wind, and it is the force of the wind which brings about his death. The other cluster of details concerns fluid: since the explosion implosion Garnet has lost the use of his "lachrymal glands"—"if I start to weep I feel a great pain in these said glands, like there were sharp rocks or millstones being drawn through raw nerves". And since the same event, Garnet's skin—hardly skin, since his whole body is an open wound or, to use his own word, an "abortion"—has been "the color of mulberry juice", where that fluid is connected with death ("mulberry night") and with his own identity (Garnet Mont*rose*, combining the dark and light aspects of red: blood and flesh). After the violent scene where Daventry slashes his veins, Garnet recovers the use of his atrophied glands, and his wounds slowly cicatrise. The connections between these lyrical patterns, of outer/inner and of blood/semen/tears begin to move towards a sexuality of penetration/being penetrated, but before examining that connection in more detail, and its place within a homoerotic discourse, some comments on the interpenetrating discourses of the text. At this point it is enough to observe that between them, Garnet and Daventry would compose a whole body, that the recognition of desire in this text is always accompanied by an awareness of mutilation, and that despite the highly polarised structure of the book's lyricism, the utopian body the text alludes to by covert hints and feints is one where the fact of difference is denied by a vision of bodily holism.

Summary of the plot makes the novel sound much more bizarre and disconnected than it is because (the reader must at this point take the antibody's word for it) the voice which narrates the text is one of such placid continuities and comforting pleasantries: a kind of Nelly Dean effect. Emergent lyrical patterns and allegorical transformations are kept at a distance from the text itself by a refusal on the part of this voice to attend to the implications of its own *recit*. The narrating voice speaks in heavy sociolect, a sort of lazy Virginian drawl which would be totally reassuring, as Nelly Dean's Yorkshire would be reassuring, if it were not so blind to the irrationality of what is in fact going on. Speaking the language of a social group, it altogether avoids idiolect, where the use of idiolect would assume a personalised speaker, from whom individual reactions would be expected. The stress on sociolect (and Purdy's Virginian is about as convincing, and at the same time unconvincing, as Emily Bronte's Yorkshire) naturalises this refusal by the *recit* to examine its own statements: dialect as alibi. Pretty soon the reader comes to view this easy, self-styled voice-of-sanity with suspicion, because at the level of the plot there is such divergence from and contradiction of the stable vocal line. The intimate, mesmerising drawl progressively assumes the guise of a malfunctioning rationality, indeed of a principle of crazy coherence committed to the production of an endless surface of continuities at all costs. I'm going to jump a few steps and characterise this register of the discourse as "isolated syntagm". The syntagmatic aspect of language is that which arranges the words of the language in sequential order, by means of the linear and recursive rules known as grammar; as opposed to the paradigmatic aspect, which concerns the selection of words from the lexicon and their interrelationships in patterns other than those of grammatical sequence (crude example, the "image pattern"). The voice which narrates *In a Shallow Grave* is blind to all forms of patterning except those of the syntagm; a blindness which drives the reader to compensate for the deficiency by eager, catalysed attention to paradigm.

Now, the paradigm is usually the critics's, or antibody's, kingdom. In a myth of writing which it is part of this novel's importance to name and challenge, the patterns of paradigm discovered by the act of reading are alleged to occur *behind the text's back*, in the same way that the lapses of the analysand's *recit* are thought of as occurring without his knowledge, through pressure on and deformation of his speech by that-which-the-subject-cannot-say (the unconscious). The paradigmatic structures that reading reveals are the text's "unconscious", and the reader who attends to those structures can establish his central elitist claim of knowing more than the text does; at the same time that he restores a semantic field broken between an area that is acknowledged and an area that is unacknowleged, into a unity surveyed as a whole from an elevated, panoptic site of the all-seeing I. Purdy upsets this satisfying myth (satisfying, among other reasons, as permission for the establishment of an industry of criticism) by presenting the syntagmatic order as already discredited and overpowered. The *writing* is obviously not occurring in the syntagm, which means that the terrain of paradigm, normally the critic's virgin territory, has been pre-ordained: the patterns of paradigm area already staked out and claimed.

The apparent orderliness of the novel as *recit* (by which I don't mean its content, but its form: its sequentiality of episode, its status as the familiar literary form of diary, its reference to known or classic narrative figures) is already challenged from within the writing by repeated acts of direct quotation from other texts. The novel historically possesses a convention which permits extensive quotation from voices other than the voice of the narrator, without threat to its narrative authority: dialogue. The supportive conventions of indentation and quotation-marks ensure that we know how to take these other voices that weave into the writing: they are contained and contextualised, they derive their meaning from the controls governing "the main text". Garnet, to pass away his lonely hours, is in the habit of reading passages at random from the books in his library, and Purdy is in the habit of transcribing those passages verbatim. But the voice of the main text, Garnet's, is one we cannot trust: the inset passages thereby lack the firm contextual over-ride of an authoritative discourse. What's more, the problem with the narrator, with Garnet, is precisely the absence of interruption in his stream of continuities: he never hesitates, loses his thread or tone, he never permits fissure or fracture in the resolute or compulsive sanity of his speech. The reader, intensifying his paradigmatic scansion to compensate for this, comes upon the inserted and quoted passages like the bird upon the worm. And Purdy makes sure that the passages inset into the text are *suggestive*, that is, diplomatically placed at sufficient proximity to the "main text" to ask for elision with it, yet sufficiently distant from it to allow the reader/antibody the pleasure of feeling he is creating a pattern behind Purdy's back. But there isn't much pleasure to come across, in the middle of a crucial exchange between Garent and Daventry, *this* quotation:

MAN AS GLYPH

Man is little more than a glyph which punctuates space, but once gone is as unrecollectable as smoke or clouds.

The text from which this is allegedly taken is called *Guide to Phrenology*, harmless enough, until one recognises that phrenology is the (discredited) science to finding meanings in the human body; which is exactly what we are asked to do with the bodies of Daventry and Garnet. To make sure no reader/antibody misses the point, Purdy makes Daventry burst into tears on hearing the passage read aloud. When asked to account for his reaction and to explain what he takes a glyph to be, Daventry makes this reply:" 'a glyph', he said, through his choking grief, 'a glyph, Garnet, must mean judging by the context of the sentence you have your finger on, a sign standing for something else' ". On one level the implications of this are clear: Daventry, whose physical beauty catalyses the projections of others, who is the blank screen or white skin on to which others project their fantasies of redemption and salvation, recognises in the word "glyph" his mark of doom. It is his fate to be forced into situations and contexts where he is "read" by others (principally by Garnet, but also by the Widow Rance, and the mysterious attackers he claims to have killed because they decided there was something about him they couldn't tolerate) as "standing for something else"; he is "smoke or clouds", lacking in Garnet's skeletal weight and resistance, and once the winds have swept him away Garnet will find him "unrecollectable". That's the obvious recuperation, but the point is that the quotation is itself one in a whole series of quoted "glyphs"—there must be at least be a dozen of them, in a short work—signs "standing for something else"; Purdy makes the reader/antibody *see* that this is what the other interruptions of the text have been, and makes it clear to him that he *knows* an interpreter is about, behind his back. And if he, Purdy, pretends not to see him, it's time for that antibody/reader to watch out.

In classical texts for classically trained readers, the province of paradigmatic pattern-making is instituted as the level of the text's truth and the reader's discovery of that truth. Purdy would seem to be just a rather irritatingly sophisticated text-producer, colonising what rightly belongs to us, if he didn't then raise the complexity of the game by creating an *inadequate paradigm*. Just as it would take someone pretty dull in the head not to see the characters of the Crucifixion standing behind the characters in *Parsifal*, it takes wilful blindness, like Garnet's, not to see the myth behind Daventry. His name, combining "entry" and "future", joins a deliberate pattern established by such words as "angle", "death", "celestial", "sky-blue", "messenger", to ensure *we* take him, even if Garnet won't, as a spiritual agent: he doesn't even die on the ground, he's spirited away, like Oedipus or Enoch. And when someone indulges in a eucharistic ritual which actually *works*, we're supposed to know where we stand. Purdy, as *In a Shallow Grave* draws to a close, gets the reader/antibody into a tightening net. The scene where Daventry takes off his shirt, slashes his skin, gets the blood to spurt into tin cups, and forces Garnet not only to drink it but not to vomit, to *digest* it, allows to the reader a gamut of all of two possibilities. Either to accept the scene as non-symbolic within the text (whatever it may tell us about symbolism within the psychology of sadism), to take it as *real*; or to take it as conforming to a symbolic pattern the text at some level agrees with. Either way, the reader is likely to refuse his predestined hermeneutic role (as he is supposed to). Viewed as a "real" event, Daventry's bloodletting is truly sickening; not only because it's possible (if you can persaude a thousand people to drink cyanide Koolaid, this one is tame), but because it wilfully destroys Purdy's subtle lyricism. Purdy is a writer of great delicacy, and all the time he respects the reader's perception of nuance; some of his effects are, to use an insufficient term meant only to indicate my genuine wonderment, magical—see, for example, the opening section of his *Narrow Rooms*. The bloodletting in *Shallow Grave* is brutal, a Peckinpah sequence inset into a Bresson film. You recoil from it into symbolism, but the "symbolism" is equally unacceptable: Daventry as a Redeemer, as sacrificial victim whose flesh is sacred, comes from a pattern only Garnet, possibly, is going to find valid. Where's an antibody to go next?

I can perhaps recapitulate the foregoing section by referring to "discursive registers", taking that word in the sense, "this organ has three registers". On the first register, all is syntagm, continuity, sanity, order, but only as a kind of aphasic disturbance in which the speaker loses the use and awareness of paradigm. Actually, the novel renounces this alibi-discourse long before its close. Garnet is rich, and can ward off the threat of his estate's dispossesion at a stroke of the pen on the cheque-book. That the text and the people within the text decide to resolve the problem at a mythical level indicates that the narrator's sane orderings and placed rationalisations have been surpassed by the text itself: that the novel actually allows the bloodletting to be magically efficacious (the storm dies down, the threat of expropriation is annulled, Garnet's wounds begins to heal) indicates that it has dropped down from that first, asymbolic register to a second level one might call "lyrical". Even before the plot itself exits from rationality, the reader's attention is likely to be working at this second register already, simply because Purdy's inset quotations have come to act as an intriguing inner text, all the more seductive because the first register's sanities seem so misplaced: when the plot renounces rationality and descends into the lyrical register, that declension is both a satisfying authorial signpost (confirming that the reader was right in moving his attention from the superficial main text towards an esoteric core); and a disturbing authorial intrusion (because it establishes the pardigmatic or esoteric core as pre-ordained by Purdy, as his terrain before it is ours). In this second register, the paradigm rushes in, establishing patterns behind Garnet's back whereby Daventry is Saviour/Eucharist/Archangel; just as in his earlier novel, *The Nephew* (1960) Purdy had established his main characters Alma and Boyd, by crude pun, as Soul and Body. Daventry is *pneuma*, spirit, Beauty, Redeemer, where Garnet is *hyle*, unformed matter or chthonic substratum ("the underground river of life"), Beast, Redeemed. *Purdy's skill lies in knowing how to anticipate the antibody's pathetic recuperations.* The lurking paradigm is established as so pre-empted, and at the same time as so useless (what is the point of reading a novel whose characters turn out to be terms in some obscure gnostic theology?), that we rush to remote corners of the text for other, pacifying reconstructions which will permit the reader/antibody to continue to function as vanquisher of the text's unconscious. We shift downwards once more, from the lyrical second register, with its diagrammatic neatness and hygienic binarism, towards a tentative third register the text seems reluctant or unable to articulate openly.

Purdy's work has often assumed as model of sexuality a homoerotic encounter of complementary masculinities. To the straight liberal reader, no problem: what he says in terms of the homoerotic relationship can be transposed to a heterosexual discourse with no more difficulty than is involved in seeing the word "lover" as both a masculine and a feminine noun. But Purdy's work raises the problem of the *nature* of a homoerotic discourse. The fact remains that there *is* no homoerotic literature; even more visibly than the related fact that there is no feminist literature. To feminists the latter absence is accountable as a necessary effect of a consolidation of institutional power in the male. The existence of Proust's Albertine or Forster's *Maurice* challenges that assumption: even within the male bastion of literature as Insitution, there must be ruse, hiding, and transposition, whenever the official gender-model is challenged. There seem to be two approaches to the problem: social, lingusitc. Socially, the repression of a homoerotic discourse has been intense: Forster's career here is exemplary. But what is the nature of a discourse based on *sameness*, within a discourse rooted in *difference*? Less generally, what is the nature of a homoerotic discourse within a governing discourse that denies its existence?

Purdy's novel indicates a possible answer to the second question: silence, secrecy, stealth. The bond between Garnet and Daventry is one of sameness, where both the exoteric and the esoteric structures of the text insist on the play of difference. In the novel's "first register", Daventry is Garnet's *negative*: where Garnet is impaired, in vocative intimacy with the reader, and the incarnation of the hideous, Daventry is potent, both unknown and unknowable to the reader, and incarnation of the beautiful. In its "second register", the characters remain polarised: Daventry is Spirit, Divinity, Saviour, Beauty, where Garnet is Body, Matter, Saved, Beast. In both registers, the structures of meaning are called into being by the crucial device—the figure Barthes claims as the master-trope of Western discourse—of Antithesis. Yet, following at any rate this antibody's reading, neither register is adequate to the text: penultimately the reader finds himself forced to choose between an asymbolic narrative of sadism and brutality and a lyrical, imginary order of equally unacceptable reductiveness. Purdy's entrapment forces the antibody to attend to those paradigmatic patternings that remain as residue after the lyrical or mythical restructurings of the narrative have been rejected. Here, the antibody searches in remote niches for possibly polarisable features: I am reminded of Levi-Strauss' more desperate searches for the figure of antithesis in his four-volume analysis of American Indian myth. Thus Garnet wears his insides outside, where Daventry is a binding force of integument; Garnet *incorporates* Daventry by drinking his blood, Daventry incorporates Garnet by possessing his secret, his "beloved", his estate; Garnet *penetrates* Daventry by forcing the Glyph, the featureless projective surface, to accept his contextual definition, and by placing Daventry in a situation where he commands him to slash himself ("Garnet, please please don't") and thereby make his "insides", "outsides"; Daventry penetrates Garnet by proxy (my making love to the Widow Rance, Garnet's possession, a surrogate Garnet) and in actual fact, by forcing his blood into Garnet's system. The figure is still antithesis, but is is antithesis that works by denying the antithesis of gender, for both Daventry and Garnet are simultaneously the penetrator and the pentrated. In penetration it can be said that outer/inner are precisely denied, but in the governing discourse this denial is itself denied by seeing both sides of "the penetration" in terms of an immutable structure of gender. Purdy's text establishes sexual fusion as a function of sameness, not difference. The two official registers, ruled by antithesis, seek to produce and to perpetuate meanings by the device of relentless opposition, but in a dim, elusive, clandestine third register, which is loyal to the somatic and disloyal to the discursive, the figure of antithesis is exactly denies as a vision of the erotic body announces itself that goes beyond the instituted, culturally policed *apartheid* of gender.

This third level exists as violation of the law of antithesis and its emergence is accompanied by violence, the violence of skin opened and fluids exchanged, in a text where each register is established through a moment of *carnage*: the "main text" set in motion by the Vietnam explosion/implosion that permits and demands the realignment of outer and inner through an acof self-expression (The diary, the voice that speaks the text); the lyrical order, taking full possession of the text at a moment when the text's world is disrupted by hurricane; and the somatic order, inaugurated in bloodshed, and abandoning the reductive antitheses of myth for an unstated bodily arena outside the law of opposition and difference, outside the speakable languages of the text, known only by implication and guile, by reading and writing between the lines between the lines: a principle of the orgiastic, where eros under the sign of the same overturns logos under the sign of difference, where what is to be represented is outside the play of differences, and where the identity of the subject is lost in elision of outside and inside, self and not-self, blood and skin.

LEONARD MICHAELS

The Men's Club

Women wanted to talk about anger, identity, politics, etc. I saw posters in Berkeley urging them to join groups. I saw their leaders on TV. Strong, articulate faces. So when Cavanaugh phoned and invited me to join a men's club, I laughed. Slowly, not laughing, he repeated himself. He was six foot nine. The size and weight entered his voice. He and some friends wanted a club. "A regular social possibility outside our jobs and marriages. Nothing to do with women's groups." One man was a tax accountant, another was a lawyer. There was also a college teacher like me and two psychotherapists. Solid types. I supposed there could be virtues in a men's club, a regular social possibility. I should have said yes immediately, but something in me resisted. The prospect of leaving my house after dinner. Blood is heavy then. Brain is slow. Besides, wasn't this club idea corny? Like trying to recapture high school days. Locker room fun. Wet naked boys snapping towels at each other's genitals. It didn't feel exactly right. To be wretchedly truthful, any social possibility unrelated to wife, kids, house, and work felt like a form of adultery. Not criminal. Not legitimate.

"Cavanaugh, I don't even go to the movies anymore."

"I'm talking about a men's club. Good company. You talk about women's groups. Movies. Can't you hear me?"

"When the phone rings it's like an attack on my life. I get confused. Say it again."

"Look, you're one of my best friends. You live less than a mile away. Do we see each other three times a year?"

"I lose over a month every year just working to pay property taxes. Friendship is a luxury. Unless you're so poor it makes no difference how you spend your time."

"A men's club. Good company."

"I hear you."

But I was thinking about good company. Some of my married colleagues have love affairs, usually with students. You could call it a regular social possibility. It included emotion chaos. Gonorrhea. Even guilt. They would have been better off in a men's club.

"What do you say? Can we expect you?"

"I'll go to the first meeting. I can't promise more. I'm very busy."

"Yeah, yeah," said Cavanaugh and gave me an address in the Berkeley flats.

The night of the meeting I told my wife I'd be home before midnight. She said, "Take out the garbage." Big sticky bag felt unpropitious and my hands soon smelled of tuna fish. After driving five minutes I found the place. The front of the house, vine covered, seemed to brood in lunatic privacy. Nobody answered when I knocked, but I heard voices, took hold of a wrought iron handle and pushed, discovering a large Berkeley living room and six men I saw dark wood paneling and potted ferns dangling from exposed beams. Other plants along the window ledges. A potted tree in a far corner, skinny, spinsterish looking. Nervous yellow leaves filled its head. Various ceramics, bowls on tabletops and plates on the walls beside huge acrylic paintings, abstractions like glistening viscera splashed off a butcher block. There was an amazing rug, but I coudn't take it in. A man was rising from a pillow on the floor, coming toward me, smiling.

"I knocked," I said.

"Come in, man. I'm Harry Kramer."

"I'm Cavanaugh's friend."

"Who isn't?"

"Really," I said, giving it the L.A. inflection to suggest sympathetic understanding, not wonder. Kramer registered the nuance and glanced at me as at a potential brother. His heavy black hair was controlled by a style, parted in the middle, shaped to cup his ears with a feeling that once belonged to little girls and now was common among TV actors and rock musicians. It was contradicted by black force in his eyes, handshake like a bite, and tatooed forearms. Blue winged snake. Blue dagger amid roses. They spoke for an earlier life, I supposed, but Kramer wore his sleeves rolled to the elbow. It was impossible to connect him with his rug, which I began to appreciate as spongy and sensuous. Orange. I felt myself wading through it as Kramer led me toward the men.

Shaking hands, nodding hello, saying my name, each man was a complex flash—eyes, hand, names—but one had definition. Solly Berliner. Tall. Wearing a suit. Dead white hair and big greenish light in his eyes. The face of an infant surprised by senility. His suit was gray polyester, conservative and sleazy. Kramer left me with Berliner beside the potted tree, a beer in my hand. A man about five foot six with an eager face came right up to us. "Care for a taste?" In his palm lay two brown marijuanas, slick with spittle. I declined. Berliner said, "Thanks, thanks", with frightening gratitude and took both cigarettes. We laughed as the dropped one back into the man's palm. The little face turned toward the other men. "Anybody care for a taste?"

The sound of Berliner's voice lingered after the joke. Maybe he felt uneasy. Out of his natural environment. I couldn't guess where that might be. He was a confusion of clues. The suit wasn't Berkeley. The eyes were worlds of feeling. His speedy voice flew from nerves. Maybe the living room affected him. A men's club would have been more authentic, more properly convened, elsewhere. What did I have in mind? A cold ditch? I supposed Kramer's wife, exiled for the evening, had cultivated the plants and picked the orange rug and the luscious fabrics on the couches and chairs. Ideas of happiness. Berliner and I remained standing as if the fabrics—heavy velvets, beige tones—were nothing to violate with our behinds. It was a woman's room, but the point of the club was to be with men, not to escape from women, so I turned to Berliner and asked what he did for a living.

"Real estate," he said, grinning ferociously, as if extreme types were into that. Wild fellows. "I drove in from San Jose." He spoke with rapid little shrugs, as if readjusting his vertebrae. His eyes were full of green distance after two drags on the cigarette. He was already driving back to San Jose, I figured, but then he said, "Forgive me for saying this, but, a minute ago when Kramer introduced us, I had a weird thought." His eyes returned.

"You did?"

I'd seen the look before. It signalled the California plunge into truth, a conversational style developed in encounter groups where sensitivity training occurs.

"I hope this doesn't bother you. But I thought you had a withered leg."

"You did?"

"I see you don't. Weird?" He giggled. His mouth was tense.

"Weird that I don't have a withered leg?"

"I thought your leg was all screwed up. Like withered."

I wiggled my legs. For my sake, not his. He stared as if into unusual depths, waiting for a truth to rise, perhaps leap into the air like a fish. I said nothing. He said, "I'm forty-seven."

"You look much younger." This was true. But, with the white hair, he also looked older.

"I stay in shape," he answered, marijuana smoke leaking from his nostrils. "Nobody," he said, sucking the leak back with crackling sheets of snot, "nobody else in the room is forty-seven. I'm oldest. I asked the guys."

He gagged a little, then released the smoke, knifing it through compressed lips. "Kramer is thirty-eight." I wondered if conversation had ever been more like medical experience, so rich in gas and mucous. "I'm always the oldest. Ever since I was a kid I was the oldest." He giggled and intensified his stare. I giggled, too, in a social way. Then the door opened and Cavanaugh walked in.

"Excuse me," I said, intimating regret but moving quickly away to greet Cavanaugh.

Cavanaugh, big and good looking, had heroic charisma. He'd once been a professional basketball player. Now he worked at the university in special undergraduate programs, matters of policy and funding. Nine to five, jacket and tie. To remember his former work—the great naked shoulders and legs flying through the air—was saddening. In restaurants and airports people still asked for his autograph.

Things felt better, more natural, healthier, with the big man in the room. Kramer reached him before I did. They slapped each other's arms, laughing, pleased at how they felt to each other. Solid. Real. I watched, thinking I'd often watched Cavanaugh. Ever since college, in fact, when he'd become famous. To see him burn his opponent and score was like a miracle of justice. Now, in civilian clothes, he was faintly disorienting. Especially his wristwatch, a golden, complicated band. A symbolic manacle. Cavanaugh's submission to ordinary life. He'd once said, "I don't want my kids to grow up like me, necks thick as their heads." He wanted his kids in jackets and wristwatches.

He'd stopped slapping Kramer's arms, but Kramer continued touching him. Kramer looked as though he might soon pee in his pants. People love athletics. Where else these days do they see such mythic drama? Images of unimpeachable excellence. I was infected by Kramer's enthusiasm. When Kramer left to get Cavanaugh a beer, we shook hands. He said, "I didn't think I'd see you tonight." There was mockery in his smile.

"It's not so easy getting out of the house. Nobody but you could have dragged me to this."

"You open the door, you're out."

"Tell me about it."

"I'm glad you're here. Anything happen yet? I'm late because Sarah thinks the club idea is wrong. I'm wrong to be here. We argued a little at dinner." He whispered then, "Maybe it isn't easy," and looked at his wristwatch, frowning, as if it were his mind. Kramer returned with the beer just as a phone started ringing.

"I'll be right back," said Kramer, turning toward the ringing.

Sarah's word "wrong" made me wonder. If something was wrong with Cavanaugh, it was wrong with the universe. Men could understand that. When Cavanaugh needed a loan to buy his house, the bank gave him no problem. You could see his credit was good; he was six foot nine and could run a hundred yards in ten seconds. The loan officer, a man, recognized Cavanaugh and felt privileged to help him with financial negotiations. He didn't ask about Cavanaugh's recent divorce, his alimony payments.

Men's clubs. Women's groups. They suggest incurable disorders. I remembered Socrates—how the boys, not his wife, adored him. And Karl Marx running around with Engels while Jenny stayed home with the kids. Maybe men played more than women. A men's club, compared to women's groups, was play. Frivolous; virtually insulting. It excluded women. But I was thinking in circles. A men's club didn't exclude women. It also didn't exclude kangaroos. It included only men. I tried to imagine explaining this to Sarah. "You see, men love to play." It didn't feel convincing. She had strong opinions and a bad temper. When Cavanaugh decided to quit basketball, it was his decision, but I blamed her anyway. She wanted him home. The king became the dean.

Kramer shouted from another room, "Is anybody here named Terry? His wife is on the phone. She's crying." Shouting again, more loudly, as if to make sure the woman on the phone would hear him, Kramer said, "Is anybody in this house named Terry?"

Nobody admitted to being named Terry. I heard Kramer, still shouting, say, "Terry isn't here. If Terry shows up, I'll tell him to phone you right away. No, I won't forget. I'll tell Terry to phone you right away."

When Kramer returned he said, "You guys sure none of you is named Terry?"

Cavanaugh muttered, "We're all named Terry."

We made a circle, some men sitting on the rug. Kramer settled into his pillow, legs folded and crossed. He began talking to us in a slow rational voice. The black eyes darkened his face. His words became darker, heavier, because of them.

"What is the purpose of this club?"

To make women cry, I thought. Kramer's beginning was not very brilliant, but he looked so deep that I resisted judgement.

"Some of us—Solly Berliner, Paul, Cavanaugh—had a discussion a few weeks ago. We agreed it would be a good idea. . . " Paul was the short, marijuana man with the eager face. Kramer nodded to him when he said his name. He went on about the good idea, but I wasn't listening.

I thought again about the women. Anger, identity, politics, rights, wrongs. I envied them. It seemed attractive to be deprived in our society. Deprivation gives you something to fight for, it makes you morally superior, it makes you serious. What was left for men these days? They already had everything. Did they need clubs? The mere sight of two men together suggests a club. Consider Damon and Pythias, Huck and Jim, Hamlet and Horatio. The list is familiar. Even the Lone Ranger wasn't lonely. He had Tonto. There is Gertrude Stein and Alice B. Toklas, but generally, two women suggest gossip and a kiss goodbye. Kramer, talking, meandered in a sea of nonexistent purpose. I said, "Why are you talking about our purpose? We're all here. Let's just say what we want to do." I'd stopped him mid-meander. He looked relieved—a little surprised, not offended. "Can you offer a suggestion?" he asked.

I glanced at the other faces, particularly Cavanaugh's. I didn't want to embarrass him. I was his guest and I'd been to aggressive maybe. He said, "Go on."

"I suggest each of us tell the story of his life."

The instant I said it I laughed, as if I'd intended a joke. What else could it be? I didn't tell the story of my life to strangers. Maybe I'd lived too long in California, or I'd given too many lectures at the University. Perhaps I'd been influenced by Berliner, becoming like him, a confessional person. Nobody else laughed. Cavanaugh looked at me with approval. Berliner grinned, his rigid ferocity. He loved the suggestion. He could hardly wait to begin. Kramer, however, said, "I'll go first."

"You want to? You do like the idea?"

"One of us can talk at each meeting. I have listened in this room to numerous life-stories." Kramer, apparently, was a psychotherapist.

"It will be good for me," he said, "to tell the story of my life, especially in a nonprofessional context. It will be a challenge. I'm going to put it on tape. I will tape each of us."

Suddenly I imagined him sitting among his plants listening to life-stories, his tape recorder going, his dark face and tatoos presiding over everything.

"Oh, come on. Let's talk to one another, Kramer. No machines."

To my dismay, Kramer yelled, "Why the hell not? I have so much talk on my tapes—friends, clients, lovers—that I don't even know what I have. So much I don't even remember."

Apparently, I'd struck at something he cherished. I didn't know him well enough to do that, but I heard myself yelling back at him, a man who looked angry, even dangerous, "If you didn't put it on tape, you'd remember."

Everyone laughed, including Kramer. He said, "That's good, that's good." No anger at all. I was strangely pleased by this violence. I liked Kramer for laughing.

"That's good," he said. "I'm going to write that down."

"Yeah," said Cavanaugh, "no tape recorder. But I want an idea of what this life-story business is like."

Berliner said, "You know what it's like, Cavanaugh. It's like in the old movies. Lauren Bacall tells Humphrey Bogart about herself. Who she is. Where she's been. Then they screw."

A blond man with plastic-framed glasses and a pastel-blue sweater strained forward in his chair, saying, "I saw that movie on *The Late Show,* right?" He looked youthful, exceptionally clean. He wore cherry-red jogging shoes.

The faces became silent. He retreated. "Maybe it was another movie."

Berliner's face seemed to swell with astonishment, then tighten into eery screeing, tortured noises, screeing, screeing. "Oh man what is your name?" He pointed at the blond, Kramer, hugging himself, contained his laughter. The blond said, "Harold." Tears, like bits of glass, formed in his eyes as he smiled.

"Oh Harold," shouted Berliner, "the name is the whole story of my life. My mother used to say, 'Solly Berliner, why can't you be like Harold.' Harold Himmel was the smartest, nicest kid in Brooklyn."

"My name is Harold Canterbury."

"Right, man, Forgive me. A minute ago when you were talking I had a weird thought. I thought—forgive me, man—you had a withered hand."

Harold raised his hands for everyone to see.

Kramer said, "Don't listen to that jackass, Harold. Nothing wrong with your hands. I'm getting more beer."

As he walked toward the kitchen, Cavanaugh followed, saying, "I don't know what this life-story business is about, but it sounds good." Kramer said, "I'll show you what it's about. You get the beers." Cavanaugh returned with the beers and Kramer with a metal footlocker, dragging it into the center of our circle. A padlock banged against the front. Kramer, squatting, tried to fit a key into the lock. His hands began shaking. Cavanaugh bent beside him. "You need a little help?" Kramer handed him the key, saying, "Do it."

Cavanaugh inserted the key and the lock snapped open as if shocked by love.

Kramer removed the lock, heaved back the lid of the footlocker, then withdrew to his pillow, quickly lighting a cigarette, his hands still shaking, "This is it, my life-story." His voice, slower than before, labored against feeling. "You guys can see my junk, my trinkets. Photos, diaries, papers of every kind." Had Kramer left the room it would have been easier to look, but he remained on his pillow, a dark pasha, urging us to look. Paul suddenly scrambled on hands and knees to the footlocker, looked, then plucked out a handful of bleary, cracked snapshots and fanned them across the rug. We could see inscriptions. Paul read aloud, "Coney Island, 1953, Tina. Party at Josephine's, New Year's, 1965. Holiday Inn, New Orleans, 1975, Gwen." He looked from the photos to Kramer, smiling. "All these pictures in your box of women?"

Kramer, in the difficult voice, answered, "I have many photos. I have my Navy discharge papers, my high school diploma, my first driver's license. I have all my elementary school notebooks, even spelling exams from the third grade. I have maybe twenty-five fountain pens. All my old passports; everything is in that box."

Paul, nodding, smiling, said, "But these photos, Kramer. All these photos women?"

"I have had six hundred and twenty-two women."

"Right on," shouted Berliner, his soul projecting toward Kramer through the big green eyes, doglike, waiting for a signal. Paul took out more photos and dropped them among the others on the rug. Over a hundred now, women in bathing suits, in winter coats, in fifties styles, sixties styles, seventies styles. Spirits of the decades. If men make history, women wear its look; even in their faces and figures. But, to me, Kramer's women looked fundamentally the same. One poor sweetie between twenty and thirty years old forever. On a beach, leaning against a railing, a tree, a brick wall, with sun in her eyes, squinting at the camera. A hundred fragments, each of them complete if you cared to scrutinize. A whole person who could say her name. Maybe love Kramer. That she squinted touched me.

Kramer, with his meticulously sculpted hair, cigarette trembling in his fingers, waited. Nobody spoke, not even Berliner. Looking at the pictures, I was reminded of flashers. See this. It is my entire crotch. Have a scream.

Berliner suddenly blurted, "Great. Great. Let's all do it. Let's all talk about our sexual experience." His face jerked in every direction, seeking encouragement.

As if he'd heard nothing, Kramer said, "I was born in Trenton, New Jersey. My father was a union organizer. In those days it was dangerous work. He was a Communist, he lived for an idea. My mother believed in everything he said, but she was always depressed and she sat in the bedroom, in her robe, smoking cigarettes. She never cleaned the house. When I was six years old I was shopping and cooking, like my mother's mother. I cannot remember one minute which I can call my childhood. I was my mother's mother. I had a life with no beginning, no childhood."

"Right," said Berliner. "You had your childhood later. Six hundred and twenty-two mothers. Right?"

"The women were women. Eventually I'll have another six hundred. I don't know where my father is, but when I hear the word "workers" or the word "struggle," I think of him. If I see a hardhat carrying a lunch pail, I think he's struggling. My mother now lives in New York. Twice a year I phone New York and get migraine headaches. Blindness and nausea. Just say the area code, 212, and I feel pain in my eyes."

I'd been looking at Kramer all evening, but now, to my surprise, I noticed that his eyes didn't focus steadily. The right eye was slightly askew. He blinked hard and brought it into line with the other eye. After a while it drifted away. He'd let it go for a moment, then blink hard again. His voice was trancelike, compulsive, as if he'd been trying to tell us something before he would be overwhelmed by doubt and confusion.

Cavanaugh said, "What about Nancy?"

"What about her?" Kramer sounded surprised, as if unsure who Nancy was.

"Nancy Kramer. These are her plants, aren't they?" Cavanaugh was looking at the photos on the rug, not the plants.

"You mean the women? What does Nancy think about my women?"

"That's right."

"We have a good understanding. Nancy goes out, too. It's cool. The plants are mine."

"Yours?" I said.

"Yes. I love them. I've even got them on my tape recorder. I could play you the fig tree in the corner." Kramer said this to me with a sly, dopey look. as if trying to change the mood, trying to make a joke.

"Too much. Too much, Kramer," said Berliner. "My wife and me are exactly the same. I mean we also have an understanding."

I said, "Let Kramer talk."

Kramer shook his head and bent toward Berliner, saying, "That's all right. Do you want to say more, Solly?"

Berliner looked down at his knees. "No. You go on, Kramer. I'm sorry I interrupted."

Cavanaugh, imitating Kramer, bent toward Berliner. "Solly, aren't you jealous when your wife is making it with another guy?"

Berliner raised his face toward Cavanaugh. "Jealous?"

"Yeah, jealous."

"No, man, I'm liberated."

"What the hell does that mean?" I said.

Looking at me now, Berliner said, as if it were obvious, "I don't feel anything."

"Yeah," said Berliner. "I'm liberated."

"Liberated means you don't feel anything?"

Harold, with a huge stare of pleasure, began repeating, "You don't feel anything. You don't feel anything."

Berliner shrugged. "Once, I felt something."

Writhing in his creamy slacks, Harold said, "Tell us about that, please."

The little tears were in his eyes again. "Tell us about the time you felt something."

"Does everyone want to hear?" said Berliner, looking at me.

I said, "Yes."

He smiled. His voice was full of accommodation. "We had a weekend in the mountains with another couple. A ski cabin near Lake Tahoe. The first night we became a little drunk after dinner and somebody—maybe me—yeah, yeah, me—I said let's trade partners. It was my own idea, right? So we traded. It was OK. It wasn't the first time we did it. But then I heard my wife moaning. I couldn't help hearing her. A small cabin. And that was OK. But she was not just moaning, you know what I mean. You know? It was love."

"Love?" said Kramer.

"Yeah, I didn't like it. She was moaning with love. Moaning is OK. But she was going too far, you know what I mean. She was doing love. I wanted to kill her."

Cavanaugh reached over and squeezed Berliner's elbow. Berliner was still smiling, the big green eyes searching our faces for the meaning of what he'd said. "Is that what you wanted to know, Harold?"

"Did it ruin your weekend?"

"It was horrible, man. I lost my erection."

Berliner began screeing again and I heard myself doing it, too, just like him, making that creepy sound.

"It was horrible, horrible. I was ashamed. I ran out of the cabin and sat on a rock. My wife started calling though the door, 'Solly, Solly, Solly Berliner.' The she came outside, laughing, and found me. I showed her what she had done to me. She said it wasn't her fault. She said it was my idea. I hit her and said that was my idea, too. She started crying. Soon as she started crying, my erection came back."

Kramer said, "What happened next?"

"But you were talking Kramer," I said. "You know what happened next. Next she hit him and then they made it together. It's a cliché. You should finish telling your story. You should have a full turn." I wanted things done according to my idea, one man at a time.

Berliner, incoherent with excitement, shouted at me, "How the hell do you know? I'm telling what happened to me. Me. Me."

"All right, all right. What happened next?"

"Next she hit me and we made it together."

Cavanaugh, with two fists, began hammering the rug until everyone quieted. Then he said, "Look at Kramer." Kramer was slumped in his pillow, elbows on his knees, the dark face hanging, glancing vaguely back at Cavanaugh.

"Let's let him alone," said Cavanaugh. "Maybe he'll want to go on later. tonight. I'll tell you guys a love story. OK?"

I said, "Kramer tells us he made it with six hundred women. Berliner says he traded his wife, then beat her up and had an erection. You call that love?"

Cavanaugh gave me a flat look, as if I'd become strange to him.

"Yeah, why not?"

"Oh God."

"Hey, man, what do you want to hear about? Toothpaste and deodorants?"

"You're right, Cavanaugh. I give up. I'll bet your story's about how you made it with ten thousand high school cheerleaders."

Cavanaugh stared at the place in the rug he had just hammered. The big body and big face were immobilized, getting things in order, remembering his story, and then his voice was simply there.

"About three months after we got married my second wife and I started having arguments. Bad scenes. We would go to bed every night hating each other. There were months with no sex. I didn't know who was more miserable. I was making a lot of money playing ball and I was playing good. It should have been good for us altogether. The marriage should have been fine. In the middle of a game with the crowd screaming, I'd think this was no fantastic deal, because I had no love at home. Soon there was nothing in my body but anger. I got into fights with my own teammates. I couldn't take a shave without slicing my face. I was smoking cigarettes. I had something against my body and wanted to hurt it. When I told my wife I was moving out, she said, 'Great.' She wanted to live alone. I moved out and stayed with a friend until I found an apartment. One day in the grocery store, I was throwing every kind of thing into my shopping cart. I was making sure nothing I needed would show up later as being not there. And this woman, I notice, is pushing her cart behind me, up and down the aisles, giggling. I knew she was giggling at me. When I got to the cashier she is behind me in line, still giggling, and then she says, very sweet and tickled, 'You must have a station wagon waiting for you.' I said, 'I have a pickup truck. Do you want a ride?' A man buying so much food, she figured, has a family. Safe to ask for a ride. She didn't have a car. I gave her a ride and carried her groceries up to her apartment. A little boy was sitting on the floor watching TV. She introduced us and offered me a drink and we sat in another room talking. The boy took care of himself. Just like in Kramer's story. He cooked dinner for himself. He gave himself a bath. Then went to bed. But his mother wasn't depressed like Kramer's. She laughed and teased me and asked a lot of questions. I talked about myself for five or six hours. We ate dinner around midnight, and then, at four in the morning, I woke up in her bed, thinking about my ton of groceries rotting in the pickup. But that wasn't what woke me. What woke me was the feeling I wanted to go home. Back to my apartment, my own bed. I hadn't left one woman to sleep with another. I didn't know what I was doing in this woman's bed. I got up and dressed and left. As I was about to drive away she comes running to the window of my pickup, naked. 'Where are you going?' she says. I told her she had nothing on. She says, 'Where are you going at this hour?' I said I wanted to go home. She says, 'Oh, OK, I'll come with you.' I told her no and said I would phone her. She said OK and smiled and said good-night. She was like that little boy. Or he was like her. Easy. OK. OK good-night. I didn't think I would phone her. Now this is my story. I woke up the next afternoon. I liked it, waking up alone. I liked it very much, but I felt something strange. I wanted something. Then I remembered the woman and I knew what I wanted wanted to phone her. So I went to the phone and I realized I didn't know her number. I didn't even know her name. Well, I showered and got dressed and stopped thinking about her. I went out for something. I didn't know what. I had everything I needed in the apartment. But I started driving and right away I was driving back to the grocery store, as if the car had a mind of its own. I was just holding the wheel. I didn't get further than the grocery store, because I didn't remember where she lived. I remembered leaving the store with her, driving toward the bay and that's all. She said, 'Turn right, turn left, and go straight,' but I never noticed street names or anything. Now I wanted to see that woman more and more. The next day I went back to the grocery store and hung around the parking lot. I did that every day for a week, at different times. I thought I remembered how she looked talking to me through the window of my pickup, how she smiled and said OK. I wanted to see her again badly. But I wasn't sure that I could recognize her in the street, looking normal. She was wearing gold loop earrings, jeans, and sandals. What if she came along in a skirt and heels? Anyhow, I never saw her again."

Cavanaugh stopped. It was obvious he had no more to say, but Kramer said, "Is that your story?"

"Yes." Cavanaugh smiled, leaning back, watching us.

"That's your love story?" I asked.

"Right," he answered, nodding. "I fell in love with a woman I couldn't find the next day. She might live around the corner, man."

"You still love her?" asked Paul, tremendous delicacy in his voice, the slight small body poised, full of tenderness and tension.

Cavanaugh smiled at him with melancholy eyes, the whole expression of his great face and body suggested that he'd been humbled by fate.

Paul said, "That can't be it, that can't be the end."

"The end."

"Cavanaugh," Paul said, pleading, "I've known you for years. How come you never told me that story?"

"I never told anyone. Maybe I'm not sure it happened."

"You did go back to the grocery?"

"So what?"

I said, "Paul means, if you looked for her, it happened."

"I still look. When Sarah sends me out to do the shopping, she doesn't know the risk she's taking."

"Cavanaugh," I said, "do you think you ever passed her in the street and she recognized you, but you didn't recognize her?"

Immediately, Kramer said, "Not recognize Cavanaugh? I'd recognize him even if I never saw him before."

"How would you recognize me?"

"From your picture in the papers."

"She didn't read the sport pages."

"Hey," said Berliner, "I have an idea. We can all look for her. What do you say?"

Paul said, "Shut up."

"Why is everyone telling me to shut up? I drove here from San Jose and everyone tells me to shut up." Berliner was sighing in a philosophical way. He'd just seen into the nature of life. "Looking for Cavanaugh's woman. To me it's a good idea. Hey, man, I have a better idea. Cavanaugh, take a quick look through Kramer's snapshots."

Cavanaugh smirked. "She wasn't one of them. She was a queen."

"Queen what?" shouted Kramer. "My women have names. What did you call her? You call her Queen; Berliner, get me my telephone directory. I'll find her. How many women in Berkeley can be named Queen?"

"I'm sorry, Kramer. Take it easy. I didn't intend to crap on your six hundred women. He thinks I crapped on his harem."

I said,"Let me talk, I want to tell a love story."

"Great," said Berliner."Everybody shut up. Go, man. Sing the blues."

"You don't want to hear my story? I listened to yours, Berliner."

"Yes he does," said Kramer. "Let him talk, Solly."

"I didn't try to stop him."

Cavanaugh said, "Just begin."

"Yeah," said Berliner, grinning in an animal way, brilliant, stiff with teeth.

"So far," I said, "I've heard three stories about one thing. Cavanaugh calls it love. I call it stories about the other woman. By which I mean the one who is not the wife. To you guys only the other woman is interesting. If there wasn't first a wife, there couldn't be the other woman. Especially you, Berliner; especially in your case. Moaning, just moaning in the other room, your wife is only your wife. Moaning with love, she's the other woman. And Kramer with the snapshots. Look at them, Kramer spent most of his life trying to photograph the other woman, not knowing that every time he snapped a picture it was like getting married. Like permanently eliminating another woman from the possibility of being the other woman. As for Cavanaugh, why can't he find his woman? Because he doesn't want to. If he finds her, she won't be the other woman anymore. This way he can protect his marriage. Every time he goes to the grocery store and doesn't see the other woman, which is every single time, his marriage is stronger."

Cavanaugh, frowning at me, said, "What are you trying to tell us? What's all this business about the other woman? Why don't you just say it, man?"

Kramer then said, "You're trying to tell us you love your wife. You think I don't love mine? You think Solly doesn't love his wife?"

Berliner cried, "If that's all you think, you're right. I hate my wife."

"Tell your story," said Cavanaugh. "Enough philosophy."

"I don't know if I can tell it. I never told it before. It's about woman who was my friend in high school and college. Her name is Marilyn. We practically grew up together. She lives in Chicago now. She's a violinist in a symphony orchestra. I spent more time with her than with any other woman except maybe my mother. She wasn't like a sister. She was like a friend, I couldn't have had such a friendship with a very close man. We'd go out together a lot and if I brought her home late, I'd stay over at her place, in the same bed.

Nothing sexual. Between us it would have been a crime. We would fight plenty, say terrible things to each other, but we were close. She phoned me every day. We stayed on the phone for an hour. We went to parties together when neither of us had a date. I liked showing up with her because she was attractive. Showing up with her increased my chances of meeting some girl. It gave me a kind of power, walking in with Marilyn, feeling free to pick up somebody else. She had the same power. Anyhow, we never analyzed our relationship, but we joked about what other people thought. My mother would sometimes answer the phone and, if she heard Marilyn's voice, she would say, 'It's your future wife.' She used to worry about us. She used to warn me that any woman I was serious about would object to Marilyn. Or she'd say it wasn't nice, me and Marilyn being so thick with each other, because I was ruining her chances of meeting a man. That wasn't true. Marilyn had plenty of affairs. All of them ended badly, but I had nothing to do with it. One of her men scissored her dresses into rags. Another flung her Siamese cat out the window. She would manage to find some man who was well educated, had pleasant manners, and turned out to be a brute. She suffered, but nothing destroyed her. She had her violin. She also had me. When I was out of a job and not going to school, she loaned me money and let me stay at her place for weeks. I didn't have to ask. I just showed up one day with my suitcase. One weekend, while I was staying at her place, she came home with a friend, a girl who looked something like her. Lean, with curly brown hair, with beautiful skin faintly olive colored, like Marilyn's. Before dinner was over, Marilyn remembered something important she had to do. She excused herself and went to a movie. Her friend and I were alone in the apartment. It was glorious. Two weeks later, when I was talking to Marilyn about this and that, I mentioned her friend. Marilyn said she didn't want to hear about her. She said that friendship was over and it was something she couldn't discuss. Furthermore, she said I had acted badly that night at dinner, driving her out of her own apartment. I said, 'I thought you left as a favor to me. I thought you did it deliberately.' She said she did do it deliberately, but only because I made it extremely obvious that I was hot for her friend and I acted like a slob. Now I began to feel angry. I told her she didn't have to leave her apartment for my sake and it was rotten of her to make me feel guilty about it two weeks after I'd started having very strong feelings about her friend, so strong in fact we had been talking about marriage. I thought this would change everything. Marilyn would laugh and give me a hug. Instead she lights a cigarette and begins smoking with quick, half-drags, flicking ashes all over her couch. Then she says, 'Why don't you just say that you consider me physically disgusting and you always have.' This was my old friend Marilyn speaking, but it seemed like science fiction. It looked like her. It sounded like her. It was her, but it wasn't. Some weird mongoose had seized her soul. Then she starts telling me about what is inside my head, things she has always known though I tried to hide them from her. Her voice is getting bitter and nasty. She says she knows I can't stand her breasts and the birthmark on her neck sickens me. I said, 'What birthmark?' She says, 'Who are you trying to kid? I've seen you looking at it a thousand times when you

Leonard Michaels

thought I didn't notice.' I sat down beside her on the couch. She says 'Get away from me, you pig.' I felt confused. Ashamed and frightened at the same time. Then she jumps off the couch and strides out of the room. I hear her slamming around in the toilet, bottles toppling out of her medicine cabinet into the sink. Smashing. I said. 'Marilyn, are you all right?' No answer. She finally comes out, wearing a bathrobe with nothing underneath and the robe is open. But she's standing there as if nothing has changed since she left the room, and she talks to me again in the same nasty voice. She sneers and accuses me of things I couldn't have imagined, let alone thought about her, as she says I did, every day, all the time, pretending I was her friend. Suddenly, I'm full of a new feeling. Feeling I've never had before. Not what a normal person would call sexual feeling, but what does a penis know? It isn't a connoisseur of normal feeling. Besides, I was a lot younger, still mystified by life, especially my own chemicals. I leap off the couch and grab her. No, I find myself leaping, grabbing her, and she's twisting, trying to hit me, really fighting. I feel she's seriously trying to hurt me, but there's no screaming or cursing, there's nothing but the two of us breathing and sweating and then she begins to collapse, to slide toward the floor. Next thing I'm on top of her. I'm wearing my clothes, she lying on her open robe. It's supernaturally exciting. Both of us are shivering and wild. We fell asleep like that and we slept at least an hour. I woke when I felt her moving. The lights were on. We were looking at each other. She says, 'This is very discouraging.' Then she went to her bedroom and shut the door. I got up and followed her and knocked at the door. She opens it and lets me kiss her. Then she shut the door again. I went home. Six months later she phoned me from Chicago to tell me about her new job and to give me her address. After a while she asked about her friend. I told her it was finished between her friend and me. I was seeing somebody else. She changed the subject. Now every few months I get a letter. I write to her also. Someday, if I happen to be in Chicago, I'll visit her."

In the silence following my story, I began to regret having told it. Then a man who had said nothing all evening asked, "Did you make it that night with Marilyn?"

"No. Nothing changed. I don't think it every will. I could show up tomorrow in Chicago with my suitcase and move into her place."

The man shook his head softly and started to say something, then stopped.

"Go on," I said. "Do you have a question?"

He smiled.

We waited. It was clear that he was a shy man. Then he said, "Was it a true story?"

"Yes."

He shrugged and smiled and said. "I liked Marilyn."

I said, "I like her, too. Maybe I can fix you up with her. What's your name?"

"Terry."

"Terry?" shrieked Berliner. "Terry, you're   osed to phone your wife."

Grinning at Berliner, Terry seemed less a shy man than a man surprised.

"It's not my wife," he said, intimating complexities. Old confusions. As if to forbid himself another word, he shook his head. Long and bald. Sandy tufts of hair beside the ears, like baby feathers. His eyes were light brown. His nose was a straight, thick pull. "I mustn't bore you fellows with my situation." He nodded at me as if we had a special understanding. "We're enjoying ourselves, telling melancholy stories about love." He continued nodding. For no reason, I nodded back.

Cavanaugh said, "Talk about anything you like, Terry. You say the woman who phoned isn't your wife?"

He grinned. "I'm a haunted house. For me, yesterday is today. The woman who phoned is my former wife. A strange expression, but what else can I call her? Ex-wife?"

"Call her by her name," I said.

"Her name is Nicki."

"How long have you been divorced?" asked Cavanaugh.

"Usually one asks how long you've been married. Nicki and I have been divorced ten years. Nicki. . . "

"It's better," said Berliner, "if you say former wife. Nicki, Nicki—you sound like a Ping-Pong game."

"All right. After ten years of divorce we're closer than during our marriage. If you don't remarry, this is natural. She phones me two or three times a week. Listen to how personal I'm becoming. Why is everything personal so funny?"

"Who is laughing?" said Berliner. "Do you sleep together? To sleep with your former wife, I think—I mean just to me—it is immoral. I couldn't do it."

"You couldn't do it," I said. "Who asked you to?"

"He's right. I'm sorry, Terry. Go on."

"It doesn't happen often. Nicki has a boyfriend. His name is Harrison. But they don't live together. Nicki can't get along with kids. She doesn't like kids. More complicated yet, Harrison's daughter, eleven years old, is a very sad fat girl. His boy, six years old, has learning problems. Harrison phones me, too. I meet him now and then to talk about his kids."

"He wants to talk to you?" I said.

"I'm a doctor. Even at parties people come up to me for an opinion. Terry, I shouldn't discuss professional matters in these circumstances, but my aged aunt Sophie has a black wart on her buttock. She wants you to know. She says to tell you it is beginning to grow hair."

"So what about Nicki? She was crying on the phone," Kramer says.

"She always does. Your Marilyn story reminded me of a fight we had when I was in medical school in Montreal. We lived in a two room flat above a grocery store. It was a Saturday morning. I was studying at the kitchen table. Can I tell this story?"

Berliner said, "Only if it's miserable."

"Anyhow, a blizzard had been building for days. I watched it through the kitchen window as it attacked the city. The sky disappeared. The streets were dead. Nothing moved but wind and snow. In this deadly blizzard, Nicki decided to go out. She had been saving money for a particular pair of boots.

Fine soft leather. Tight. Knee-high. They had a red brown tone, like dried blood, but slightly glossy. Totally impractical and too elegant. The wind would tear them off her legs. Nobody in our crowd owned such boots. Our friends in Montreal were like us—students, poor, always working, always worried about money. Nicki had worked as a secretary all that year and she never bought presents for herself. Her salary paid for our rent and food. I had a tiny scholarship that covered books and incidental tuition fees. We were badly in debt, but she wanted these boots. I don't know how she saved a penny for them. I pleaded with her not to go out in the blizzard. Something in my voice, maybe, suggested more anxiety about the price of the boots than her safety. The more I pleaded the more determined she became."

"Why didn't you go with her?" I asked.

"I wanted to. But the idea of the boots—so trivial, such a luxury—and her wanting to go get them that morning—made me furious. I could sympathize with her desire for beautiful boots. She deserved a reward. But why that minute did she have to go get them? I was trying to study. My papers and books were on the kitchen table. Also a box of slides and a microscope I carried home from the laboratory. Today, though I own a house with ten rooms, I still use the kitchen table when I read medical journals or write an article. Anyhow, I was trying to study. I needed the time. It's difficult for me to memorize things, but I can do it if there is peace and quiet and no bad feelings in the air. You don't have to be a genius to be a doctor. But now I was furious. I yelled, 'Go on, do what you like. Buy the stupid boots. Just leave me alone.' She slammed the door.

"For a while I sat with my papers and books. Outside the blizzard was hysterical. Inside it was warm and quiet. I worried about her, but my fury cancelled the worry. Soon I began really to study and I forgot about Nicki. Maybe three hours passed and, suddenly, she's home. Pale and burning and happy I didn't say hello. My fury returned. She had a big shoe box under her arm. She had returned with her boots. While she put them on, I continued trying to study. I didn't watch her, but I could tell she needed help. The boots were tight. After a while she managed to get them on by herself, then she walked up to my table and stood there, in blood colored legs, waiting for me to notice. I could feel her excitement. She was trembling with pleasure. I knew what expression was in her face. Every muscle working not to smile. She waited for me to look up, collapse with approval, to admit she was magnificent in those boots. But the blizzard was in my heart. I refused to look. Suddenly, my paper, books, slides, microscope—everything on the table was all over the kitchen floor. Nicki is strong. She plays tennis like a man. I jumped up. I felt I had been killed, wiped out of the world.

"She still claims, I hit her. I don't remember. I remember rushing out into the blizzard with no coat or hat. Why? To buy a gun. I didn't really know what I wanted until I happened to pass a pawnshop. I saw guns in the window. I had a pocket watch that my father gave me when I left for medical school. A Waltham Premier worth about two hundred dollars. Gold case. Gothic numericals. A classic watch. Also a heavy gold chain. In exchange for that watch I got a rifle. Then I asked the man for a bullet. I couldn't pay for it, but I told him the deal was off unless he gave me a bullet. He said, One bullet?' I screamed. 'Give me a bullet.' He gave it to me. If I'd asked for a ton of bullets, he would have thought nothing. But ask for one bullet and there's trouble."

"The police were waiting for you," said Berliner, "when you got home."

"I noticed the police car in front of the house, its light blinking through the storm. So I entered an alley behind the house and went up to the roof and loaded the rifle. I intended to go to the flat and blow my brains out in front of Nicki."

"I thought you were going to shoot her," I said.

"Her? I'd never shoot her. I'm her slave. I wanted to make a point about our relationship. But the police were in the flat. I was on the roof with a loaded rifle, freezing in the storm. I aimed into the storm, toward the medical school, and fired. How could I shoot myself? I'd have been on that roof with a bullet in my head, covered by snow, and nobody would have found me until spring. What comes to mind when you commit suicide is amazing. Listen, I have a question. My story made me hungry. Is there anything to eat?"

Kramer rose from his pillow with a brooding face. "Men," he said "Terry is hungry. I believe him because I too am hungry. I suppose all of us could use a little bite. Any other night I would suggest we send out for pizza. Or I myself would make us an omelet. But not tonight. You are lucky tonight. Very lucky. Tomorrow, in this room, Nancy is having a meeting of her women's group. So the refrigerator happens to be packed with good things. Let me itemize. In the refrigerator there is three different kinds of salad. There is big plates of chicken, turkey, and salmon. There is also a pecan pie. I love pecan pie. There is two pecan pies and there is two lemon pies. There is a chocolate cake which, even as I speak of it, sucks at me. I am offering all this to you men. Wait, Berliner. I have one more thing to say, Berliner. In the alcove behind the kitchen, rests a case of zinfandel. It is good, good California. Men, I offer to you this zinfandel."

Berliner was already in the kitchen. The rest of us stayed to cheer Kramer. Even I cheered. Despite his tatooed arms, which reminded me of snakes, I cheered. His magnanimity was unqualified. No smallest doubt or reluctance troubled his voice. Every face in the room became like his, an animal touched by glee. We were "lucky," said Kramer. Lucky, maybe, to be men. Life is unfair business. Whoever said otherwise? It is a billion bad shows, low blows, and number one has more fun. Nancy's preparations for her woman's group would feed our club. The idea of delicious food, taken this way, was thrilling. Had it been there for us, it would have been pleasant. But this was evil, like eating the other woman. We discovered Berliner on his knees before the refrigerator, door open, his head inside. We cheered again, crowding up behind him as he passed things out to us, first a long plate of salmon, the whole pink fish intact, then the chicken, then a salad bowl sealed with a plastic sheet through which we saw dazzling green life. It would be a major feast, a huge eating. To Cavanaugh, standing beside me, I said, "I thought you had to leave early." He didn't reply. He pulled his watch off, slipped it into his pocket, and shouted, "I see pâte in there. I want that, too."

The cheers came again. Some of the men had already started on the salmon, snatching pieces of it with their fingers. Kramer, who had gone to the alcove, reappeared with black bottles of zinfandel, two under his arms, two in his hands. He stopped, contemplated the scene in his kitchen, and his dark eyes glowed. His voice was all pleasure. "This is a wonderful club. This is a wonderful club."

JAMES PURDY

Summer Tidings

There was a children's party in progress on the sloping wide lawn facing the estate of Mr. Teyte and easily visible therefrom despite the high hedge. A dozen school-aged children, some barely out of the care and reach of their nursemaids, attended Mrs. Aveline's birthday party for her son Rupert. The banquet or party itself was held on the site of the croquet grounds, but the croquet set had only partially been taken down, and a few wickets were left standing, a mallet or two lay about, and a red and white wood ball rested in the nasturtium bed. Mr. Teyte's Jamaican gardener, bronzed as an idol, watched the children as he watered the millionaire's grass with a great shiny black hose. The peonies had just come into full bloom. Over the greensward where the banquet was in progress one smelled in addition to the sharp odor of the nasturtiums and the marigolds, the soft perfume of June roses; the trees have their finest green at this season, and small gilt brown toads were about in the earth. The Jamaican servant hardly took his eyes off the children. Their gold heads and white summer clothing rose above the June verdure in remarkable contrast, and the brightness of so many colors made his eyes smart and caused him to pause frequently from his watering. Edna Gruber, Mrs. Aveline's secretary and companion, had promised the Jamaican a piece of the "second" birthday cake when the banquet should be over, and told him the kind thought came from Mrs. Aveline herself. He had nodded when Edna told him of this coming treat, yet it was not the anticipation of the cake which made him so absentminded and broody as it was the unaccustomed sight of so many young children all at once. Edna could see that the party had stirred something within his mind for he spoke even less than usual to her today as she tossed one remark after another across the boundary of the privet hedge separating the two large properties.

More absent-minded than ever, he went on hosing the peony bed until a slight flood filled the earth about the blooms and squashed onto his open sandals. He moved off then and began sprinkling with tempered nozzle the quince trees. Mr. Teyte, his employer and the owner of the property which stretched far and wide before the eye with the exception of Mrs. Aveline's, had gone to a golf tournament today. Only the white maids were inside his big house, and in his absence they were sleeping most of the day, or if they were about would be indifferently spying the Jamaican's progress across the lawn, as he labored to water the already refreshed black earth and the grass as perfectly green and motionless as in a painted backdrop. Yes, his eyes, his mind were dreaming today despite the almost infernal noise of all those young throats, the guests of the birthday party. His long black lashes gave the impression of having been dampened incessantly either by the water from the hose or some long siege of tears.

Mr. Teyte, if not attentive or kind to him, was his benefactor, for somehow that word had come to be used by people who knew both the gardener and the employer from far back, and the word had come to be associated with Mr. Teyte by Galway himself, the Jamaican servant. But Mr. Teyte, if not unkind, was undemonstrative, and if not indifferent, paid low wages, and almost never spoke to him, issuing his commands, which were legion, through the kitchen and parlor maids. But once when the servant had caught pneumonia, Mr. Teyte had come unannounced to the hospital in the morning, ignoring the rules that no visits were to be allowed except in early evening, and though he had not spoken to Galway, he had stood by his bedside a few moments, gazing at the sick man as if her were inspecting one of his own ailing riding horses.

But Mrs. Aveline and Edna Gruber talked to Galway, were kind to him. Mrs. Aveline even "made" over him. She always spoke to him over the hedge every morning, and was not offended or surprised when he said almost nothing to her in exchange. She seemed to know something about him from his beginnings, at any rate she knew Jamaica, having visited there three or four times. And so the women—Edna and Mrs. Aveline—went on speaking to him over the years, inquiring of his health, and of his tasks with the yard, and so often bestowing on him delicacies from their liberal table, as one might give tidbits to a prized dog which wandered in also from the great estate.

The children's golden heads remained in his mind after they had all left the banquet table and gone into the interior of the house, and from thence their limousines had come and taken them to their own great houses. The blond heads of hair continued to swim before his eyes like the remembered sight of fields of wild buttercups outside the great estate, stray flowers of which occasionally cropped up in his own immaculate greensward, each golden corolla as bright as the strong rays of the noon sun. And then the memory came of the glimpsed birthday cake with the yellow center. His mouth watered with painful anticipation, and his eyes again filled with tears.

The sun was setting as he turned off the hose, and wiped his fingers from the water and some rust stains, and a kind of slime which came out from the nozzle. He went into a little brick shed, and removed his shirt, wringing wet, and put on a dry one of faded pink cotton decorated with a six-petaled flower design. Ah, but the excitement of those happy golden heads sitting at a banquet—it made one too jumpy for cake, and their voices still echoed in his

Summer Tidings

ears a little like the cries of the swallows from the poplar trees.

Obedient, then, to her invitation, Galway, the Jamaican gardener, waited outside the buttery for a signal to come inside, and partake of the brithday treat, bemusing however, about the party and all the young children, the sounds of their gaiety, their enormous vitality, lung power, their great appetites, the happy other sounds of silverware and fine china being moved about, added to which had been the song of the birds now getting ready to settle down to the dark of their nests, a kind of memory, a heavy nostalgia had come over him, recollection deep and far-off weighted him down without warning like fever and profound sickness. He remembered his dead loved ones. ... How long he had stood on the back steps he could not say, until Edna suddenly laughing as she opened the door on him, with flushed face, spoke: "Why, Galway, you know you should not have stood on ceremony. . . Of all people, you are the last who is expected to hang back. . . Your cake is waiting for you. . ."

He entered and sat in his accustomed place where so many times past he was treated to dainties and rewards.

"You may wonder about the delay," Edna spoke more formally today to him than usual. "Galway, we have, I fear, bad news. . . A telegram has arrived. . . Mrs. Aveline is afraid to open it. . ."

Having said this much, Edna left the room, allowing the swinging door which separated the kitchen from the rest of the house to close behind her and then continue its swing backwards and forwards like the pendulum of a clock.

Galway turned his eyes to the huge white cake with the yellow center which she had expressly cut for him. The solid silver fork in his hand was about to come down on the thick heavily frosted slice resting sumptuously on hand-painted china. Just then he heard a terrible cry rushing through the many rooms of the house and coming, so it seemed, to stop directly at him and then cease and disappear into the air and the nothingness about him. His mouth became dry, and he looked about like one who expects unknown and immediate danger. The fork fell from his brown calloused muscular hand. The cry was now repeated if anything more loudly, then there was a cavernous silence, and after some moments, steady prolonged hopeless weeping. He knew it was Mrs. Aveline. The telegram must have brought bad news. He sat on looking at the untasted cake. The yellow of its center seemed to stare at him.

Edna now came through the swinging door, her eyes red, a pocket handkerchief held tightly in her right hand, her opal necklace slightly crooked. "It was Mrs. Aveline's mother, Galway. . . She is dead. . . And such a short time since Mrs. Aveline's husband died too, you know. . ."

Galway uttered some words of regret, sympathy, which Edna did not hear, for she was still listening to any sound which might try to reach her from beyond the swinging door.

At last turning round, she spoke: "Why, you haven't so much as touched your cake. . ." She looked at him almost accusingly.

"She has lost her own mother. . ." Galway said this after some struggle with his backwardness.

But Edna was studying the cake. "We can wrap it all up, the rest of it,

Galway, and you can have it to sample at home, when you will have more appetite." She spoke comfortingly to him. She was weeping so hard now she shook all over.

"These things come out of the blue," she managed to speak at last in a neutral tone as though she was reading from some typewritten sheet of instructions. "There is no warning very often as in this case. The sky itself might as well have fallen on us. . ."

Edna had worked for Mrs. Aveline for many years. She always wore little tea aprons. She seemed to do nothing but go from the kitchen to the front parlor or drawing room, and then return almost immediately to where she had been in the first place. She had supervised the children's party today, ceaselessly walking around, and looking down on each young head, but one wondered exactly what she was accomplishing by so much movement. Still, without her, Mrs. Aveline might not have been able to run the big house, so people said. And it was also Edna Gruber who had told Mrs. Aveline first of Galway's indispensable and sterling dependability. And it was Galway Edna always insisted on summoning when nobody else could be found to do some difficult and often unpleasant and dirty task.

"So Galway, I will have the whole 'second' cake sent over to you just as soon as I find the right box to put it in. . ."

He rose as Edna said this, not having eaten so much as a crumb. He said several words which hearing them come from his mouth startled him as much as if each word spoken had appeared before him as letters in the air.

"I am sorry. . . and grieve for her grief. . . A mother's death. . . It is the hardest loss."

Then he heard the screen door closing behind him. The birds were still, and purple clouds rested in the west, with the evening star sailing above the darkest bank of clouds as yellow as the heads of any of the birthday children. He crossed himself.

Afterwards he stood for some time in Mr. Teyte's great green backyard, and admired the way his gardener's hands had kept the grass beautiful for the multimillionaire, and given it the endowment of both life and order. The wind stirred as the light failed, and flowers which opened at evening gave out their faint delicate first perfume, in which the four-o'clocks' fragrance was pronounced. On the ground near the umbrella tree something glistened. He stooped down. It was the sheepshears, which he employed in trimming the ragged grass about trees and bushes, great flower beds, and the hedge. Suddenly, stumbling in the growing twilight he cut his thumb terribly on the shears. He walked dragging one leg now as if it was his foot which he had slashed. The gush of blood somehow calmed him from his other sad thoughts. Before going inside Mr. Teyte's great house, he put the stained sheepshears away in the shed, and then walked quietly to the kitchen and sat down at the lengthy pine table which was his accustomed place here, got out some dicarded linen napkins, and began making himself a bandage. Then he remembered he should have sterilized the wound. He washed the quivering flesh of the wound in thick yellow soap. Then he bandaged it and sat in still communion with his thoughts.

Summer Tidings

Night had come. Outside the katydids and crickets had begun an almost dizzying chorus of sound, and in the far distant darkness tree frogs and some bird with a single often repeated note gave the senses a kind of numbness.

Galway knew who would bring the cake—it would be the birthday boy himself. And the gardener would be expected to eat a piece of it while Rupert stood looking on. His mouth now went dry as sand. The bearer of the cake and messenger of Mrs. Aveline's goodness was coming up the path now, the stones of gravel rising and falling under his footsteps. Rupert liked to be near Galway whenever possible, and like his mother wanted to give the gardener gifts, sometimes coins, sometimes shirts, and now tonight food. He liked to touch Galway as he would perhaps a horse. Rupert stared sometimes at the Jamaican servant's brown thickly muscled arms with a look almost of acute disbelief.

Then came the step on the back porch, and the hesitant but loud knock.

Rupert Aveline, just today aged thirteen, stood with outstretched hands bearing the cake. The gardener accepted it immediately, his head slightly bowed, and immediately lifted it out of the cake box to expose it all entire except the one piece which Edna Gruber had cut in the house expressly for the Jamaican, and this piece rested in thick wax paper separated from the otherwise intact birthday cake. Galway fell heavily into his chair, his head still slightly bent over the offering. He felt with keen unease Rupert's own speechless wonder, the boy's eyes fixed on him rather than the cake, though in the considerable gloom of the kitchen the Jamaican servant had with his darkened complexion all but disappeared into the shadows, only his white shirt and linen trousers betokening a visible presence.

Galway lit the lamp, and immediately heard the cry of surprise and alarmed concern coming from the messenger, echoing in modulation and terror that of Mrs. Aveline as she had read the telegram.

"Oh, yes, my hand," Galway said softly, and he looked down in unison with Rupert's horrified glimpse at his bandage—the blood having come through copiously to stain the linen covering almost completely crimson.

"Shouldn't it be shown to the doctor, Galway?" the boy inquired, and suddenly faint, he rested his hand on the servant's good arm for support. He had gone very white. Galway quickly rose and helped the boy to a chair. He hurried to the sink and fetched him a glass of cold water, but Rupert refused this, continuing to touch the gardener's arm.

"It is your grandmother's death, Rupert, which has made you upset. . ."

Rupert looked away out the window through which he could see his own house in the shimmery distance; a few lamps had been lighted over there, and the white exterior of his home looked like a ship in the shadows, seeming to move languidly in the summer night.

In order to have something to do and because he knew Rupert wished him to eat part of the cake, Galway removed now all the remaining carefully wrapped thick cloth about the birthday cake and allowed it to emerge yellow and white, frosted and regal. They did everything so well in Mrs. Aveline's house.

"You are. . . a kind. . . good boy," Galway began with the strange musical accent which never failed to delight Rupert's ear. "And now you're on your way to being a man," he finished.

Rupert's face clouded over at this last statement, but the music of the gardener's voice finally made him smile and nod, then his eyes narrowed as they rested on the bloodstained bandage.

"Edna said you had not tasted one single bite, Galway," the boy managed to speak after a struggle to keep his own voice steady and firm.

The gardener, as always, remained impassive, looking at the almost untouched great cake, the frosting in the shape of flowers and leaves and images of little men and words concerning love, a birthday, and the year 1902.

Galway rose hurriedly and got two plates.

"You must share a piece of your own birthday cake, Rupert... I must not eat alone."

The boy nodded energetically.

The Jamaican cut two pieces of cake, placed them on large heavy dinner plates, all he could find at the moment, and produced thick solid silver forks. But then as he handed the piece of cake to Rupert, in the exertion of his extending his arm, drops of blood fell upon the pine table.

At that moment, without warning, the whole backyard was illuminated by unusual irregular flashing lights and red glares. Both Rupert and Galway rushed at the same moment to the window, and stared into the night. Their surprise was, if anything, augmented by what they now saw. A kind of torchlight parade was coming up the far greensward, in the midst of which procession was Mr. Teyte himself, a bullnecked short man of middle years. Surrounded by other men, his well-wishers, all gave out shouts of congratulation in drunken proclamation of the news that the owner of the estate had won the golf tournament. Suddenly his pals raised Mr. Teyte to their shoulders, and shouted in unison over the victory.

Listening to the cries growing in volume, in almost menacing nearness as they approached closer to the gardener and Rupert, who stood like persons besieged, the birthday boy cautiously put his hand in that of Galway.

Presently, however, they heard the procession moving off beyond their sequestered place, the torchlights dimmed and disappeared from outside the windows, as the celebrators marched toward the great front entrance of the mansion, a distance of almost a block away, and there, separated by thick masonry, they were lost to sound.

Almost at the same moment, as if at some signal from the disappearing procession itself, there was a deafening peal of thunder, followed by forks of cerise lightning flashes, and the air so still before rushed and rose in furious elemental wind. Then they heard the angry whipping of the rain against the countless panes of glass.

"Come, come, Rupert," Galway admonished, "your mother will be sick with worry." He pulled from a hook an enormous mackintosh, and threw it about the boy. "Quick, now, Rupert, your birthday is over..."

TILLIE OLSEN

Requa-I

It seemed he had to hold up his head forever. All he wanted was to lie down. Maybe his uncle would let him, there in that strip of pale sun by the redwoods, where he might get warm.

I got those sitting kinks, too, his uncle said, but you don't see *me* staggerin round like an old drunk. . . Here, shake a leg and let's get wood for a fire. Dry pieces if there is any such. I'll catch the fish.

But he had to heave. Again.

How can you have 'any a shred left to bring up. Remind me not to take you noplace but by street car after this. . . Alright, stretch out: you'll see you're feeling better.

Everything slid, moved, as if he were still in the truck. He had been holding up his head forever. The spongy ground squished under him, and the wet of winter and spring rains felt through the tarp. He was lying on the ground, *the ground*. There might be snakes. The trees stretched up and up so you couldn't see if they had tops, and up there they leaned as if they were going to fall. There hadn't even been time to say good-bye to the lamppost that he could hug and swing himself round and round. Round and round like his head, having to hold it up forever. Being places he had never been. Waiting moving sliding trying. Staying up to take care of his mother, afraid to lie down even when se was quiet, 'cause he might fall asleep and not hear her if she needed him.

Even the sun was cold. Wes took off his mackinaw and threw it over to him. He squinched himself together to try and fit under it. Moving sliding. The road was never straight, the pickup bumped and bumped and he had to hold up his head. Even when he threw up, his uncle wouldn't stop. Maybe it was the

---

"Requa" (originally Rek-woi) is a native American place name just inside the Oregon border in Northern California. It is situated on a hill, looking down on the mouth of the Klamath River and the split rock Oregos, traditionally sacred to the Yurok Indians who lived in the area. The story printed here is the first third of a novella which Tillie Olsen is near completing.

GRANTA/111

whiskey they'd had when they got back from   that place, made him sick. Or the up all night, up-down sorting and packing, throwing away and loading. Then that wet hoohoo wind on the auto ferry, and the night so dark he didn't even get to see the new bridge they were building.

The trees *were* red, like blood that oozied out of old meat and nobody washed the plate. Under them waved—ferns?   Baddream giant ones to the bay kind they put around flowers for too sick people.

He had been holding up his head forever. The creek was slipping and sliding too. His uncle came from nowhere and put three fishes too close to him on a rock. They flopped and moved their sides, trying hard to breathe like too sick people.

He pulled the tarp farther down to the next stripe of sun. A wind made the skinny fire cough gallons of smoke and him shiver even more. Curling and curling till he got all in a ball under the mackinaw and didn't have to see

or smell

When we woke up, he was warm. Fog curled high between the trees, the light shone rosy soft like a bedroom lamp lit somewhere. By the fire, a harmonica in his hand, his uncle was sleeping. Across the creek, just like in the movie show or in a dream, a deer and two baby deers were drinking. When he lifted his head, they lifted theirs. For a long time he and the doe looked into each other's eyes. Then swift, beautiful, they were gone—but her eyes kept looking into his.

Wes was mad to have conked out like that. Six more hours to go—that's if this heap holds up and we don't get stuck 'hind a load going up a grade. I'll have to put out at work like always tomorrow, and it's sure not any restin we been doin these gone days.

Just like before, but colder. Moving sliding. Having to hold up his head. Bumproad twisty in a dark moving tunnel of trees. The lumber trucks screamed coming round the bends, and after it was dark their lights made the moving fog look scary. Sometimes he could sleep, sagged against his uncle who didn't move away. Cold or jolts would wake him. He didn't understand how it was that he was sitting up or why he didn't have a bed to lie down in or why or where he was going. All he wanted was to lie down

forever

•

A long bridge with standing stone bears. His uncle said: Klamath, almost there, (*Underneath in the night, yearling salmon slipped through their latest fresh water, making it easy to the salt ocean years.*) When the car stopped, there wasn't even a street lamp to see by. A lady came out to help. The light from the open door made the dark stand taller than even the redwoods and *that* leaned like it might fall on him too.   The wind or something blew away her words and his uncle's words. His feet were pins and needles   too many boxes and bundles   too many trips down and back a long hall like a cave. A feather cape or something hanging got knocked down. His head gasped back and forth like the sides of the fish on the rock   Something about: we didn't throw away nothin   well I'm sure not goin to miss where I've been   hot milk or coffee? but he didn't answer, just lay down on a cot with the bundles stacked around him and went into a dream.

So he came to Requa   March, 1932   13 years old.

•

He stands with his back clamped hard against the door Wes has left open, and he has jumped up from the cot to close.

Hey. Leave it open. My can's still draggin. A block behind.

(*No smile. Skinny little shrimp. Clutching at the door knob, knuckles white, nostrils flaring. Funny animal noises in his throat.*)

Sleeping—all day? Cmon, you had to at least take a leak and put something into that belly. . . Mrs. Ed or Yee didn't stick their nose in? You didn't see nobody?. . . Well (looking around), one thing, you sure weren't neating up the place.

(*Pale. Ol Ghostboy. Silent Cal.*) (*Natural—it's plenty raw yet.*)

I been sleepin too—on my feet AND gettin paid for it. That's talent. (*No smile*) I wasn't bawlin you out, we can get squared away tonight or tomorrow . . . Sure you have to come to eat. It'll only be them that stays here. We all get along. You don't bother them, they don't bother you.

•

They are taking away the boxes and bundles, his low little walls.

That one on top: left over groceries. Into the kitchen, Yee. Forget takin it off the week's board, Mrs. Ed, they didn't cost me nothin. Bedding stuff, Bo; up to the attic. Pots and kitchen things, High. Attic.   . . . Well who'd I leave them for and I thought they might be worth a dime or two. Listen, you'd be surprised how many's been in tryin to sell Evans their pots and blankets and everywhich things. Even guns and fishin gear, and thats get-by when nobodys workin. (Lowered voice) Just her clothes, Mrs. Ed, you know anybody? Mrs. Ed's room. Lamps and little rugs, Stevie *said* they was theirs. Sure lay it down, save me a splinter. Looks good.   . . . Anyone for a lamp? (Funny noises in the kid's throat.)   Gear. *He'll* put 'em away, Mrs. Ed. The bottom drawer, kid, yours and room to spare. Just a mitt? no ball, no bat?   . . . Oddsies, endsies. Yah, a radio. Even works: Kingfish and Madam Queen, here we is. Stevie, Mrs. Edler is talking at you: you got clean stuff for school or does Yee have to wash? No, we never talked is he goin to school or what.   . . . I'll tell you this, though, he's not going through what me and Sis did: kicked round one place after another, not havin nobody. Nobody. Right, Stevie? Can you use a clock, High? Attic.   . . . Was you startin to say something, Stevie? (*Ghostboy!* Swallowing, snuffling.) Naw, that last box stays: our ketchall; it'll take time, goin through it.

Wait, Bo, maybe I'll chase along after all   IF you got the do-re-mi. Sattiday night, isn't it? and I feel the week. (*What am I doing, what am I goin to do with this miserable kid?*) Stevie's for the shuteye anyway, aren't you, kid?

GRANTA/113

Tillie Olsen

Are you for the shuteye, Stevie?
Scratch of a twig on the window. All he has to lull to, who has rocked his nights high on a tree of noise, his traffic city.

Blind thick dark, whose sleep came gentled in streetlamp glow.

And the head on his pillow bulging, though still he is having to hold it up somewhere   And the round and round slipping   sliding   jolting   moved to inside him, so he has to begin to rock his body; rock the cot gently, down and back.

Down and back. It makes a throb for the dark. A clock sound.

That man Highpockets who stuck his hand out at supper and said "Shake, meet the wife" and everybody laughed, he had their clock that stood by the bamboo lamp. A tiny lady in a long dress leaned on it and laughed and held up a tinier flower branch. It had been one of his jobs to wind it and it wheezed while he was winding it.

Jobs.

He couldn't remember, was it Bo had taken the lamp? Telling everybody at the table like it was a joke or important. Would you believe it? He's never been fishin never been huntin never held a gun never been in a boat.

Never Forever

Down and back. The army blanket itched. When he was a kid he'd really believed that story about they were that color and scratchy because of blood and mud and poo and powdered licy things from the war that never could get washed out

Down and back   A clock sound   It keeps away

What had happened with the bloody quilt? Soft quilt   She hadn't even asked how he was when they let him in after all that waiting and waiting to see her   Just: *did you   soak   my quilt?* Burning eyes

Gentle eyes that looked long at him   blood dripping from where should be eyes   Out in the hall swathed bodies floating like in bad movies   never touching the ground   At the window

down and back   down and back

If he had the lamp   the boxes

You promised   and see I'm someplace else again   dark and things that can get me and I don't know where anything is. Don't expect *me* to be 'sponsible

they should have put the clock and lamp in with her   the boxes and bundles and wall and put them round her   everything would be together   he wouldn't have to try and remember   or hold up his head that wouldn't lay down inside the one on the pillow so he could sleep

down and back   down and back

•

All that week he would be lying on the cot in the half dark when Wes got home from work; jump up to re-close the door; lie down again until Wes made him wash up, go in to supper.

At the table he looked at no one, answered in monosyllables, or seemed not to hear at all, stared at the wall or at his wrist, messed the food on his plate into the form of one letter or another, hardly ate

Supper over, he would walk somnanbule back to the gaunt room, take off his shoes, get under the covers and lie there, one hand over his eyes.

Bo, Hi, crowded in chattering alongside the radio or playing a quick round of cards; Wes oiling his boots for work, tinkering with fishing-hunting gear, playing the harmonica; or the room empty: lying there, his arm over his eyes snuffling scratching swallowing

One Monday (let him be a while, Mrs. Ed had said), Wes, on his way to work, left the boy at the Klamath crossroads to wait the school bus.

He stands motionless in the moist fog that is almost rain, in Bo's too big fishing slicker. Blurs of shapes loom up and pass. Once a bindle stiff plods by. The across-the-road is blotted out.

When the bus stops and the door snorts open, he still does not move. The driver tries three honks, pokes his head out and yells: c'mon New, whatever your name, I'm late. You can do your snoozing inside.

Laughter from in the bus. In hoots.

Slowly, as if returning from an infinite distance, the boy focusses his eyes on the driver, shaking his head and moving his lips as if speaking. He is still mutely shaking "No," as the faces at the grimy windows begin to slip by fast and faster contorted or vacant or staring.

On *his* face, lifted to the fog, is duplicated one by one, the expressions on the faces of his fellow young. Still he stands, his lips moving. When he has counted thirteen cars passing (a long while), he crosses and goes back down the road, the way his uncle had brought him.

•

Days.

This time when Wes got home, his neatly made bed was torn up, its blanket bunched round the boy stretched out in dimness near the window.

At the expected convulsive jumpup, Wes stepped back and grabbed the doorknob himself. Alright, alright, I'm closin it. The law ain't chasin *me*. Are they chasin you?

(but the boy had not moved at all)

He felt like yelling: why do you do that   or: look at me for once, say hello.

Instead he sat down heavily in the big chair, unlaced his boots. No, I won't ask what he's been doin. Nothin. He'll say it in nothin, too.

Night scratched at the window and seeped from the room corners. No other sound but rising river wind.

The work of the day (of the week, of years) slumped onto Wes. For a minute he let go, slept: snored, great sobbing snores. In a spasm of effort, jerked awake, regarded the shadows, the rumple on the floor by the window.

Something about the light, the radio, not being snapped on; the absence of the usual attempted pleasantries; some rhythm not right, roused the boy from the trancing secret tremble of leaves against the low glowing sky. Was that his mother or his uncle sagged there in the weight of weariness, and why were her feet on the floor?

Get back he said implacably Your footstool's gone too In a box or throwed away or somebody else resting their tootsies on it Serves you right How you going to put up your feet and rub on the varicose like you like to, now?

(*Blue swollen veining*) (*Are you tired, Ma? Tired to death, love.*)

What are you twitchin your muscles like a flybit horse for? asked Wes. And stop swallowin snot.

He slept again This man he hardly knew who came and took everything and him and put him in a place he did not know where he was. Slumped sagged, like . . .

Wes, if you set your feet up on something. *WES*

If I what?

If you set your feet up on a box

A box. For Crizake

Or a chair and rub where your feet hurt

A box Say, did you do up that box today like I told you?

It rests them, Wes. You rub up, not down

Answer me, Did you? No. You leave the only thing I ask you to do, for me to do, on my day off My one day Just look at this place You didn't help High neither when I asked you You think the candlefish run is goin to last forever? Maybe you might of brung in a basket or two Mrs. Ed would've took it into consideration You cost boy ghostboy don't you know that? My Saturday night for one thing my one night to howl you're costin

(Shrimp!) (I'd better watch it; I'm really spoiling tonight.) A rancorous: What's goin to be with you, you dummy kid? raps out anyway.

Sounding a long plaintive mockcowboy howl, switching on the light, yanking him up (God, he's skinny) and with a shove that is half embrace, steers him in to dinner.

Where he'd pushed the boiled salt salmon and potatoes away, the crack on his plate said: *Y. You cost, boy, you cost.* In his wrist a little living ball pushed, as if trying to get out Where the visiting nurse put her pinky and counted too sick people

Sagged with weariness   like Wes   her stockings rolled down rubbing rubbing where the blue veins swoll

On the wall the bottom of the Indian bow made: *U.* No, a funny *V. Y. V.* Vaude-e-ville. He'd stay for it twice and the feature twice and maybe the serial too while the light the silvery light Face bigger and bigger on the screen Closer Vast glutinous face Sour breath *IS YOU DERE, CHARLIE?* Bo. Only Bo. Everybody at the table laughing

And now the faces start up bigger than the room   on the fast track Having to hold up Hurry

At the door, Wes heard it again, that faint rhythmic creak. The first time, nights ago, he had thought: is the little bastard jacking off? but it wasnt that kind of a sound. Switching the light on, he saw the boy—as usual—lying on the cot, arm over his face—yes, and rolled into *his* blanket. The sound had stopped.

Sit up. Don't you know enough to excuse yourself when you leave a table sudden? Mrs. Edler was askin me, could you go upriver with her tomorrow to the deer or jumpdance or some such Indian thing they're having at Terwer. She must want somebody else white to come along with her pretty bad.

Is you dere, Charlie? You jumped a mile when Bo yelled that into your mug. Serves you right, sitting there night after night like you're no place at all, hardly answerin if people talk to you. Why are you such a snot?   *Why?* (*savagely*) IS YOU DERE?

> *(Somewhere.*
>
> *But the stupor, the lostness, the torpor)   (the safety)*
>
> *Keep away you rememorings   slipping   slidings having to hold up my head   Keep away you trying to get me's*
>
> *Become the line on a plate, on a wall   The rocking and the making warm   the movement of leaves against sky*
>
> *I work so hard for this safety   Let me a while   Let me)*

—C'mon. Set up like you belong. We're going to get shed of that box. Right now. But first you make up my bed. Just *keep* that blanket you dragged round the floor, and give me yours.

—C'mon, tuck those corners in. We keep things neat around here. Monday you're starting school. For sure this time. No more of this laying around.

—Neat, I said. Now, where's that goddamn box. And quite making those damn noises.

Scooping onto the bed:
>   boy-sitting-on-a-chamber-pot ash tray   Happy Joss Hollywood California painted fringed pillow cover kewpie doll green glass vase, cracked

Jesus, what junk
>   tiny India brass slipper ash tray   enamel cigarette case, Fujiyama scene (thrown too close to the edge of the bed, it slithers off, slips down behind) pencils, rubber banded

Junk is right. We sure throwed it in in a hurry
>   Plush candy box: sewing stuff: patches buttons in jars   stork scissors   pincushion doll, taffeta bell skirt glistening with glass pinheads

Tillie Olsen

Now you got a dolly to play with   Ketch   Can't you even ketch?
Red plush valentine box: nestled in the compartments: brown baby hair, ribbon tied   perfume bottle, empty   china deer miniature, the fawn headless   heart locket, stone missing   and sand dollar   gull feather

                              close quick
Now why did we . . . ?
            tarnished mesh purse: in it a bright penny   lipstick   rouge-powder compact, slivered mirror   powder sifts
                              close quick
      Pictures:
            palm size, heart shaped frame
                                          onto the bureau
            celluloid frame, tin laddered back stand
                                          onto the bureau
            stained oblong cardboard, smaller snapshots clipped round the large center one (His hand falters, steadies
                                          onto the bureau
            More boxes, slender, rubber banded: in the first: letters tied in a man's handkerchief   tin collar button   red garter band   ribboned medal pinned to a yellow envelope   In the second: (vicious the rubber band snaps)

                                    D O N ' T
      The boy rigid on the floor, eyes glazed, mouth open, fixed; face contorted. A fit?
      Steve? Stevie?
      Crawling now, a snake. Rising. With the pillow batting the box out of Wes's hands, flailing at him. *Put it back*. With the pillow shoving everything off the bed into the box. *Put it back. If you was dead   you'd put it back*   With the pillow pushing the box into the hall   slamming the door   *all of it   dead   bury   buried*   Runs to the chamberpot   vomits   jabs at Wes when he tries to help him   Runs to the door to run out   sees the box   runs back   takes the coverlet to him and rocks
      Alright   alright   Easy   Some other day   Where was my marbles?   Phew   Just a bad day, Stevie   mine was a Lulu   Alright, it's over   It was too soon, I know   All her things   Alright   Easy
      Heaving again .
      You through? I'll get it out of here (Almost falling over the box on his way to empty the slop.) (No, nobody home I can bum a drink off of. Sattiday night . . .) *(What am I doing   what am I going to do with this miserable kid?)*
      Bawling now like a girl.
      Alright! It's over, Stevie   It got to me too   Easy   You got to grab

hold . . . It's no good for you, layin round   never going out like normal   Monday you're going to start school   Keep you busy   You'll be with other kids, play ball, have somebody to fish with   Not lay around all the time thinkin about her, feelin bad.

Stopping his rocking. I don't. I don't.

Easy. It's all right; it's natural. But now you got to take hold.

Shut up bastard. Jabbing at him. Shut up. I told you I don't think about her, I don't feel bad. She's dead. Don't you know she's dead, don't you know?

Fending him off   nodding wordlessly   (*don't I know?*) Edging him back to the cot   Easy   Do I have to paste you one?   Forget it, try to sleep, fella   There's just so much I can stand   Easy   I'm so tired I could drop   I'll help you to catch hold, Steve, I promise I'll help   Stop now   Try to sleep   Holding him down to the cot   I'm tryin. Doing the best I can, even if it turns out worse like usual   But tryin. You try too. You hear that, Stevie? You try too.

Having to hold up

The pictures stayed, untouched, face down on the dresser. Whereever the box went, Wes assumed it was to the attic. Days later, making his bed, he found the cigarette case, slipped it into a drawer against that far time he might no longer have to roll his own, could afford tailor-mades.

The boy would not rouse. Shaken awake, would not come to breakfast, refused to go out with him and Bo. "We was goin to start you practice shootin today, try for some fish, maybe even let you take the wheel awhile. *You're* the loser." But Wes did not do much urging, wanting to get away from the incomprehensible moil of with-that-boy.

Before he went, he left instructions: Don't lay down *once*, not once. Neat up this room. If there's going to be any hot water, get yourself scrubbed up for school tomorrow   squeak clean. Find out has Yee got some work you can do; God,   in hell CAN you do. Get outside even if it's raining   down to the river   throw rocks or something. Keep yourself moving   Hear? And don't try to con me.

Asleep in the big chair when Wes got back; no, not asleep (hair still wet and an almost phosphorescent shine on his face) (*ghostboy*) So   *gone*   Wes's breath stops for a moment. Maybe I ought to get a doc, or ask Mrs. Ed to look in the doctor book. But what would she look for? laying around?   throwin up? actin nuts?

Then the tranced, shocked eyes looked at him   but the voice said, perfectly normal: I did everything like you told. Yee cooked him and me rice chow yuk so I don't have to go in for supper tonight, do I. How was your fishing, Wes?

•

He did not go to school.

Clean to his one white shirt with its streaks of blueing, clutching his and Wes's lunch pails, he sat silent in the pickup till Wes slowed for the crossroads stop where, three weeks before, he had been left for the school bus. Quickly he is over the side.

Hey, *I'm* takin you. You forget? *WAIT!* Where do you think you're heading?

Plodding back towards Requa.

Get back here. Listen, don't pull no girl tantrum. Get in.

Having to pull over to the shoulder, park, run after him. His violent grab missing, so that he tears the sleazy jacket, half yanking down the boy.

I'm not going, Wes.

Get up, you're going all right. If I have to drag you.

I'd leave soon as you were gone, Wes.

Starting down the road again.

Spinning him around, socking him a good one, steering him back into the car. (*What am I doing, what am I going to do*)

—What you got against school anyway?

—You're headed straight for the nuthouse, layin round like you've been doing. Just nuttier every day. I'm not goin to let you.

—I'll have the truant officer, see? Wait, is 14 or 16 the limit?

—You're goin, see. What the hell else you got to do? C'mon, dust yourself off. I can't be late.

Starting to climb out again.

Really hurting him; pinning him back, banging and banging his head against the wheel, against the seat. You *have* to go, see?

Wes   (In a strangled voice) Wes you're hurting.   If I find me a job?

A job!   Releasing him in disgust. You ARE in a nutworld. Half the grown men in the county's not working, High's down to two days, and this dummy kid talks about a job.

In Frisco then, Wes? Maybe set up pins again. Or ship?

In Frisco, my God. It's worse there, you know that. And how you goin to make that 500 miles? And who you got in your corner there? Nobody. You NEED learnin.

Starting up the motor.

Wes, I'll jump.

Socking him again. Hard.

Wes, if I go with you? Ask Mr. Evans, can I help? A learn job, Wes. By you.

Something in the boys voice . . . This time Wes's hands on his shoulders are gentle. Steve, don't fight it no more. It's five, maybe six weeks to vacation . . . fishin. You'll have buddies. Maybe you'll even like school. And even if you don't, sometimes in this life you got to do what you *don't* like. (*Sometimes!*) Evans ain't about to put anybody on—if he did, Ez would be first choose; every week Ez is in askin: can he have his job back . . . Evans don't have it, Stevie. Sometimes its slow even for me. And everythings credit or trade-in; when we get a nickel, he bites it, makes sure its real. I'm surprised he pays *me.*

Ask him, Wes. You said: I'll help you, Steve. You said it. He don't have to pay me. You hurt me bad, Wes. A learn job. By you. You promised.
Not school
Never
Forever

•

NEW USED

U NAME IT—WE GOT IT
U ASK IT—WE FIX IT

Gas   Butane   Sportsmens Goods
Auto Parts   Fittings   Tools
Lumber   Rags   Scrap iron
Electric/plumber/builder supply
Housefurnish things

Auto Repair   Towing   Wrecking
Machine   Soldering   Welding
Tool & Saw Sharping
Glass work   Boat caulking/repair

(Leaky, appraising eyes) Sure, why not? Favor to you, Wes. Anything he gets done, we're that much ahead. But if he's in the way, or it don't work out, that's it. And he's *your* headache. Anybody stick their nose in, he's helping you, not working for me. Don't get him expecting anything for the piggy bank, either. Used stock sometime maybe, whatever I think it's worth and he's worth. Catch?

Tumble of buildings and sheds, stockpiles and junk—a block from the bridge—sprawled in the crotch between 101 going north/south and the short crooked upriver road to game and Indian country.

Landscape of thinghillocks and mounds innumerable. Which shed is which? The wind blows so. Too close: scaly, rapid river; too close: dwarfing, encircling: dark massive forest rise.

Stumbling the mounds in his too thin jacket or Bo's too big slicker after Wes. *(got to figure out what's simple enough he can do. Keep him up. Moving. Paying attention.)* Helping haul drag break apart; find the right sized used tire generator lumbersash; hand the measure   the part   the tool

I said the red devil   Red devil glass cutter   Your ears need reaming?

Does that even *look* like a 16 x 120? Why the thing they throw peanuts at could figger it

What you breathin like that for? I showed you: if you lift it this way, she goes easy. Easy. A right way and a wrong way— easy is the right way

Is that a shimmy or a shiver? I ought to take me a razor cut, see is it blood or icewater runs in your carcass

The mess heap. Your baby to red up when I'm not needin you. Stack everything, that's what's here, everything—with its own kind. If theys a pile or shed already for it, get it over there   Whats too far gone or cant be burnt, leave. Get them rotten carpets   mattresses out first. Then them batteries   Pile 'em so.   Where I expect to spot you when you're not workin with me, see?

Into the toolshed when it rains. Sort outa the bins into these here washboilers: like, pipe fittins: brass here   copper there: elbows flanges unions   couplings   bends   tees. Check out the drawers, see just what belongs is in 'em; get acquainted: like this row: wing nuts   castellated   slotted quarter inch   *Pay attention!*

> Heaps piles glut accumulation
> Sores cuts blisters on his hands
> Don't look: scaly rapid river   dark forest encircling

Cold   hardly comprehending   wearing out so quick

Didn't you hear me calling? Answer me. What you staring at? You paralyzed? (*ghostboy*) Drop that carpet and get out of sight till you can come to   Do I have to paste you one?

(The stiff mouldy rug breaks like cardboard in his hands. Underneath maggot patterns writhe)

Can't you tell the difference between taper and spiral fluted? (lock or finish washer?) (adapter, extension?)   can't you? can't you?

Who said you could come in here and lay down? You sure tire instant   Get yourself back to the burn pile and throw that filthy ragquilt out of here. No wonder you're always scratching.

Is that all you got done and I let you alone all mornin for it? What's there goin to be to show Evans you're of use   Yah, as much use as a tit on a bull   O for Crizake you're not here at all

More and more wrapped in the peacock quilt, rocking, scratching, snuffling. Rain on the toolshed roof; the little kerosene stove hissing warmth through its pierced crown. Wes looming in the doorway, the gray face of evening behind him. C'mon, useless. 6:30. You killed another day. I *knowed* this was never going to work.

And once, in the most mournful of voices: Can't you do no better? I can't stand it, Stevie. You're ending up in the dummy or loony house, for sure.

But the known is reaching to him, stealthily, secretly, reclaiming.
Sharp wind breath, fresh from the sea. Skies that are all seasons in one day. Fog   rain. *Known weather of his former life.*

Disorder twining with order. The discarded, the broken, the torn from the whole: weathereaten weatherbeaten: mouldering, or waiting for use-need. *Broken existences that yet continue.*

    Hasps   switches   screws   plugs   tubings   drills
    Valves   pistons   shears   planes   punchers   sheaves
    Clamps   sprockets   coils   bits   braces   dies

How many shapes and sizes; how various, how cunning in application. Human mastery, human skill. Hard, defined, enduring, they pass through his hands—link to this city life of manmade marvel.

Wes: junking a towed-in car, one hundred pieces out of what had been one. Singing—unconcious, forceful—to match the motor hum as he machines a new edge, rethreads a pipe. Capable, fumbling; exasperated, patient; demanding, easy; uncomprehending, quick; harsh, gentle: *concerned* with him. *The recognizable human bond.*

The habitable known, stealthily, secretly, reclaiming.
The dead things, pulling him into attention, consciousness.
The tasks: coaxing him with trustworthiness, pliancy, doing as he
    bids

                                        having to hold up

Rifts:
Wes sets the pitch, the feed, the slide rest to chase a thread.
"Wes, *let* me. We're learning it in shop. It's my turn again Monday."
(Monday! What Monday? A Monday cobweb weeks miles gone life ago) Hard, reassuring, the lathe burrs; spins under his hands. (Somewhere in cobweb mist, a school—speck size. Somewhere smaller specks that move speak have faces)
Watch it! O my God, you dummy. How'm I going to explain *this* one to Evans.

Wheat wreathes enamelled on a breadbox he is tipping to empty of rain Remembered patter; forgotten hunger peanut butter, sour french bread Remembered scene, face, hand, wavering through his face, reflected in the rusty agitated water.
He lifts the wrecking mallet, pounds. Long after the spurting water has dried from his face and the tin is shreds in great muddy earth gouges, he still mindlessly pounds.
Later, dragging a mattress to the burn pile, his face contorts, fixes rigid, mouth open. The rest of the day in the toolshed, to lie immobile, and will not get up even to Wes's kick of rage.

Rags stiff and damp Green slime braids with the rope coils, white grubs track his palm
    Bottle fly colors lustre the rotting harness rusty tongueless bells fall

Only the rain saves him—otherwise, before lunch, he practices shooting. Buckets, cans, are spotted in a semicircle for targets, the rococo scroll of carpet beater nailed to a post. Sight. Squeeze. Splat. Shuddering rock of the recoil.

Who barks more, Wes or the gun? If you'd been concetrating if you'd just been concetrating. I want you good as me, Stevie. See? 200 yards right on target everytime.

The bruise on his shoulder—from when? Wes's beating the day he would not go to school?—purples, spreads.

Maybe this is better'n school for you Stevie   Keep you outdoors, build you up   I got so much to learn you   All your life you can use it.

He is warmer now. An old melton coat with anchor buttons that Evans let Wes take from the clothes shed. Faint salt of a seaman's many voyagings seems to nest in it, and deep in the pockets, mysterious graininesses crumble. Afternoons, if the strong northwest winds of May have cleared the sky an hour or two, the coat distills stores the sun about him as he moves through mound-sheltered warmth in and out of the blowing cold;   or sits with Wes, poncho over the muddy ground, eating their baloney and bread lunch in the sun-hive the back of the scrapiron pile makers.

Weeds, the yellow wild mustard and rank cow parsnip, are already waist high, blow between him and the river. Blue jays shrill, swoop for crumbs; chipmunks hover. Wes gabs, plays his harmonica. The boy lies face down in his pool of warmth. In him something keeps trembling out in the wind with the torn whirled papers, the bending weeds, the high tossed gulls.

Helping at the gas pump, he keeps his head lowered so that he knows the grease spots on the ground and how they change from day to day, but not who is in the cars. Even when the speech comes glottal, incomprehensible, Indian, he will not look up on the faces, nor on those of the riggers and swampers checking the chains tight around the two-three giant logs that make up their load.

Grease spots, and how they change from day to day; loggers muddied boots, flowerets and pine needles embedded; plaint redwood hair strands loosened from the logs and blowing across the road; the cars of the regulars; Evans dry ghost cough from the store, and that a certain worn-to-bareness tire tread will bring him watchfully into hearing distance; these he comes to know—but never faces.

Once, checking tires (young swaggering voices in the car), a girl steps out on the running board, so close he can smell her, round his hand to her bared thigh, the curve of her butt.

Relentless, vehement: clamor congests   engorges. Gas bit, the soaked rag held to his nostrils, will not help.

Wes, don't call me to the pumps any more.
You'll do as you're told, you snotty kid   Snotty's right   Everytime I look you. Wipe that nose. You need a washer in there?

> relentless
> engorged
> clamorous
> *stealthily secretely reclaiming*

Terrible pumps:
Evans out more and more.
Davis does what *I* say, see? Pay on the line or no *tow*. You heard me, no dough, no go. I don't care *how* many kids you got stuck in your jalopy, or how far you had to hitch to get here. Sure we got a used transmission. We got a used everything. But for do-re-mi. Don't ask *me* how you're going to manage without a heap . . . Well, you can junk it.

No, not even for five gallons trade, I won't take that mattress. I got a shed full now. There's maybe four hundred families the fifty miles around; they're sleeping on something already; who's going to buy 'em off me? No. That spare hasn't got a thousand miles left. Well maybe the gun.

Ten gallons gets you up—say—Grants Pass. How do *I* know how you'll make it to your brothers in Chehalis. One thing we *don't* sell here is a crystal ball.
. . . You'd think it was me knocked up their old ladies and lost 'em their jobs.

Whisper: Over here, Wes. I don't want ol Skinflint to spot me. You think you might have some link chain like this? An /8th or maybe a quarter inch. I got this idea, see? Sports season coming, and you know how they like to bring back a souvenir. Well, Christmas we didn't know what to do, so I whittled the boys up little lumber trucks—load of logs, chain and all—they're still playing with 'em. I thought till the woods open up again, I might pick up some loose change makin 'em to sell. Esty's doing up dolls out of redwood hair. Real cute. Evans won't help me out, but you will, won't you Wes. I'm about out of my mind.

When I call you I don't mean tomorrow sometime next week. If I catch you cuddlin up to that stove again, I'll turn you every which way but loose

•

The smell of the whiskey is making him sick   is making him happy   is making him sleepy   The brights and the ragtime making him happy   lights lights little lights over the fireplace going on and off and on and off and on if you wink your eyes in time in time   I love you lights   Are you howling Wes   is that how you howl your night to howl?   O Wes   in the blue of smoke and breaths tapdancing with Bo and that lady Esty in the middle and that fatso man   Stop you don't know how to tap, Wes   The keys on the player piano nickel in the slot piano know how   jigging and tapping and nobody's playing them because I'M playing them   long distance   knowing how   tapping and dancing (luxurious round the table   round the dollars   his fingers tapping) round and round

What you going to do with those two big beautiful cartwheels honey? Tapdance my fingers round and round them   what he didn't answer her and should have   because   because   and here the breathblue smokeblue clouds into his head   And on and off and round   tiniest sparkle on the wall   calendar snow scene, moose locking horns   sparkly I love you O I like that ragtime kitten on the keys   I *am* the keys   What did you say that's so ha ha Wes? wave   wave   dance my hand (no nobody's looking) highstep fingers   o highstep and off and on and round   I wanta go to a movie show   And round   Red light that squiggles to you in the fog and when you get closer says   E A T   but nobody's eating   they're dancing they think its dancing   chewing the rag and swiggling   and off and on and sparkle and round and fire jumping and Wes howling

    Stop that, Bo

                                              sticky and cold, the whiskey doused over him.   *Best hair tonic there is, I'm tellin you, kid, use it myself every celebratin night   and it stinks so purty*

It doesn't   it doesn't   and it doesn't wipe off and the smell is on his sleeve now so when he has to wipe his nose or wave his arm is making him sick   and off and on   and round   o put another nickel in   reeling waltz   I wanta go to a picture show   A man crying (Fatso)   *sobby sentimental stew*   O ma, that's funny, a sobby sentimental stew

Liar   You promised   and see I'm another place again   no movies and no stores and no Chinatown and cold water in the faucet you have to pump not even lights   just tonight   little prickle kind and one squiggle sign   just tonight

and round and round and off and on · push on the keys   dance tap float on the sadness   sleep pushing down clouding and   Sure   I'm listening Wes   No thanks you just gave me another nip   Yah *how you keep Evans from catching on that I'm not all there*   Yah and round   sparks like blows from a fist   the fire?   over the fireplace, branching antlers, sad deer eyes   in the fire, branching antlers glowing eyes   am going to be sick

                                                      aaagh
                                                      aaagh

•

Requa-I

A dream? The yard   lithe Bo tapdancing the mounds   Wes in the furnish shed handing out bottles   gurgling from one himself bootleg   he don't know I know he's peddlin hooch but I do, gettin in on it just when it's goin to get legal   end hard times   Turning round and round a musical saw wheel   dry whispery papery sad sound   *they have taken her to Georgia*   Wes's harmonica prowl papery sad   *there to wear her life away*   making his saddest train-whistle sounds   round   and   round

•

The damp rushing air slaps the boys face: *wake up*   the lurching in his belly, the pitching truck: *wake up.* Wes slapping too, jabbing him away with his elbow every lurch he is thrown against him; waves of drunk smell from Wes's breath or is it his own sleeve: *wake up.* Wes driving jolty, not like Wes at all: shouting   singing   mumbling   beating on the dash. Crooning: poor ol shrimp cant sit up   poor ol shrimp passin out   Take him out to celebrate Evans shakin loose two smackers and he cant take it   cant celebrate   FOO-derackysacky want some seafood momma shrimpers and rice are very nice poor old shrimp (pounding on the dash)   YOU'RE A SHIT EVANS YOU HEAR ME   he don't know though does he (elbow jab)   he don't know you're not all there (jab) cause I cover up good don't I Stevie? We'll have a heaver on that, hey? Me, not you, shrimp. Am taking care of you like I promised. Right?

Vamp me honey kitchaleecoo   anything you'll want we'll do   Jab. Forever long to get to Mrs. Eds. Not the same way they came. Jolt, jolt. Is it even a road? Headless shadows in the carlights. Stumps. *Not all there*   Sparks like blows   Hurtled, falling   falling   Wet on his face   fir needles? leaves   Blood?

C'mon, up, up. See if you're hurt. Well, I did stop sudden. You're fine, kid, sound as a dollar. Go ahead, puke. I got to go to this place down here, see? Thick   oblivious   Laughing   mumbling   Pawing the floor of the truck for something, throwing the poncho at him, hard   *Cover up*   Dont want you ketching cold. You're running out of snot as is. Counting, recounting his silver by the light of a flash. Expansively: Keep'em, Stevie, keep'em; don't need 'em.

Need what? Thick black   His trembling body redoing the hurtling fall over and over   all scraped places burning.   His shoulder . . . Far down in trees a weak light   whorled, spectral, veined   Eyes

Wes, wait, wait for me. Tripping over the poncho. On the ground again, his nose bubbling blood.

Easier to just lie there   roll into the poncho   shrink into the coat   Cry (In one soft pocket his fingers tap round and round the silver dollars; in the other, hold the tongueless bell.) Put another nickel   Some celebrating!   *Not all there*

Faint salt smell   from drying blood?   the coat?   Warm.   Round and round   not even minding the dark

Sudden the knowledge where Wes has gone. *Annie Marines*, she sells it. Nausea. Swelling, swollen aching. Helpless, his hand starts to undo the coat layer (*meet the wife, meet the wife*).

Slap. On his face. Another slap. Great drops. *Rain.* Move, you dummy. Pushing himself up against a tree, giant umbrella in the mottled dark. Throb sound and around him (his own excited blood beat?) Rain, hushing, lapping

City boy, he had only known rain striking hard on unyielding surface, walls, pavement; not this soft murmurous receiving: leaves, trees, earth. In wonder he lay and listened, the fir fragrance sharp through his caked nostrils. Warm. Dry.

Far down where Wes was, a branch shook silver into the light. Rain. *His mothers quick shiver as the rain traced her cheek. C'mon baby, we've got to run for it.*

Laughing. One of her laughing times. Running fast as her, the bundles bumping his legs. Running up the stairs too. Tickling him, keeping him laughing while she dried his face with the rough towel.

Twisting away from the pain: trying to become the cocoa steam, the cup ring marking the table, the wheat wreathed breadbox. *Her shiver.* How the earth received the rain, how keen its needles. Don't ask *me* where your umbrella got put, don't expect *me* to be sponsible, you in your leaky house.

Rain underneath, swelling to a river, floating her helpless away *Her shiver*

Twisting away from the pain: face contorted, mouth fallen open: fixed to the look on her dying, dead face.

When Wes lurched down the path, he still did not move. The helpless pain came again. For Wes this time, drunk, stumbling, whispering: O my God, I've had better imagines

Stevie! Where the hell are you? You scared the hell out of me. . . Let's get going. I feel lower than whale shit, and that's at the bottom of the ocean.

The light was still on. Wes must have carried or walked him in, been too drunk to make him wake up, undress. Wes hadn't undressed either, lay, shoes muddy on his bed, he, who was always the neat one.

The boy stared at the bulb staring at him; then, painfully, got up, pulled off his clothes, went over and knelt by Wes's bed to tug off the offending shoes and cover him.

One of Wes's fists trembled; a glisten of spit trickled out of the corner of his mouth. His fly was open. How rosy and budlike and quiet it sheathed there.

The blanket ends wouldn't lap to cover. He had to pile on his coat, Wes's mackinaw, and two towels, patting them carefully around the sleeping form. *There now you'll be warm*, he said aloud, *sleep sweet, sweet dreams* (though he did not know he had said it, nor in whose inflections.)

He was shivering with cold now. *Dummy or crazy house not all there* Though he put his hands out imploringly to protect himself, the blows struck at him again. His uncle moaned, whispered something; he leaned down to hear it, looked full on the sleeping face. Face of his mother. *His* face. Family face.

For once he was glad to turn off the light and have the shutting darkness: hugged the pillow over his face for more. At the window spectral shapes tapped; out in the hall, swathed forms floated, wrung their hands. Later he hurtled the fall over and over in a maggoty sieve where eyes glowed in rushing underground waters and fire branched antlers, fir needle after shining needle.

•

    accurately threaded, reamed and chamfered

        Shim   Imperial flared

            cutters benders grinders beaders
              shapers notchers splicers reamers

                                how many shapes and sizes,
                                how various, how cunning in
                                        application

What did Toots and Casper want? Did I hear them asking for two gallons of gas? *Two* gallons? Where they coming from anyway? I thought that kind were all riding 99.

Tentacle weeds pierce the dishpan he is trying to pry up. Orange rust flowerings flake, cling to the quivering stalks, embroider the gaping pan holes.
    Beauty of rot   rust   mold

    Wing ding anchors   bearing sheaves   plated, crackle, mottle blue, satin finish

Are your dreamin or workin? That carbon should of been clean chipped off by now. I *promised* that motor. O for Crizake, you ain't here at all.

Something is different at Mrs. Eds. Is it the longer light? How clear everyone is around the table, though still he does not look into their faces. The lamps, once so bright and hung with shadows, are phantom pale; the windows, once black mirrors where apparitions swam, show green and clear to heads of trees, river glint, dark waver of hill against sunset sky.
    Highpockets is gone. When had he gone, and why? The blurredness will not lift. A new man, thready, pale, sits in his place and has his room.
    The talk eddies around him: ain't going to *be* no season, not in Alaska Vancouver or Pedro . . . like crabs feedin on a dead man, like a lot gulls waitin for scraps . . . the Cascades the Olympics the Blues . . . nickel snatchin bastards
    He sees that it is not shadows that hang on the wall around the bow, but Indian things: a feathered headdress, basket hats, shell necklace. Two faces dream in shell frames. One, for all the beard, Mrs. Ed's.
                                            family face

Tillie Olsen

    sharping   hauling   sorting   splicing
    burring   chipping   grinding   cutting
    grooving   drilling   caulking   sawing

the tasks, coaxing

rust gardens

Nippers. You bring nippers. Did you thing I was going to *bite* the wire? Try it with *your* choppers.

Pilings on pilings. Rockers. victrolas, flyspecked mirrors, scroll trundle sew machines, bureaus, bedsteads. baby buggies.
Wes, I can't hardly open the door, it won't go in, there's no room.
No room, you make room, dummy. That's the job. You good for *any*thing?

The wind blows the encircling forest to a roar. Papers fly up and blind; a tire is blown from his hand. He scrambles the scrapiron pile to the shelter side, stands, coat flapping, blown riverspray wet on his face, hallooing and hallooing to the stone bears on the bridge, the bending trees.
Loony, loony, get down. You see that canvas needs tackin? Tack.

Miming Wes's face Sounding Evans dry ghost cough Gentling his bruised shoulder. Sometimes stopping whatever he is doing, his mouth opening: fixed to the look on her dying face
We'll be able to start burnin today or tomorrow if the wind stays down, says Wes. Don't this sun feel good? Just smell.
Brew of rose bay, forest, river, earth dryings, baked by the sun into a great fragrant steaminess. In it, every metal scrap, every piece of glass, glances, flashes, quivers, spangles, ripples light.
Wes stands in fountains of light: white sparkles as he moves the wheel for knife sharpening; blue jettings as he welds a radiator.
I didn't know you could sing, Stevie. You practicing for the Majors Amateur Hour?
It's for my head, Wes.
Outa your head, you mean.
The baking warmth, the vapor, the dazzle, the windlessness.

Toward the noon the next day, they set the burn pile. Wes lets him douse on the gasoline, but the boys look is so unnatural—spasms of laughing and spastic body dance as the flames spurt—Wes cuffs him away.
You a firebug nut or something? Get away, loony.
The wordless ecstasy will not contain. Quiver and dazzle are magnified in the strange smoking air. Baking mud sucks at his shoes as he runs from flash to flash. Stench of burning rubber and smoldering wet rags layer in with the heady sweet spring vapors. How vast each breath. Wreaths of yellow and black smoke rise. A stately rain of ash begins. *And still the rippling, glancing,*

magnifying light. It drives him down by the river, but the stench and dazzle are there too, and flashing rainbow crescents he does not know are salmon leaping.

There, on a sandy spit, where the blue water greens the edging forest, the climbing fir trees blue the sky, he lays himself down.

Only when they turn at Panther Creek for the Requa cutoff do they leave the smoke. They ride west into setting sun blare. The road is gold, black leaves shake out sungold, and from the low deer brush—outlined too in gilt—there reels a drunken wild-lilac smell.

Ten more days to huntin, Stevie. You don't know how much I want them few days . . . I shouldn't have got so mad; you're doin almost o.k. lately, sometimes as much help as trouble. Even your shootin

Four days in a half stupor, pumping for breath.

What do you have to pull something like this for? Now I got to work Decoration Day, be far enough ahead so he'll give me them three days off. . . Mrs. Ed, come here, isn't there anything you can do to help this poor kid catch his breath?

•

He stands beside her negligently, as if he is not there at all, stooping his newly tall, awkward body into itself while she introduces him to the preacher, families, other young.

Better go in, Stephen, you shouldn't be standing here in this strong wind. Betty'll show you where to sit, won't you, Betty?

his Dad . . . never knew him . . . before he was
born . . . AEF . . . his mother, a young woman, real sudden
. . . Wes Davis   his uncle . . . all he has

His sleeves don't pull down to cover   ugly scabs *That these dead shall not peely walls* Mrs. Edler's arm light on his hurt shoulder   *He breaketh the bow and snappeth the spear asunder*   cobwebs   under the backless benches Spiders?   his skin crawls. Scratching the itch places he can reach   scratching blood. Dead fly in hymn book   Somebody giggling whispering
There is a fountain filled with blood
sweet voice   a girl or lady in back
and there may I, as vile as he wash all my sins away
somebody giggling whispering   The sleeves don't pull down

•

At the first cemetry, he waits for her under the Requiescat in Pace gate. People come by, carrying wreaths and flowers and planting flags. If you were a dead soldier, you got a flag. The flags made crackle noises in the wind—like shooting practice—and kept getting blown down and having to be planted again.

A girl—that Betty maybe?—called his name, so he had to walk to a tangled part where nobody else was. His foot kicked over something—a glass canning jar—rust and dried things that might once have been flowers in it. Did it belong to the marble hand pointing to the sky, Leo Jordan, 1859-1911, He is Not

Dead but Sleeping, or to the kneeling stone lamb, almost hidden by the tall blowing weeds?

He bent down and stood it by the lamb. Milena Willet was carved on it,
1 yr. old   Budded on earth
                Blooming in Heaven

He had to pull away the weeds and scratch out the sandy dirt to read the rest:
        Thy mother strives in patient trust
        Her bleeding heart to bow
        For safe in God the Good the Just
        Her babys sleeping now

That part was sunk in the ground.

How warm it felt down there in the weeds where nobody could see him and the wind didn't reach. The lamb was sun warm too. He put his arm around its stone neck and rested. Red ants threaded in and out; the smell was sweet like before they set the burn pile; even the crackling flags sounded far away.

The sleep stayed in him all the way to the second cemetry. Other people were in the car, they had stopped at back dirt roads to get them. You always get out and open the car door for ladies, Stephen, Mrs. Edler had said. But they weren't ladies, they were Indians.

The sun baked in through the car window and their trouble talk floated in haze He says the law on his side Legal *but it's ours* The Sheriff bones don't prove it he says the law

This cemetery he didn't get out of the car. It trembled all the time, pushed and rattled by the wind. Trees, bent all their lives that one way, clawed toward the windows. There were firing sounds here too, but maybe they were ocean booms. He thought he could see ocean, lashing beyond the trees.

•

What did you do to him? Wes asked Mrs. Edler. When I heard where you went, I expected sure he'd get back near dead, bad as in the beginning. But he's been frisky as a puppy all day. Chased me round the junk heaps. Rassled went down to the river on his own throwed skimmers sharped a saw perfect Paid attention Curled up and fell asleep on the way home.

That's where he is—still sleeping. Lay down second we got home and I can't get him up. Blowing out the biggest bubble of snot you ever saw. Just try and figger that loony kid.

stealthily secretly reclaiming

John Updike

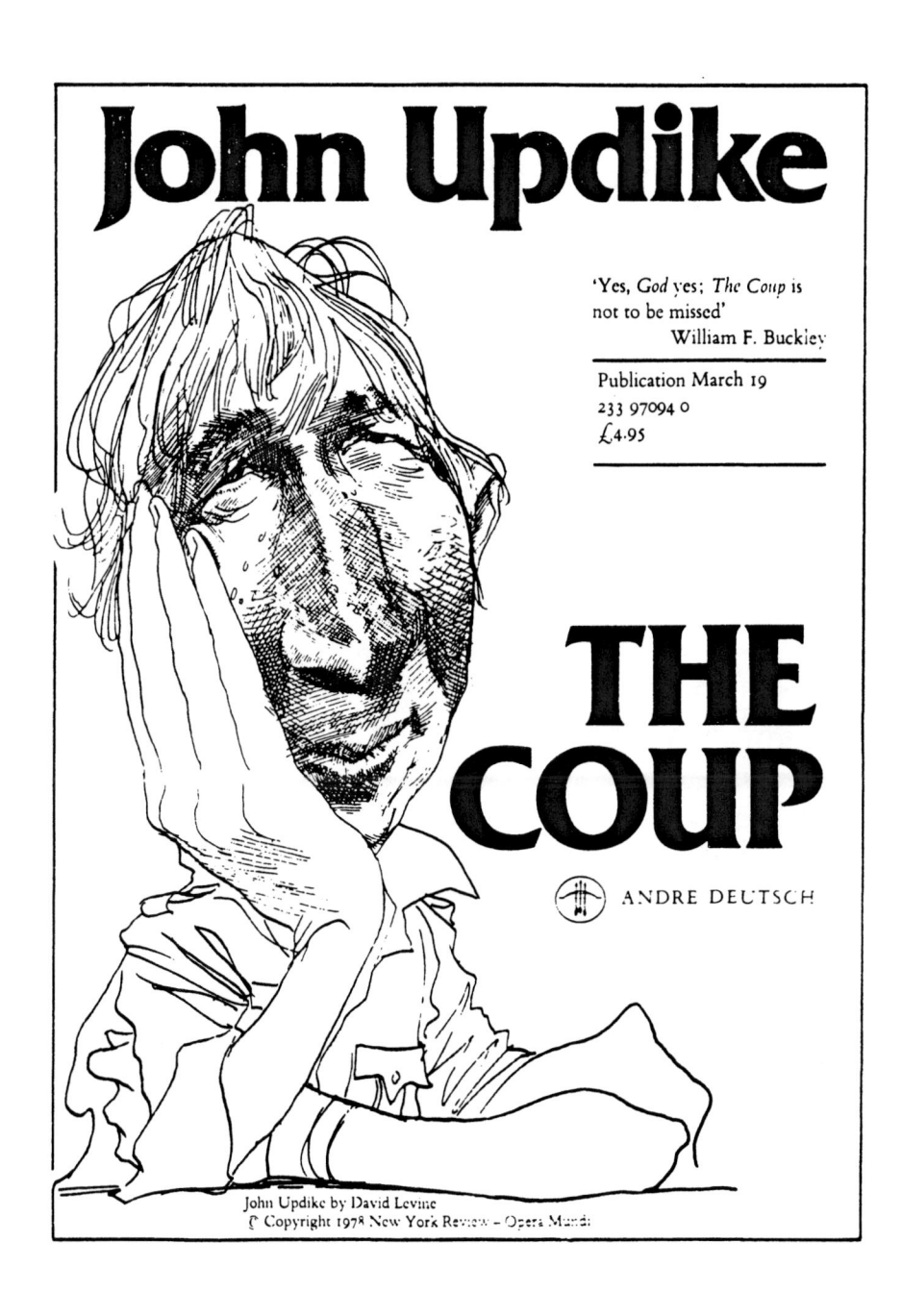

'Yes, *God* yes; *The Coup* is not to be missed'
William F. Buckley

Publication March 19
233 97094 0
£4.95

THE COUP

ANDRE DEUTSCH

John Updike by David Levine
© Copyright 1978 New York Review – Opera Mundi

DONALD BARTHELME

The New Music

—What did you do today?
—Went to the grocery store and Xeroxed a box of English muffins, two pounds of ground veal and an apple. In flagrant violation of the Copyright Act.
—You had your nap, I remember that—
—I had my nap.
—Lunch, I remember that, there was lunch, slept with Susie after lunch, then your nap, woke up, right?, went Xeroxing, right?, read a book not a whole book but part of a book—
—Talked to Happy on the telephone saw the seven o'clock news did not wash the dishes want to clean up some of this mess?
—If one does nothing but listen to the new music, everything else drifts, goes away, frays. Did Odysseus feel this way when he and Diomedes decided to steal Athene's statue from the Trojans, so that they would become dejected and lose the war? I don't think so, but who is to know what effect the new music of that remote time had on its hearers?
—Or how it compares to the new music of this time?
—One can only conjecture.
—Ah well. I was talking to a girl, talking to her mother actually but the daughter was very much present, on the street. The daughter was absolutely someone you'd like to take to bed and hug and kiss, if you weren't too old. If she weren't too young. She was a wonderful-looking young woman and she was looking at me quite seductively, very seductively, *smoldering* a bit, and I was thinking quite well of myself, very well indeed, thinking myself quite the— Until I realized she was just practicing.
—Yes, I still think of myself as a young man.
—Yes.
—A slightly old young man.
—That's not unusual.
—A slightly old young man still advertising in the trees and rivers for a

mate.
—Yes.
—Being clean.
—You're very clean.
—Cleaner than most.
—It's not escaped me. Your cleanness.
—Some of these people aren't clean. People you meet.
—What can you do?
—Set an example. Be clean.
—Dig it, dig it.
—I got three different shower heads. Different degrees of sting.
—Dynamite.
—I got one of these Finnish pads that slip over the hand.
—*Numero uno.*
—Pedicare. That's another thing.
—Think you're the mule's eyebrows don't you?
—No. I feel like Insufficient Funds.
—Feel like a busted-up car by the side of the road stripped of value.
—Feel like —*I don't like this!*
—You're just a little down, man, down, that's what they call it, down.
—Well how come they didn't bring us no ring of roses with a purple silk sash with gold lettering on that mother? How come that?
—Dunno baby. Maybe we lost?
—How could we lose? How could we? We!
—We were standing tall. Ready to hand them their asses, clean their clocks. Yet maybe—
—I remember the old days when we almost automatically—
—Yes. Almost without effort—
—Right. Come in, Commander. Put it right there, anywhere will do, let me move that for you. Just put that sucker down right there. An eleven-foot-high silver cup!
—Beautifully engraved, with dates.
—Beautifully engraved, with dates. That was then.
—Well. Is there help coming?
—I called the number for help and they said there was no more help.
—I'm taking you to Pool.
—I've been there.
—I'm taking you to Pool, city of new life.
—Maybe tomorrow or another day.
—Pool, the revivifier.
—Oh man I'm not up for it.
—Where one can taste the essences, get swindled into health.
—I got things to do.
—That lonesome road. It ends in Pool.
—Got to chop a little cotton, go by the drugstore.

The New Music

—Ever been to Pool?
—Yes I've been there.
—Pool, city of new hope.
—Get my ocarina tuned, sew a button on my shirt.
—Have you traveled much? Have you traveled enough?
—I've traveled a bit.
—Got to go away 'fore you can get back, that's fundamental.
—The joy of return is my joy. Satisifed by a walk around the block.
—Pool. Have you seen the new barracks? For the State Police? They used that red rock they have around there, quite a handsome structure, dim and red.
—Do the cops like it?
—No one has asked them. But they could hardly... I mean it's new.
—Got to air my sleeping bag, scrub up my canteen.
—Have you seen the new amphitheater? Made out of red rock. They play all the tragedies.
—Yeah I've seen it that's over by the train station right?
—No it's closer to the Great Lyceum. The Great Lyceum glowing like an ember against the hubris of the city.
—I could certainly use some home fries 'long about now. Home fries and ketchup.
—Pool. The idea was that it be one of those new towns. Where everyone would be happier. The regulations are quite strict. They don't let people have cars.
—Yes, I was in on the beginning. I remember the charette, I was asked to prepare a paper. But I couldn't think of anything. I stood there wearing this blue smock stenciled with the Pool emblem, looked rather like a maternity gown. I couldn't think of anything to say. Finally I said I would go along with the group.
—The only thing old there is the monastery, dates from 1720 or thereabouts. Has the Dark Virgin, the Virgin is black, as is the Child. Dates from 1720 or around in there.
—I've seen it. Rich fare, extraordinarily rich, makes you want to cry.
—And in the fall the circus comes. Plays the red rock gardens where the carved red asters, carved red phlox, are set off by borders of yellow beryl.
—I've seen it. Extraordinarily rich.
—So it's settled, we'll go to Pool, there'll be routs and revels, maybe a sock hop, maybe a nuzzle or two on the terrace with one of the dazzling Pool beauties—
—Not much for nuzzling, now. I mostly kneel at their feet, knit for them or parse for them—
—And the Pool buffalo herd. Six thousand beasts. All still alive.
—Each house has its grand lawns and grounds, brass candlesticks, thrice-daily mail delivery. Elegant widowed women living alone in large houses, watering lawns with whirling yellow sprinklers, studying the patterns of the grass, searching out brown patches to be sprinkled. Sometimes there is a grown

child in the house, or an almost-grown one, working for a school or hospital in a teaching or counseling position. Frequently there are family photographs on the walls of the house, about which you are encouraged to ask questions. At dusk medals are awarded those who have made it through the day, the Cross of St. Jaime, the Cross of St. Em.

—Meant to be one of those new towns where everyone would be happier, much happier, that was the idea.

—Serenity. Peace. The dead are shown in art galleries, framed. Or sometimes, put on pedestals. Not much different from the practice elsewhere except that in Pool they display the actual—

—Person.

—Yes.

—And they play a tape of the guy or woman talking, right next to his or her—

—Frame or pedestal.

—Prerecorded.

—Naturally.

—Shocked white faces talking.

—Killed a few flowers and put them in pots under the faces, everybody does that.

—Something keeps drawing you back like a magnet.

—Watching the buffalo graze. It can't be this that I've waited for, I've waited too long. I find it intolerable, all this putter. Yet in the end, wouldn't mind doing a little grazing myself, it would look a little funny.

—Is there bluegrass in heaven? Make inquiries. I saw the streets of Pool, a few curs broiling on spits.

—And on another corner, a man spinning a goat into gold.

—Pool projects positive images of itself through the great medium of film.

—Cinemas filled with industrious product.

—Real films. Sent everywhere.

—Film is the great medium of this century—hearty, giggling film.

—So even if one does not go there, one may assimilate the meaning of Pool.

—I'd just to rest and laze around.

—Soundtracks in Burmese, Italian, Twi, and other tongues.

—One film is worth a thousand words. At least a thousand.

—There's a film about the new barracks, and a film about the new amphitheater.

—Good. Excellent.

—In the one about the new barracks we see Squadron A at morning roll call, tense and efficient. "Mattingly!" calls the sergeant. "Yo!" says Mattingly. "Morgan!" calls the sergeant. "Yo!" says Morgan.

—A fine bunch of men. Nervous, but fine.

—In the one about the amphitheater, an eight-day dramatization of Eckermann's *Conversations with Goethe.*

—What does Goethe say?

The New Music

—Goethe says: "I have devoted my whole life to the people and their improvement."
—Goethe said that?
—And is quoted in the very superior Pool production which is enlustering the perception of Pool worldwide.
—Rich, very rich.
—And there is a film chronicling the fabulous Pool garage sales, where one finds solid-silver plates in neglected bags.
—People sighing and leaning against each other, holding their silver plates. Think I'll just whittle a bit, whittle and spit.
—Lots of accommodations in Pool, all of the hotels are empty.
—See if I have any benefits left under the G.I. Bill.
—Pool is new, can make you new too.
—I have not the heart.
—I can get us a plane or a train, they've cut all the fares.
—People sighing and leaning against one another, holding their silver plates.
—So you just want to stay here? Stay here and be yourself?
—Drop by the shoe store, pick up a pair of shoes.
—Blackberries, buttercups, and wild red clover. I find the latest music terrific, although I don't generally speaking care much for the new, qua new. But this new music! It has won from our group the steadiest attention.
—Momma didn't 'low no clarinet played in here. Unfortunately.
—Momma.
—Momma didn't 'low no clarinet played in here. Made me sad.
—Momma was outside.
—Momma was *very* outside.
—Sitting there 'lowing and not-'lowing. In her old rocking chair.
—'Lowing this, not-'lowing that.
—Didn't 'low oboe.
—Didn't 'low gitfiddle. Vibes.
—Rock over your damn foot and bust it, you didn't pop to when she was 'lowing and not-'lowing.
—Right. 'Course, she had all the grease.
—True.
—You wanted a little grease, like to buy a damn comic book or something, you had to go to Momma.
—Sometimes yes, sometimes no. Her variously coloured moods.
—Mauve. Warm gold. Citizen's blue.
—Mauve mood that got her thrown in the jug that time.
—Concealed weapons. Well, what can you do?
—Carried a .357 daytimes and a .22 for evenings. Well, what can you do?
—Momma didn't let nobody work her over, nobody.
—She just didn't give a hang. She didn't care.
—I thought she cared. There were moments.
—She never cared. Didn't give pig shit.
—You could even cry, she wouldn't come.
—I tried that, I remember. Cried and cried. Didn't do a damn bit of good.

—Lost as she was in the Eleusinian mysteries and the art of love.
—Cried my little eyes out. The sheet was sopping.
—Momma was not to be swayed. Unswayable.
—Staring into the thermostat.
—She had a lot on her mind. The chants. And Daddy, of course.
—Let's not do Daddy today.
—Yes, I remember Momma, jerking the old nervous system about with her electric *diktats.*
—Could Christ have performed the work of the Redemption had He come into the world in the shape of a pea? That was one she'd drop on you.
—Then she'd grade your paper.
—I got a C, once.
—She dyed my beard blue, on the eve of my seventh marriage. I was sleeping on the sun porch.
—Not one to withhold comment, Momma.
—Got pretty damned tired of that old woman, pretty damned tired of that old woman. Gangs of ecstatics hanging about beating on pots and pans, trashcan lids—
—Trying for a ticket to the mysteries.
—You wanted a little grease, like to go to the brothel or something, you had to say, Momma can I have a little grease to go to the brothel?
—She was often underly generous.
—Give you eight when she knew it was ten.
—She had her up days and her down days. Like most.
—Out for a long walk one early evening I noticed in the bare brown cut fields to the right of me and to the left of me the following items of interest: in the field to the right of me, couple copulating in the shade of a car, tan Studebaker as I remember, a thing I had seen previously only in old sepia-toned photographs taken from the air by playful barnstormers capable of flying with their knees, I don't know if that's difficult or not—
—And in the field to your left?
—Momma. Rocking.
—She'd lugged the old rocking chair all that way. In a mauve mood.
—I tipped my hat. She did not return the greeting.
—She was pondering. "The goddess Demeter's anguish for all her children's mortality."
—Said my discourse was sickening. That was the word she used. Said it repeatedly.
—I asked myself: Do I give a bag of beans?
—This bird that fell into the back yard?
—The south lawn.
—The back yard. I wanted to give it a Frito?
—Yeah?
—Thought it might be hungry. Sumbitch couldn't fly you understand. It had crashed. Couldn't fly. So I went into the house to get it a Frito. So I was trying to get it to eat the Frito. I had the damn bird in one hand, and in the other the Frito.

—She saw you and whopped you.
—She did.
—She gave you that "the bird is our friend and we never touch the bird because it hurts the bird" number.
—She did.
—Then she threw the bird away.
—Into the gutter.
—Anticipating no doubt handling of the matter by the proper authorities.
—Momma. You'd ask her how she was and she'd say, "Fine." Like a little kid.
—That's what they say. "Fine."
—That's all you can get out of 'em. "Fine."
—Boy or girl, don't make a penny's worth of difference. "Fine."
—Fending you off. Similarly, Momma.
—Momma 'lowed lute.
—Yes. She had a thing for lute.
—I remember the hours we spent. Banging away at our lutes.
—Momma sitting there rocking away. Dosing herself with strange intoxicants.
—Lime Rickeys.
—Orange Blossoms.
—Rob Roys.
—Cuba Libres.
—Brandy Alexanders and Bronxes. How could she drink that stuff?
—An iron gut. And divinity, of course.
—Well. Want to clean up some of this mess?
—Some monster with claws, maybe velvet-covered claws or Teflon covered claws, inhabits my dreams. Whistling, whistling. I say, Monster, how goes it with you? And he says, Quite happily, dreammate, there are certain criticisms, the Curator of Archetypes thinks I don't quite cut it, thinks I'm shuckin' and jivin' and when what I should be doing is attacking, attacking, attacking—
—Ah, my bawcock, what a fine fellow thou art.
—*But on the whole*, the monster says, I feel fine. Then he says, Gimme that corn flake back. I say, What? He says, Gimme that corn flake back. I say, You gave me that corn flake it's my corn flake. He says, Gimme that corn flake back or I'll claw you to thread. I say, I can't man you gave it to me I already ate it. He says, C'mon man gimme the corn flake back did you butter it first? I say, C'mon man be reasonable, you don't butter a corn flake—
—How does it end?
—It doesn't end.
—Is there help coming?
—I called that number and they said whom the Lord loveth He chasteneth.
—Where is succor?
—In the new music.
—Yes, it isn't often you heard a disco version of *Un Coup de Dés.* It's strengthening.

Donald Barthelme

—The new music is drumless, which is brave. To make up for the absence of drums the musicians pray nightly to the Virgin, kneeling in their suits of lights in damp chapels provided for the purpose of the corridors of the great arenas—
—Momma wouldn't have 'lowed it.
—As with much else. Momma didn't 'low Patrice.
—I remember. You still see her?
—Once in a way. Saw her Saturday. I hugged her and her body leaped. That was odd.
—How did that feel?
—Odd. Wonderful.
—The body knows.
—The body is perspicacious.
—The body ain't dumb.
—Words can't say what the body knows.
—Sometimes I hear them howling from the hospital.
—The detox ward.
—Tied to the bed with beige cloths.
—We've avoided it.
—So far.
—Knock wood.
—I did.
—Well, it's a bitch.
—Like when she played Scrabble. She played to kill. Used the filthiest words insisting on their legitimacy. I was shocked.
—In her robes of deep purple.
—Seeking the ecstatic vision. That which would lift people four feet off the floor.
—Six feet.
—Four feet or six feet off the floor. Persephone herself appearing.
—The chanting in the darkened telesterion.
—Persephone herself appearing, hovering. Accepting offerings, balls of salt, solid gold serpents, fig branches, figs.
—Hallucinatory dancing. All the women drunk.
—Dancing with jugs on their heads, mixtures of barley, water, mint—
—Knowledge of things unspeakable—
—Still, all I wanted to do was a little krummhorn. A little krummhorn once in a while.
—Can open graves, properly played.
—I was never good. Never really good.
—Who could practice?
—And your clavier.
—Momma didn't 'low clavier.
—Thought it would unleash in her impulses better leashed? I don't know.
—Her dark side. They all have them, mommas.
—I mean they've seen it all, felt it all. Spilled their damn blood and then

The New Music

spooned out buckets of mushy squash meanwhile telling the old husband that he wasn't number three on the scale of all husbands...

—Tossed him a little bombita now and then just to keep him on his toes.

—He was always on his toes, spent his whole life on his toes, the poor fuck. Piling up the grease.

—We said we weren't going to do Daddy.

—I forgot.

—Old Momma.

—Well, it's not easy, conducting the mysteries. It's not easy, making the corn grow.

—Asparagus too.

—I couldn't do it.

—I couldn't do it.

—Momma could do it.

—Momma.

—Luckily we have the new music now. To give us aid and comfort.

—And Susie.

—Our Susie.

—Our darling.

—Our pride.

—Our passion.

—I have to tell you something. Susie's been reading the Hite Report. She says other women have more orgasms than she does. Wanted to know why.

—Where does one go to complain? Where does one go to complain, when fiends have worsened your life?

—I told her about the Great Septuagesimal Orgasm, implying she could have one, if she was good. But it is growing late, very late indeed, for such as we.

—But perhaps one ought *not* to complain, when fiends have worsened your life. But rather, emulating the great Stoics, Epictetus and so on, just zip into a bar and lift a few, whilst listening to the new, incorrigible, great-white-shark, knife, music.

—I handed the tall cool Shirley Temple to the silent priest. The new music, I said, is not specifically anticlerical. Only in its deepest effects.

—I know the guy who plays washboard. Wears thimbles on all his fingers.

—The new music burns things together, like a welder. The new music says, life becomes more and more exciting as there is less and less time.

—Momma wouldn't have 'lowed it. But Momma's gone.

—To the curious: A man who was a Communist heard the new music, and now is not. Fernando the fish-seller was taught to read and write by the new music, and is now a leper, white as snow. William Friend was caught trying to sneak into the new music with a set of bongos concealed under his cloak, but was garroted with his own bicycle chain, just in time. Propp the philosopher, having dinner with the Holy Ghost, was told of the coming of the new music but also informed that he would not live to hear it.

—The new, down-to-earth, think-I'm-gonna-kill-myself music, which unwraps the sky.

―Succeed! It has been done, and with a stupidity that can astound the most experienced.
―The rest of the trip presents no real difficulties.
―The rest of the trip presents no real difficulties. The thing to keep your eye on is less time, more exciting. Remember that.
―As if it were late, late, and we were ready to pull on our red-and-gold-striped nightshirts.
―Cup of tea before retiring.
―Cup of tea before retiring.
―Dreams next.
―We can deal with that.
―Remembering that the new music will be there tomorrow and tomorrow and tomorrow.
―There is always a new music.
―Thank God.
―Pull a few hairs out of your nose poised before the mirror.
―Routine maintenance, nothing to write home about.

Why should the illiterate poor care about anything beyond the next meal?

The Indian electorate acted as if it knew the answer: the chance of there being a next meal is not increased but lessened when critics are silenced, when political expression is confined to courtiers, when power can be abused without exposure and check ....
(Prof. WH Morris-Jones in his introduction to *The Emergency, Censorship & the Press in India 1975 - 7* by Soli Sorabjee, published by Writers & Scholars/Index on Censorship)

"In many parts of Latin America the problems which are the closest reality for people are not discussed freely and analysed in public but are usually denied and silenced." Mario Vargas LLosa in *Index* 6/1978.

"The peoples of Argentina, Chile, Uruguay, Paraguay and Bolivia (and Brazil) find themselves in the position of prisoners deprived not only of communication with the outside world but also with their fellow men." Julio Cortazar in *Index* 6/1978.

INDEX on Censorship is a magazine about freedom of expression; it publishes banned manuscripts and detailed reports. It is available on subscription from OUP Journals, Press Rd., London NW10 at £8 for six issues. Or you can inspect a copy at HEFFERS bookshop; but search hard for it.

Index on Censorship

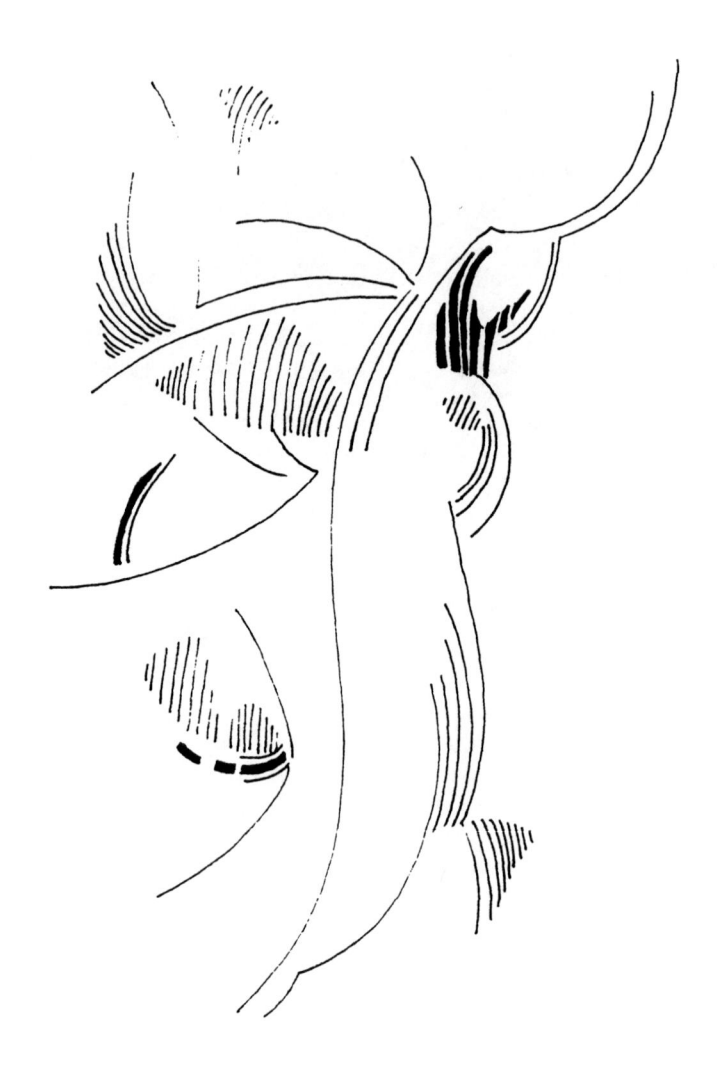

DONALD GUTTENPLAN

The Wor(l)ds of William Gass

A World of Words

The world is the totality of facts, not of things.
Wittgenstein, *Tractatus Logico-Philosophicus, 1.1*

Polonius: What do you read, my Lord?
Hamlet: Words, words, words.

Ah, what bliss to be a word. Cool and shimmering in blue or black on a white page as pristine and inviting as any world before the first day of creation. To live a life measured not in coffee spoons, but in sentences, for a word alone is as timeless as "tick", while to sit snugly in a sentence would be truly to live the life of Riley, or rather, "to live the life of Riley". In fact, to be perfectly safe perhaps we ought to say "to live the life of 'Riley' ", for "Riley" is not just any old run of the mill collection of plausibly arranged letters, no pedestrian passel of phonemes, but a name, proper as Prospero, even if fictitious as Huckleberry Finn, or Romeo Montague, or Hieronymous Fensterwald.

What's in a name? Be careful how you anwer that one; Juliet tried and died in the attempt. The connection between name and named, word and thing, has been a problem ever since Adam woke up in Eden to find a world in his bedroom, if not longer.

The world is all that is the case.
Tractatus

One might say that the world is hardly more ancient than the art of making the world.
Valery, "On Poe's Eureka"

Gutman: Well, frankly, sir, I'd like to have you along, you're a man of nice judgements and many resources.
Sidney Greenstreet in *The Maltese Falcon*

If Wittgenstein is right, then world-making is easy. The earliest philosophers went about making theirs geometrically: point, line, square, cube, cosmos- — and if that all seems a bit rushed we can start smaller. If we were William Gass (a name) we'd start with a hand (a name of another kind):

A Five Finger Exercise

Let's make a hand. That seems simple enough. Nothing should be easier. A hand. Then we can make the hand do whatever else we want done. "The figure, in greeting, thrust forth a hand." There — the work's complete. I told you nothing was easier. (WWW,317)[1]

Right away several things suggest themselves: a wrist, an arm, gloves, even another hand. A whole world of associations, all of them beside the point: the hand is all that *is* in this world one sentence long, but it is sufficient for Gass's purpose. In fact the sentence "The figure, in greeting, thrust forth a hand" is not only a convincing example, it is a brilliantly conceived one as well, fitting the task like, oh, like hand and glove, and it is not at all true that nothing could be easier. In fact Nothing could be harder. Compare the persuasive power of Gass's sentence with Martin Heidegger's "The Nothing nothings", for example. Gass is a master world-maker; a word-user of nice judgements and awesome resources. Watch him make a man, from the top of the page on down:

> Brackett Omensetter was a wide and happy man. He could whistle like the cardinal whistles in the deep snow, or whirr like the shy white rising from its cover, or be the lark a-chuckle at the sky. He knew the earth. He put his hands in water. He smelled the clean fir smell. He listened to the bees. And he laughed his deep, loud, wide and happy whenever he could—which was often, long, and joyfully. (OL, 31)

So there he is, Brackett Omensetter, as big as "life". We might notice that in a novel called *Omensetter's Luck* it takes thirty-one pages to get to this description. In another age we'd have met Omensetter on the first page, just as in another age he'd be described as an object of vision ("He was an inch, perhaps two, under six feet, powerfully built, and he advanced straight at you with a slight stoop of the shoulders") or pictured in action ("Joe Williams put on the secondhand suit and dropped his uniform, with a cobblestone wrapped up in it, off the edge of the dock and into the muddy water of the basin"). Instead we are given a catalogue of capabilities and senses; the actions put in the past tense become frozen and habitual, become attributes. Omensetter is not described so much as made: "a wide and happy man".

The presence of all this potential action makes us impatient; we want something to happen. The paragraph is somehow restless as well, and since Omensetter *is* (insofar *as* he is) the paragraph, his decision to move in the next paragraph makes sense to us.

The subtlety and grace with which Bracket Omensetter was made (a neutral word, balancing incarnated and fabricated) in no way diminishes the grandeur of Gass's achievement. The jump from hand to man isn't enough, of course, but Gass does it all. Here he is making a scene "In the Heart of the Heart of the Country":

The Church

Friday night. Girls in dark skirts and white blouses sit in ranks and scream in concert. They carry funnels loosely stuffed with orange and black paper which they shake wildly, and small megaphones through which, as drilled, they direct and magnify their shouting. Their leaders, barely pubescent girls, prance and shake and whirl their skirts above their bloomers. The young men, leaping, extend their arms and race through puddles of amber light, their bodies glistening. In a lull, though it rarely occurs, you can hear the squeak of tennis shoes against the floor. Then the yelling begins again, and then continues: fathers, mothers, neighbors joining in to form a single pulsating ululation—a cry of the whole community—for in this gymnasium each body becomes the bodies beside it, pressed as they are together, thigh to thigh, and the same shudder runs through all of them, and runs toward the same release. Only the ball moves serenely through the dazzling din. Obedient to law it scarcely speaks but caroms quietly and lies at peace. (HOC, 222)

There are worlds and worlds, just as there are roses and roses, names and names, bodies and bodies. Making a world from words may be easy; after all, any god is good enough for treeing, but worlds—and words—as beautiful as Gass's are rarer than ebony. This is because he know; Gass knows words the way a cabinet maker knows wood; he knows the language the way a lover knows the body of his beloved—that is to say, not ideally or romantically, but *intimately*.

"That novels should be made of words, and merely words, is shocking, really. It is as though you had discovered that your wife were made of rubber" (FFL, 27). Although expressed blithely, it is an idea whose implications Gass takes quite seriously, and one which he takes up often: "Death will not fill up any empty life and in a line of verse it occupies only five letters of space" (WWW, 12).

The impossible wordness (an awkward, but necessary alternative to wordiness) of fictional worlds is vexing to Gass, but he realizes (as some do not) that it was just as much of a problem for Shakespeare; yet "Hamlet has a history in his heart, and none of us will ever be as real, as vital, as complex, as he is" (FFL, 283). He may be interested in different questions than those which occupied Shakespeare, but in any (fictional) case, "It [art] can only succeed through the cooperating imagination and intelligence of its consumers, who fill out, for themselves, the artist's world and make it round, and whose own special genius partly determines the ultimate glory of it" (FFL, 22).

> Man can believe the impossible, but man can never believe the improbable.
> Oscar Wilde, "The Decay of Lying"

Exactly what Gass is doing in his peculiar river is difficult to say (aside from groping for trout, of course[2]), but we can be certain of two things: that he is definitely fishing and that he knows how to fish. In the middle of "Mrs. Mean", the least successful story in *In the Heart of the Heart of the Country*, Gass stops and meditates on the extent to which the narrative has become formless and uninteresting: "Against the mechanical flutter of appearance I failed to put the glacial movement of reality" (132). Further down the page he formulates the problem: "To be the bait, to carry the harpoon down and in that round and previously unshaken belly stick it, then escape—that would be the trick." What Gass hopes to catch is still far from clear, but a clue, as well as an indication of the recurrent significance of the fishing metaphor, can be found in this passage from *Omensetter's Luck*:

> He, Olus Knox, Chamlay and Mat were fishing, not getting much, but fishing; trying the rocky point past the big bend, not getting much, but fishing in the very early morning; the boat passing the long shale crop opposite the clay bank, bringing their bait from the deep to shallow, but with no success but fishing; and he, Olus Knox, Chamlay and Mat had nearly given up hope of fish, and had got to that fine point of enjoying, as much as any fish they might have caught, the drops of water clinging to their lines, and the slowly widening rings they made on the surface of the river. (OL, 113)

This is more than luscious, lazy prose; it is more even than a shameless parable, a set of instructions from Gass to his readers. Read in the light of Gass's use elsewhere of the fishing metaphor to signify writing, the shift in value to reading in this passage demonstrates neatly the extent to which reading and writing implicate one another (literature is a reflexive activity), while the lyrical beauty of the prose entices us into participation (try it my way, you'll like it).

To be the bait—and to escape: to acknowledge the extent to which consciousness must consent for literature to happen, and to lure that consent anyway; to seduce without deception; to make a world, not with spurious things but with words.

> At the bank a young man freshly pressed is letting himself in with a key. Along the street, delicately teetering, many grandfathers move in a dream. During the murderous heat of summer, they perch on window ledges, their feet dangling just inside the narrow shelf of shade the store has made, staring steadily into the street. Where their consciousness has gone I can't say. It's not in the eyes. Perhaps it's diffuse, all temperature and skin, like an infant's though more mild. Near the corner there are several large overalled men employed in standing. A truck turns to be weighed on the scales at the Feed and Grain. Images drift on the drugstore window. The wind has blown the smell of cattle into town. Our eyes have been driven in like the eyes of old men. And there's no one to have mercy on us. (HOC, 195)

A world made without sweeping consciousness under the rug is not always a cheerful place. The Feed and Grain in that paragraph sells no corn for our kind, so why do we bother to hang around? What is there in it for *us*? Gass asks just such a question regarding the similarly scrupulous prose of Samuel Beckett, and the reply he gives applies with equal force to his own exquisite fictions:

> It is [his] wonderful rhythms, the way he weighs his words, the authority he gives to each, their measured pace, the silences he puts between them, as loving looks extend their objects into the surrounding space; it is the contrapuntal form, the reduced means, the

simple clear directness of his obscurities, and the depth inside of every sentence, the graceful hurdle of every chosen obstacle, everywhere the lack of waste. (OBB, 44)

This may sound like a prescription for austerity. It is not. At his best, in *Willie Masters' Lonesome Wife*, the stories "Order of Insects" and "In the Heart of the Heart of the Country", and some of *Omensetter's Luck*, Gass finds forms large enough to contain multitudes, and makes worlds large enough to fill them as fitly as our old friends the hand and the glove, or two lovers in an embrace.

Meaning and Saying

"When I use a word," Humpty Dumpty said in a rather scornful tone, "it means just what I choose it to mean, no more, no less."
Lewis Carroll, *Through the Looking Glass*

Vivian: My dear fellow, I am prepared to prove anything.
Oscar Wilde, "The Decay of Lying"

I said earlier that Gass knows the language the way a lover knows the body of his beloved. There are, however, lovers and lovers. Any Mary you might imagine could be the beloved of almost any John, unless one or both are nun or priest or not-interested-in-the-opposite-sex. The finite possiblities of exception are fascinating, but what concerns us here is love. Specifically the question is: can a boy from a small town in the Midwest find love (and knowledge) of language as a fiction writer while at the same time seeking knowledge (as well as love, though of a different kind) as a philosopher in a medium-sized urban university? My answer to this question is a heavily qualified "Maybe", significant mainly in that it differs from Gass's even more heavily qualified "Yes". I shall examine Gass's performance as a philosopher, and then, after a brief exploration (theoretical but not philosophical) of a few related issues, turn to a discussion of the effect of philosophy on Gass's writing, and to the fiction itself.

Logic is not a body of doctrine, but a mirror image of the world.
Tractatus, 6.13

In one of the blurbs on *The World Within the Word*, William Gass is described as being "a trained philosopher". A curious expression, "trained philosopher". The phrase conjures up kindred; almost immediately we wonder at the nature of the nature of the beast. Does the reviewer mean to suggest a subtle affinity with a trained seal, for instance, so that we picture Gass flopping around on a platform and barking philosophically, stressing thereby the performative aspects of the pursuit? Or perhaps, the phrase was meant to suggest "trained" in the sense that a dog can be made a "trained killer", with attendant connotations of involuntary viciousness not as a personality trait, but rather inculcated; the product of an education which, although resulting in an occasional unfortunate incident, is on the whole necessary and/or useful.

This sounds a little more plausible, especially given the fact that the label is applied almost uniquely to analytic philsophers, whose hostile tendencies would seem to warrant some word of warning.

More likely than either of these two alternatives, however, is the possiblity that the reviewer's choice of words, insofar as it was a choice, was determined by the desire to convey status coupled with at least a primitive recognition of the singular nature of philosophy as a profession, if not as a pursuit.

We would think it strange, for instance, to refer to a physician as a "trained doctor"; but the philosophy departments of our universities are full of people who are no more philosophers than Plato was a parachutist. So "philospher" by itself won't do, besides the word has connotations of homosexuality and the generally disreputable. "Professional philospher", on the other hand, may claim too much.

From the purists who insist that there are but one or two men who do "real work" in any given period, to the ultrapurists who insist that John Dewey was the last professional philosopher in America, to the fanatics who point to Plato and Aristotle and have their doubts about Aristotle, it doesn't take much to see that almost no one gets paid for doing philosophy (whatever that means); rather people get paid for teaching or writing. Leaving aside entirely the strong possiblity that "trained philosopher" exists solely as a euphemism for "salaried academic" or the equally strong likelihood of its being as redundant a formulation as "highly trained specialist", we are left with the safe and single observation that philosophers make their living the same way writers make their worlds: with words, words, words.

This coincidence is expressed with characteristic *elan* by Gass in the essay "Philosophy and the Form of Fiction", where he goes on to add "there are no descriptions in fiction, there are only constructions, and the principles which govern these constructions are persistently philosophical" (FFL, 17).

> There are more things in heaven and earth, Horatio,
> Than are dreamt of in your philosophy.

The journey from language to metalanguage is not one that comes naturally to men; we can find a suggestion of Gass's motives for embarking upon it at the end of "The Concept of Character in Fiction". Gass talks about the novelist's need to inspire credulity in his reader, to elicit a sympathetic response:

> and then to return him, like a philosopher liberated from the cave, to the clear and brilliant world of concept, to the realm of order, proportion, and dazzling construction. . . to fiction, where characters unlike ourselves, freed from existence, can shine like essence, and purely Be.(FFL, 54)

Although "to shine like essence" is an attractive enough, if imprecise, concept, it is nonetheless true that the reader's experience proposed here smells suspiciously like the old bait and switch of object lesson, didacticism, and moral uplift. We are all sufficiently Freud's grandchildren to wonder about the motives behind any such ambition, and we are not made any easier by statements such as "words were superior; they maintained superior control; they touched without your touching; they were at once the bait, the hook, the pole, the line, the water in between" (OL, 113).

Although these are putatively the thoughts of the Rev. Jethro Furber regarding his choice of vocation, we've learned too much from Gass to be able to leave it at that. They suggest a concern for distance and invulnerability which can be nothing but harmful to one who has a stated desire "to be the bait". I would suggest that it is precisely philosophy's (or at least a certain type of philosophy's passionate committment to dispassion which acted as a mirror image of whatever phantom Gass would fish for in fiction. The particular danger of his chosen mirror (the Wittgenstinian one) is that it expresses a relationship between a language and a language object, rather than the relationship between two langauages (that of the author and that of the reader).

> There is no such thing as the subject that thinks or entertains ideas.
> *Tractatus*, 5.631

Without a responding subject the elusive phantom of art is like a vampire in Wittgenstein's mirror, it casts no reflection. In other words, it doesn't signify.

> Philosophy aims at the logical clarification of thoughts.
> *Tractatus*, 4.111

It can with some justice be maintained that the chief concern of philosophy is philosophy. Philosophers, however, are not entirely to blame for this state of affairs. The problem with philosophy is that it was such a great success, dropping off disciplines like a prodigal parent. This image of philosophy as the mother of sciences is a cliché, of course, but in using it I'm running roughshod over intellectual history in order to get to the present, and the point that no matter how one feels about the state of contemporary philosophy, Wittgenstein's proposition remains noncontroversial.

Construed narrowly, he can be seen as asserting the radical independence of the pursuit; construed broadly, as Gass does, Wittgenstein can be viewed as asserting that "what is exactly central to philosophy is the effort to propose and argue views whose validity will transcend their occasion. . .*If that effort cannot succeed (as we know in many cases it does not) then philosophy becomes a form of conceptual fiction, and new determinants of quality, equally harsh and public, must be employed" (WWW, 183). However broadly one construes Wittgenstein, it ought first of all be said that (in his published essays at least) William Gass does not do much philosophy.

Lest I seem unduly harsh, I hasten to point out that only one of Gass's books—*On Being Blue*—actually declares itself to be "a philosophical inquiry". Yet none of his other essays (the memoirs excluded) eschew the suggestion of philosophical intent.

Quite the contrary, in fact. Gass's use of titles like "Philosophy and the Form of Fiction" or "The Ontology of the Sentence" lay explicit claim to the domain and method of the philosopher, while their inclusion in the same volumes, respectively, as "Pricksongs and Descants" (a review of Robert Coover) and "Mr. Blotner, Mr. Feaster, and Mr. Faulkner" (a study of literary biography) suggests that Gass views himself as a triple-threat man, commuting back and forth between identities as talented fiction writer and "trained philospher" with literary criticism filling up the time on the train.

It doesn't work. The situation is similar to Gass's own admirable illustration of the difference between literary and ordinary language use:

> The scribbles of the poet and the clerk, the novelist or biographer: they are not different the way eating soup and eating steak are, or even as two activities necessary to life like moving one's bowels or fucking one's spouse. . . Rather they are opposed like people playing chess and checkers on the same board. (WWW, 284)

Only in Gass's case someone is trying to play backgammon as well, using the checkers and the back side of the board. Perhaps, though, I am hoist on my own counterexample? Not so, for I do not mean to assert that we can never function in more than one capacity at a time. One of the things art does is add to the number of ways in which we see the world. My main objection is not that when Gass does pull it off (as he does brilliantly in "Carrots, Noses, Snow, Rose, Roses" (WWW) and the preface to *In the Heart of the Heart of the Country*) he does so mainly as an illustrator of other men's idea; good teachers are as rare in philosophy as anywhere else. The problem with Gass is not that he is often wrong, but that he is often dishonest.

In his "philosophical inquiry" on blueness, for example, Gass interrupts his discussion with a plea: "If color is one of the contents of the world, as I have been trying to get someone—anyone to claim. . ."(OBB, 76). The problem here is not that the hypothesis is faulty—to underscore this point I have truncated it in the middle—but that any philosophy professor who pretends ignorance of G. E. Moore's use of colour as a "primitive" in *Principia Ethica* is a liar.

Similarly, when Gass says, in "Fiction and the Figures of Life": "In a sense yet to be fully discovered, the technique of the artist is like that of a scientist," he is idea dropping, engaging in pratful profundities for the amusement of his audience. When he states, "We may indeed suspect that the real power of historical events lies in their descriptions; only by virtue of their passage into language can they continue to occur" (FFL, 126), and then leaves it at that, he is not being suggestive, he is being irresponsible. [3]Footnotes, indices, the whole paraphernalia of scholarship which are largely absent from Gass's criticism, may be tedious, but they help keep a critic honest.

For a twentieth century philosopher to pretend ignorance of phenomenology is to show a shocking contempt for his readers, yet there is only one other explanation for a sentence like "Although we are alert to changes in our physical and mental health, and have catalogued their causes and conditions, little has been done to describe adequately states of consciousness themselves or evaluate their qualities" (FFL, 269). If Gass is not playing dumb here, and the emphasis is on "describe adequately" as a standard to which phenomenology doesn't measure up, he is still being dishonest, sneaking his value judgement past us by disguising it as historical generalization.

Why Gass does these things is difficult to explain. Part of the answer is strategic, I think. By seeming to know less than he does Gass renders himself less likely to be read critically; we allow ourselves to be carried along on the strength (considerable) of his rhetoric. By leaving out the intellectual background of his suggestions, he makes each reader into a Monsieur Jourdain, and amazes us by demonstrating that we speak prose. This use of "tricks" to score rhetorical points is a constant of Gass's style, a means of establishing his "hipness". Here is an example from "Sartre on Theater", where a relatively rarified discussion of the entitlements of passion is followed by a supporting quote from one of Sartre's essays, and then:

> Let us take a case and see what we can determine within it. I am furious because this nigger's dog has just shit on my lawn. I strike him smartly across his sassy black face with a length of sprinkler hose. Then it turns out that it was not his dog but a neighbor's. Man. . . am I mad at that nigger now. (WWW, 190)

Even leaving aside the extent to which Gass's casual use of "Nigger" to establish his "hipitude" implicates him in the very discourse of racism his exemption from which was being demonstratively taken for granted (although the phrase "sassy black face" is strong evidence on the side of bad faith), leaving all of this aside, we are still confronted with the upsetting glibness of the transition.

Gass is a writer of considerable verbal facility, and his characteristic throw-aways—"Well, what's the point of being born in Oak Park if you're going to kill yourself in Ketchum?" or "As a space, the present has been oversold. It is simply what the future, pushed roughly by the past, falls flat in. That is rather nice, I think. So shall I say that I believe it?"—may simply be the result of a kind of rhetorical restlessness. This does not excuse them, however, and the fact that Gass is aware of his tendency to glibness only increases the aggravating vulgarity of "My genes had guaranteed I should never in my life commit an act of Marx".

Gass has a meanness in some of his writing which, although confined mostly to and, I believe, arising out of his philosophy, also accounts for the occasional deficiencies of his fiction. Gass himself provides a parable of the connection:

> When, with an expression so ill-bred as to be fatherless, I enjoin a small offensive fellow to 'fuck a duck', I don't mean he should. Nothing of the sort is on my mind. . . Although the expression *says* 'hunt up a duck and fuck it,' the command quite routinely *means* 'go away; pursue some activity suitable to your talents,

something disgusting and ineffectual like fucking a duck. (OBB, 47-48)

There are many ways of not meaning what you say. Poetry is one of them, the novel is another. Philosophy is not.

A Dogma (and some nice distinctions)

What can be said at all can be said clearly, and what we cannot talk about we must pass over in silence.

Tractatus, preface.

In the essay "A Memory of a Master", Gass describes a graduate school encounter with Wittgenstein as "the most important intellectual experience of my life". He recalls being fascinated by "the funny, shabby man:

> Without cant, without jargon, and in terms of example, this abstract mind went concretely forward; and is it any wonder that he felt impatient with twaddle and with any emphasis on showy finish, with glibness, with quickness, with polish and shine, with all propositions whose hems were carefully the right length, with all those philosophies that lean on one another, like one in a stupor leans against a bar? (FFL, 248)

The passage is extremely interesting; not only an evocation of the scene, it is symptomatic of the tension caused by Gass's very fascination with "the total naked absorbtion of the mind in its problems". Glibness, quickness, polish, and shine—to what do these qualities belong if not Gass's own prose? We need look only as far as the end of the paragraph to see his facility at work.

That any incompatibility between Wittgenstein's account of language and Gass's use of it is Wittgenstein's problem ought to be obvious to Gass. The *Tractatus* says that "all philosophy is a critique of language"; fiction such as Gass's is not only a far more radical critique of langauge; it is a work of art and hence a critique of life. The *Tractatus* says that both logic and philosophy are activities, not bodies of doctrine. *Willie Master's Lonesome Wife* is not only a body of doctrine it is a world, a world whose insistent claims on existence are absolutely dogmatic.

> One must admit that Esthetics is a great, even an irresistable temptation.
>
> Valery, "Leonardo and the Philosophers"

Anyone who writes about literature has an aesthetic. It may not be consistent, it may not be pretty, but it *is*, lurking behind every observation, peering cautiously past each pronouncement. What is an aesthetic? A mythical beast, graceful as a unicorn or grim as a gryphon, through whose eyes the critic sees. Another way to think of it is as a dogma that's been domesticated. Valery, for instance, had an aesthetic like a leopard—proud, lean, and hard to domesticate. "Poetry is a survival", he said, and he meant it. "A poem must be a holiday of Mind. It can be nothing else." He meant that too. It is easy to keep house with a leopard; Valery stopped writing poetry for fifteen years. Pound had an aesthetic like a bad tempered, slightly down at the heels boxer. "There's no high road to the Muses", he said in "Homage to Sextus Propertius". And he could hit below the belt:

> La beaute, "Beauty is difficult, Yeats" said Aubrey Beardsley
>   when Yeats asked why he drew horrors
>   or at least not Burne-Jones
>   and Beardsley knew he was dying and had to
>   make his hit quickly
>
> hence no more B-J in his product.
>
>   So very difficult, Yeats, beauty so difficult.
>
> From CANTO LXXX

Aesthetics are normally retiring creatures, however, and can usually be recognized only by the judgements they trail behind them and which litter the landscape like the tailfeathers of a profligate peacock. When an aesthetic does go abroad, it is frequently in the company of an ethic, for whom it is often confused. In writing about literature, at least, the ethic can be distinguished by the sharpness of its tail, called a moral judgement. The rounded tail of the aesthetic is called a judgement of taste. The assertion that the two creatures, however similar, related, and often cross-bred, are not the same, is dogma—at least in this discussion.

The nice distinctions come in because the words we use to talk about literature are so imprecise. Fiction, for instance. Do we mean fiction as opposed to fact—or poetry? If we let alliteration deal the cards, we end up with three pairs: fact/fiction, prose/poetry, life/literature. The first and last are easy:

> The peculiar literary function of fiction, from at least Boccaccio, and certainly to the present, has been first of all the transformations of life into language, and then the further metamorphosis of that language into literature. . . still another, much remoter, squarer sphere. (WWW, 285)

Fiction here is in part used to stand for storytelling, but it is also used to mean art-made-of-language-that-is-not-poetry. As for art-made-of-languge-that-is-poetry, Gass has this to say: "Unlike prose, poetry is not a communication, but a construction in consciousness" (WWW, 173).

The implication is that whereas in prose the fictionalness of fiction detaches language from the world and allows it to be used for literature (koshers it, you might say), it is the literariness of poetry which detaches it from the world, and fashions it into art. "Against what do the great lines of poetry reverberate, if not the resoundings of other lines?" (WWW, 301), he asks. To which I would reply, "Against what do the lines of Homer resound? Or those of Shakespeare?" The only thing long enough for Homer is History;

and the only thing wide enough for Shakespeare is Life. Which is in no way an insistence on literature as imitation or sociology. It is simply that Gass's description of language-into-art via koshering (literally purification or cleansing) makes for kosher art, which is all too likely to be bloodless, bland, and over-cooked. Writing and reading are rituals all right; but they are rituals performed not for purification but for pleasure.

Words in literature derive their power not from their purity, but from their impurity. The closest we can come to Gass's version of poetic language is by writing/reading in a language we don't understand. Words separated completely from the world become pure sound; at best we'd end up with music.

On the other hand, if words and world fit exactly, we'd have the truth, or at least logic. And although literature may contain both truth and music, they are not the sources of its art.

The power of literature is not logical or musical, but rhetorical. The truth of this assertion becomes evident when we consider the way in which, after reading Shakespeare, we tend to think in "Shakespeare". His rhetorical force is so great that, even over a distance of four centuries, his language in some sense replaces our own. The authorized version of the Bible is a prose work which has much the same effect. How this happens is difficult to say. How it can happen, though, is easier.

Literature can happen because literary language neither means what it says nor says what it means. Prose fiction and poetry are different, not because one is purer than the other, but in the ways they are impure. The distinction is not hard and fast, of course, but in general poetry means more than it says, and prose (prose fiction) says more than it means.

When a poet baffles us we ask "what does this mean?" because what he says is right there. In a novel, on the other hand, although the words are there, and the meaning is generally accessible as well, we want to know what's going on, "what's it saying?". The fact that neither of these questions can be answered definitively is what makes literature possible. A couple of examples ought to suffice:

> For how to the heart's cheering
> The down-dugged ground-hugged grey
> Hovers off, the jay-blue heavens appearing
> Of pied and peeled May!

This is a piece of a poem. Here is a piece of prose:

> It's been terribly hot in Cleveland. Dry. Well, we've the lake. And you've the river. Dry. Yes ma'am. Dry. Like lava. Yes ma'am, indeed. Like lead in the sunlight, yes indeed. A Prussian Helmet's head. Like the River Styx. Oh like. . . Oh very like. . . They'll find us in our pederastic postures like Pompeii. (OL, 107)

Now here is a whole poem.

IN A STATION OF THE METRO
The apparition of these faces in the crowd;
Petals on a wet, black bough.

And a whole prose:

PEOPLE

Aunt Pet's still able to drive her car—a high square Ford—even though she walks with difficulty and a short stick. She has a watery gaze, a smooth plump face despite her age, and jet black hair in a bun. She has the slowest smile of anyone I ever saw, but she hates dogs, and not very long ago cracked the back of one she cornered in her garden. To her vigor she will tell you this, her smile breaking gently while she raises the knob of her stick to the level of her eyes. (HOC, 213)

We notice right away a bigger difference between whole and part in poetry than prose. The meaning of the first prose is: "hot and dry", but the interest is all elsewhere, from helmeted heads to Hamlet. It is incomplete, of course, but only in an additive sense. The Hopkins, however, suffers intrinsic damage by being excerpted. It can be identified but not construed.[4]

This difference points to a number of other contrasts. Time in prose is linear, or at least made up of duration; time in poetry tends toward stasis.[5] Prose is discursive, it thrives on elaboration. Poetry is focused, it gains by concentration. The rhetorical force in prose is like an earthworm—cut off a piece and whatever is left still has enough wiggle to bait your hook. The force of a poem is different; "shatter a stone and the bits you make are simply further stones, but break a seashell or a poem and every piece will declare itself a fragment of some whole" (WWW, 173).

Poetry and prose are both more senses of direction than anything else. Poetry moves through silence towards space, sustained by a vision of form. Prose moves through time towards meaninglessness, held in place by the demands of style.

Here is a tender button:

A carafe, that is a blind glass. A kind in glass and a cousin, a spectacle and nothing strange a single hurt color and an arrangement in a system to pointing. All this and not ordinary, not unordered in not resembling. The difference is spreading.

Gertrude Stein, *Tender Buttons*

Virginia Woolf said that human nature changed around 1910 and you can go to the Courtauld Gallery and look at the Fry collection and see what she had in mind. Or you can read Gertrude Stein. Here is what Gass has to say on the subject:

Flaubert and Cezanne taught the same lesson; and as she [Stein] examined the master's portrait of his wife she realized that the reality of the model had been superseded by the reality of the composition. Everything in the painting was related to everything else in the painting, and to everything else equally (there were no lesser marks or moments) while the relation of any line or area of color in the painting to anything outside the painting (to a person in this case) was accidental, superfluous, illusory. (WWW, 74)

I used to think it was one of art's little ironies that both Gertrude Stein and Ernest Hemingway claimed to have learned how to write from Cézanne.

Then one day I wised up. There are few things less true of Cezanne than that everything in any painting of his related equally to everything else. In fact as he becomes less interested in Mont Blanc and more interested in the lines that make up the mountain the style stands more on its own, and the effect of the most subtle variation in emphasis is enormous.

> You can reach us by crossing a creek. In the spring lawns are green, the forsythia is singing, and even the railroad that guts the town has straight bright rails which hum when the train is coming, and the train itself has a welcome horning sound.
> Down the back streets the asphalt crumbles into gravel. Then there's Westbrook's, with the geraniums, Horsefall's, Mott's. The sidewalk shatters. Gravel dust rises like breath behind the wagons. And I am in retirement from love. (HOC, 191)

What I finally figured out was the difference between telling a world and making one. Strangely enough, in making a world its the telling that matters. What both Hemingway and Stein got from Cezanne was nothing more or less than style. Style—the word comes from the Latin *stylus*, for "writing tool", which may *be* one of art's little ironies.

Hemingway might have said he was telling the truth, but his style said he was making a world, and in prose writing style talks louder than words. William Gass might think he's engaged in a "pure pursuit", but he's got a writing tool on him that gives the lie to his words. Making a world or telling one, as Gertrude Stein said, "The difference is widening". Gass's fictions hit home not because they are pure—his style is closer to Mencken or Whitman than to Mallarme to Wittgenstein—but because they are real. And in a word-made world, "Reality is not a matter of fact, it is an achievement". (FFL, 282).

---

[1] *The World Within the World, p. 317. Similarly, HOC means* In the Heart of the Heart of the Country; *FFL means* fiction and the Figures of Life; *OBB means* On Being Blue *and OL means* Omensetter's Luck.

[2] *See the essay on metaphor, "Groping for Trouts", in* The World Within the Word, *pp. 262-80.*

[3] *Gass's suspicion has been explored in some depth, and with considerable verbal brilliance in the works of Michael Foucault, especially* The Order of Things *and* The Discourse on Language.

[4] *Note that neither one can be adequately paraphrased. In literature, as in cricket, there are no substitutions.*

[5] *For a discussion which anticipates Gass's use of spatial metaphors and his treatment of Stein, see William V. Spanos's "Modern Literary Criticism and the Spatialization of Time" in* The Journal of Aesthetics and Art Criticism. Vol. XXIX, no.1. Fall 1970, p.96.

JON LEVI

John Cheever in the Bourgeois Tradition

For John Cheever, all gall is divided into three parts. Geographically, the world is the cultural East Coast of America; Cleveland, Ohio; or Europe. Emotionally, his characters are unhappily married, separated, or divorced. Economically, they are lower-middle class, middle-middle class, or upper-middle class. *The Stories of John Cheever* aim at ordering life's joys into 61 neat, analytical, and specious bundles.

"The Geometry of Love" is a representative story with an emblematic title. Charlie Mallory, like most of Cheever's men, is a moderately successful businessman, working in New York and commuting to his suburban nest. It's a slow day at the office, so he shops for a screwdriver to mend his filing cabinet.

> It was one of those rainy late afternoons when the toy department of Woolworth's on Fifth Ave is full of women who appear to have been taken in adultery and who are now shopping for a present to carry home to their youngest child.

To his moderate surprise, a fur coat he recognizes is attached to his wife, Mathilda. He greets her, she turns and accuses him of spying, threatens to call the police, pays for a wooden duck, and storms out. Back in his office, Mallory is stunned. "It was not that he had lost his sense of reality but that the reality he observed had lost its fitness and symmetry." He gazes out the window and spots a small truck advertising EUCLID'S DRY CLEANING & DYEING. A Cheeverish thought strikes him:

> "What he needed was a new form of ratiocination, and Euclid might do. If he could make a geometric analysis of his problems, mightn't he solve them, or at least create an atmosphere of solution."

So, slide rule in hand, poor Mallory plunges on, with the optimistic desperation of a man arranging his empty martini glasses at the Oyster Bar in Grand Central

The Short Stories of John Cheever *is published by Alfred A. Knopf in New York.*

Station.

And cataloguing comes easily to the reader of Cheever. His are the comfortable people: the established families from the right side of Boston; the successful businessmen from the best suburbs or the proper part of the City—New York has only an East Side. They vacation on Cape Cod, do business in Cleveland, and separate to Rome or Turino. These are the people you'd love to trap in some pigeonhole and then kick in their teeth—if they weren't already involved in self-imposed root canal work. This is not to say that Cheever's people are self-deprecating or that Cheever damns them simply because they have 43% fewer cavities than the rest of mankind. He neither curses the apple nor paints the worm. He is excellently moderate. His people find only half the worm.

Take Johnny Hake, from "The Housebreaker of Shady Hill". Let him take himself:

> We have a nice house with a garden and a place outside for cooking meat, and on summer nights, sitting there with the kids and looking into the front of Christina's dress as she bends over to salt the steaks or just gazing at the lights in heaven, I am as thrilled as I am thrilled by more hardy and dangerous pursuits, and I guess this is what is meant by the pain and sweetness of life.

"Nice" damns him before we get a glimpse of cleavage. But there's something about his simple thrilling that endears him to us beyond the banal things that thrill him. Like Albee's New York executive, he is "possessed with a truly enviable innocence". Yet this innocence in the face of financial disaster, marital insecurity, and rampant middle-class values allows him merely to continue leading such a disastrously insecure banal life.

Cheever, for all his condemnation, prefers these sentimentalists. Abel is his reasoned candidate, but in his heart he knows Cain's right. He often makes the job tough on himself by putting his anti-middle class message in the mouths of workers. Cheever's writing of workers is real only in its comment on a middle-class view of workers. They are niched, kicked in the teeth, and fed rabbits:

> The purchase would make that weekend the weekend when they had bought the rabbits and distinguish it from the weekend when they had transplanted the Christmas fern or the weekend when they had removed the dead juniper. They could put the rabbits into the old duck house, Virginia said, and when they went back to the city in the fall, Kasiak could eat them. Kasiak was the hired man. ("The Country Farmer")

Back in the city, Cheever's doormen are hokey, his superintendents dull, and his elevator operators two-bit button pushers: their backdoor view is simplified and contrived; they are functions rather than people. Indeed, all Cheever's message carriers are functions—disapproving brothers, malcontented wives, pompous college kids. The message that Cheever sends through the mouths of these undesirables is tempered not only by their lack of dimension but by their very undesirability, plus the feeling that Cheever doesn't really see their message as a solution. He hopes for the neat garden, the lawn without crabgrass or brown spots. And he's at his best and most depressing when he's hopeful.

These are Cheever's people. With cigarette holder tip hidden, yet firmly cheek-implanted he blesses them:

> the last of that generation of chain smokers who woke the world in the morning with their coughing, who used to get stoned at cocktail parties and perform obsolete dance steps like "the Cleveland Chicken", sail for Europe on ships, who were truly nostalgic for love and happiness, and whose gods were as ancient as yours and mine, whoever you are.

The moonlighting cat-burglar, the potential rapist. These are the meek. These are they who shall inherit Cheever's earth, or Uncle Perry's 100 shares of Xerox—whichever comes first.

JOHN DUGDALE

Updike's Nabokov

> Maybe I'm like Sherman Adams and Fats Domino and other, you know semi-remote figures who have acquired a certain historical interest
>
> John Updike (1968)

From John Updike a new novel: it arrives moist and carmine from the co-ed kisses of the *New York Review of Books*. Set in the fictional sub-Saharan nation of Kush, it concerns the deposing of the Islamic Socialist President Felix Ellelou, who narrates his fall in the first and third persons. Travelling in Africa as a Fulbright Lecturer in 1973, Updike clearly coveted some of the qualities he noted in the African novels he reviewed for *The New Yorker* between 1971 and 1973—classical tragic form, openness to the possiblities of the marvellous, and the inclusion of characters whose lives are "a synopsis of human history". However, if one skims off a Koranic layer most apparent in the Ustinovian exchanges of the first scene ("that Kismet crap", Felix's American wife calls it), the master tonality of *The Coup* is derived not from Jilali, Achebe or Awoonor, but from the candied utopian language of a mind so pure that no general idea can violate it. The influence of Nabokov can be recognized throughout American fiction of the last two decades, notably in Barth, Hawkes, Gass and even Robbins, but *The Coup* is the first time to my knowledge that this dominance has been thematized.

A sceptical judgement would be that having done a Bellow (*Bech*), a Mailer-Sammler (*Rabbit Redux*), a late Vidal (*Buchanan Dying*), and an Updike (*Marry Me*), the greatest novelist to come out of Pennsylvania believed he should go after number one. But in fact the position of Nabokov in this novel is subtle and equivocal. "Novels ought to have secrets", Updike said once,

John Updike's The Coup *is published by Andre Deutsch.*

by which he meant, contextually, something as dull as star signs: whereas now, "the air of Kush is transparent; there are no secrets, only reticences". Thus Russian control of Kush is represented by a missle base run by Colonel Sirin (Nabokov's interwar pseudonym) knowing that the rockets may be "dummies, sacks of local sand"; and , while Ellelou is out performing the traditional chores of the postwar American male lead (i.e. quim and quest), the Minister of the Interior, Michaelis Ezara, is inflitrating America consumer goods into his country. Felix's gradual realization of this process is the occasion for a number of sharp effects:

> Ellelou sat down and sipped his chocolate which had grown cool: but no mere tepidity had subverted its taste: there was something added and subtracted, something malty, ersatz, adulterate, mild, mellow, vitaminized. Ambushed by recognition, Ellelou blurted out to Ezara the one word 'Ovaltine'!

Further into the novel the Islamic-African-Russian stylistic coalition is disclosed as an impossible enterprise, expelled and dispersed into America, as are Felix's similar plans for Kush. Updike seems to me to have seized upon not only an inversion, in writing an African novel, of Nabokov's reinvention of the American novel, but also the relation between that reinvention and expatriation—the discovery, in James and Fitzgerald, that through the use of inventory and precise rendition of the surfaces of the alien, those "inessential houses" of sensuous materiality and social infrastructure may be peeled away like decals from a windscreen. Compare the disconcerting data of Updike's opening and his scintillating evocations of the dungs and musks of Kush, which in one movement proffer and retract their object (the "Disneyesque eyelashes" of the camels come to mind). Pynchon woz 'ere, of course, and I feel duty bound to remark that what I find most admirable in *The Coup*—the attempt to synthesize an unstable, polyglot, post-colonial discourse in which a new American style may be baptized—was also the aim of the Fausto Maijstral section of *V*, the chapter referred to by C. Ricks as "pretentious maundering". It is pleasant to observe Updike adopting this mode of transport rather than the Jumbo Jets of John Barth, whom I take to be spoofed in the passage where Ellelou visits, in the most barren zone of Kush, the talking head of executed King Ezara.

The finest scenes in *The Coup* occur during the journey to this monstrosity, and are also the most distincitvely HMV—shuttling, *Pale Fire*-like, between Felix with his transparently Lolitan fourth wife Sheba and his memories of McCarthy College, Wisconsin, in the middle bulge of the 1950s. This is a conceit which itself plays on Nabokov—the place of forfeited bliss is not the kingdom of semblances but the country of exile—and the section constitutes an exhibition catalogue of Nabokovian *Lazzi*. Yet somehow in applying this nacreous coating Updike describes a lunar version of Eisenhower America which resembles only the landscapes of Dick and Heinlein.

It might be observed that *The Coup* elides Angola, a disgrace equidistant between the years of its setting and its writing, as *Couples* straddles and secretes Vietnam escalation. This is conceivably the case; just as the black man in *Rabbit Redux* turns out to be of the bad ass Superfly variety, so here the American "subversion" reported in the blurb is only as deplorable as Colonel Sanders and the nurses at the end of *Streetcar Named Desire*—certainly nothing to offend the shade of Sirin, whose politics were a little to the right of the sledded Brzesinski. The explicit comparison with the fall of Nixon, by proposing a historical break, conceals the continuity of interventionism. My own feeling is that the political language which square-bashes awkwardly across the unusual parade ground of an Updike novel is as distracting an installation as the Soviet Missiles, and basically subordinate to literary objectives. It is part of Updike's new coquetry to refuse the vulgarity of progressive and humanist solutions to his audience, whatever ideological consequences this entails. I freely admit, however, that I may be over-reading by misjudging Updike's constituency and the Forsythe voters he would hope to pick up this time, whose opinions may be confirmed rather than disturbed.

I find myself fondest of those occasions in *The Coup* on which Updike demurely contemplates his anachronistic status—churchgoing, registered Democrat, monogamist—in contemporary American fiction. Unable to consider a Barthelme a writer, rather "an operator on a cultural scene", because he does not produce "an expression of human spirit" which can be poured out and inhaled. Updike is menaced on his other flank by the apparition of Nabokov, which forecloses the *betise* of orthodox narration. One such occasion is the final "Note on the Type" as character, in which he observes that this "excellent example of the influential and sturdy Dutch types that prevailed in England up the time of William Caslon", was in fact designed by a Hungarian, although he had been taught by a Dutchman—a line of succession of obvious connection with the question of indebtedness raised in this review. More relevant, perhaps, to *The Coup* is Updike's description of the attractions of the title type of *The New Yorker*, "evocative of the Twenties and Persia and the future all at once". The Fats Domino comparison was right for '68 but now I'm more reminded of the juggler who supported Jonathan Richman at Hammersmith '77—a permission of irony which nonetheless did not efface the mastery of a gaudy and nostalgic art.

STANLEY ELKIN

from The Franchiser

He'd been driving for hours, on his way from his St. Cloud, Minnesota, Dairy Queen to his Mister Softee in Rapid City, South Dakota—his milk run, as he liked to call it. His right hand had fallen asleep and there was a sharp pain high up in the groin and thigh of his right side.

Mornings he'd been getting up with it. A numbness in his hand and hip, bad circulation, he thought, which left these damned cold zones, warm enough to touch when he felt them with the freely circulating blood in the fingers of his left hand or lifted his right hand to his face, but, untouched, like icy patches deep in his skin. Perhaps his sleeping habits had changed. Almost unconsciously now he found the right side of the bed. In the night, sleeping alone, even without a twin or triplet beside him, the double bed to himself, some love-altered principle of accommodation or tropism in his body taking him from an absent configuration of flesh to a perimeter of the bed, a yielding without its necessity or reason, a submission and giving way to—to what? (And even in his sleep, without naming them, he could tell them apart.) To ride out the night sidesaddle on his own body. (No godfather Julius he, not set in *his* ways, unless this were some new mold into which he was pouring himself.) Pressing his head—heavy as Gertrude's marrowless bones—like a nightmare tourniquet against the flesh of his arm, drawing a knee as high up a diver's against his belly and chest, to wake in the morning cut off, the lines down and trailing live wires from the heavy storm of his own body. Usually, as the day wore on, the sensation wore off, but never completely, some sandy sensitivity laterally vestigial across the tips of his fingers, the sharp pain in the region of his thigh blunted, like a suction cup on the tip of a toy arrow. Bad circulation. Bad.

Unless. Unless—Unless from Wolfe's mouth to God's ears.

He checked into the Hotel Rushmore in Rapid City and asked the clerk for a twin-bedded room. And then, seeing the width of the single bed, requested a rollaway be brought, narrower still. This an experiment. In the narrow bed no place to go, his body occupying both perimeters at once, returned as it had been in the days before he'd shared beds, the pillow beneath his head almost the width of the bed itself, tethered by a perfect displacement, lying, it could be, on his own shadow. But in the morning the sensation still there, if anything worse, not to be shaken off. (Never to be shaken off.)

And a new discovery. At Mister Softee handling the tan cardboard carton of popsicles, as cold to the touch of his right hand as dry ice. He thought his blood had thickened and frozen. Something was wrong.

He got the name of a doctor from his Mister Softee manager, saw Dr. Gibberd that afternoon, and was oddly moved when the doctor told him that he would like him to go into Rapid City General for observation.

A black woman took him in a wheelchair to his bed.

It was very strange. Having voluntarily admitted himself to the hospital, having driven there under his own steam—his 1971 Caddy was parked in the Visitors' lot—and answered all the questions put to him by the woman at the Admissions Desk, showing them his Blue Cross and Blue Shield cards, his yellow Major Medical, he had become an instant invalid, something seductively agreeable to him as he sat back in the old wheelchair and allowed himself to be shoved up ramps and maneuvered backward—his head and shoulders almost on a level with his knees—across the slight gap between the lobby carpet and the hard floor of an elevator and pushed through what he supposed was the basement, past the kitchens and laundry rooms, past the nurses' cafeteria and the vending machines and the heating plant, lassitude and the valetudinarian on him like climate, though he had almost forgotten his symptoms.

"Where are we going? Is it much farther?"

"No. We almost there." She shoved the brass rod on a set of blue fire doors and they moved across a connector through a second set of fire doors and past a nurses' station, and entered a long, cinderblock, barracks-like ward in which there were perhaps fifteen widely spaced beds down each side of a broad center aisle. Except for what might be behind a folding screen at the far end of the ward, the beds were all empty, the mattresses doubled over on themselves.

"This is the boondocks," Ben said. "Is it a new wing?"

"You got to ask your doctor is it a new wing," she said and left him.

A young nurse came and placed a hospital gown across the back of the wheelchair. She asked Ben if he needed help. He said no but had difficulty with his shirt buttons. Unless he actually saw his fingers on them, he could not be sure he was holding them.

"Here," she said, "let me." She stooped before him and undid his buttons. She unfastened his belt. "Can you get your zipper?"

"Oh sure." But touching the metal was like sticking his hand into an electric socket. The nurse made up the bed. He sat back down in the chair and, watching the fingers on his right hand, carefully attempted to interlace them with the fingers on his left.

"Modest?"

The Franchiser

Ben nodded. It was not true. In sickness he understood what he never had in health, that his body, anyone's, everyone's, was something for the public record, something accountable like books for audit, like deeds on file in county courthouses. If he was ashamed it was because he couldn't work his fingers. He stood to take off his pants and shorts. Then he smiled.

"Yes?"

"I was just thinking," he said.

"Yes?"

"I'm Mister Softee." She turned away and completed the last hospital corner. "No," Ben said, "I am. I have the local Mister Softee franchise. It's ice cream." She folded the sheets back. "It's true. Anytime you want a Mister Softee, just go down and ask Zifkovic. Zifkovic's my manager."

"Please put your gown on."

"Tell him Ben Flesh sent you," he said and burst into tears.

"What is it? What's wrong?"

"I don't know," Ben said, "I don't know what's happening to me."

"That's why you're here," she said, "so we can find out." She helped him out of the chair gently, unfolded and held open the gown for him. "Just step into it," she said, "just put your arms through the sleeves." He had to make a fist with his right hand so his fingers wouldn't touch the rough fabric. She came toward him with the gown. His penis moved against her uniform. "Can you turn around?" she said. "I'll tie you up the back."

"I can turn around." He was crying again.

"Please," she said, "please don't do that. You mustn't be afraid. You're going to be fine."

"I can turn around. See?" he sobbed. "Is it smeared? My ass? What there is of it. All belly, no ass. Is it smeared? Is it smeared with shit? Sometimes, I don't know, I try, I try to wipe myself. Sometimes I'm careless."

"You're fine," she said. "You're just fine. Please," she said, "if you shake like that, I won't be able to tie your gown for you."

"No? You won't?" He couldn't stop sobbing. He was grateful they were alone. "So I'd have to be naked. How would that be? This—this body na-naked. Wouldn't that be something—thing? No ass, just two fl-flabby gray pouches and this wi-wide tor-tors-*torso*. They say if you can squeeze a half inch of flab between your forefinger and thumb you're—you're too fat. What's this? Three in-*in-inch-ches*? What does that make *me*? I never looked like you're supposed to look on the—on the beach. I've got this terrible body. Well, I'm not the franchise man for nothing. It's—it's like any middle-age man's. I'm so *white*."

"Stop," she demanded. "You just control yourself."

"Yeah? What's that? Shock therapy? **Thanks, I needed that?** Well, why not? Sure. Thanks, I needed that." He turned to face her. He raised his gown. "*Flesh the flasher!*" He was laughing. "See? I've got this tiny weewee, this undescended cock."

"If you can't control yourself," she said.

"What? You'll call for help? Lady, you just saw for yourself. You don't *need* help. *You* could take me." He sat on the side of the bed, his legs spread wide, his elbows on his thighs, and his head in his palms. But he was calm. "I just never took care of the goddamn thing, my body. I just never took care of it. And the only thing that counts in life is life. You jog?" he asked suddenly.

"What's that?"

"Do you jog?"

"Yes."

"I knew. I knew you did. You smoke?"

"No."

"Right. That's right. Ship-fucking shape."

"I think one of the interns. . ."

"No," he said calmly, "I'm okay now. No more opera. But you know? I hate joggers. People who breathe properly swimming, who flutter kick. Greedy Maybe flab is a sign of character and shapelessness is grace. Sure. The good die young, right?"

"Why do you loathe your body so?"

"What'd it ever do for me?"

"Will you be all right now?"

"I told you. Yes. Yeah." He got into bed. When he pulled the covers up his hand tingled. The nurse turned to go. "Listen," he said.

"Yes?"

"Tell Gibberd he can skip the preliminaries, all the observation shit. Tell him to get out his Nation's Leading Crippler of Young Adults kit. The kid's got M.S."

"You don't know what you have."

"Yes. Wolfe the specialist told me. He gave me egg salad and set me straight."

The nurse left him. He tried to feel his pulse with the fingers of his right hand and couldn't. He did five-finger exercises, reaching for the pulse in his throat, his hand doing rescue work, sent down the carefully chiseled tunnels of disaster in a mine shaft, say, to discover signs of life. He brought the fingers away from his dick and waved to the widows. He placed three fingers of his good hand along a finger of his right and, closing his eyes, tried to determine the points where they touched. He couldn't, felt only a suffused, generalized warmth in the deadened finger. He took some change the nurse had put with his watch and wallet in the nightstand by his bed and distributed it on his blanket around his chest and stomach. Still with his eyes closed, he tried to feel for the change and pick it up. He couldn't. He opened his eyes, scooped up a nickel, a dime, and a quarter with his left hand and put them in the palm of his right hand. Closing his eyes again, he very carefully spilled two of the coins onto the blanket—he could determine this by the sound—and made a fist about the coin still in his hand. Concentrating as hard as he had ever concentrated on anything in his life, and trapping the coin under his thumb, he rubbed it up his forefinger, trying to determine the denomination of the remaining coin. It's the dime, he decided. He was positive. Yes. It's the dime. The inside of this thumb still had some sensitivity. (Though he couldn't be sure, he thought he had felt a trace of pulse under his thumb when he had held the dead necklace of his right hand against his throat.) Definitely the dime. He opened his eyes. His hand was empty. He shoved the change back in the nightstand and closed the drawer.

"I say, are you *really* Mister Softee?" The voice was British and came from behind the screen at the far end of the ward.

"Who's that? Who's there?"

"Are you?"

"Yes."

"Jolly good. They're rather splendid."

"Thanks."

"Mister Softee." The name was drawn out, contemplated, pronounced as if it were being read from a marquee. "Apropos too, yes?"

"Why's that?"

"*Well*, after your performance just now for Sister, I should have thought that would be obvious, wouldn't it?"

"I'm sick."

"Not to worry," the invisible Englishman said cheerfully. "We're all sick here." Ben looked around the empty ward. "Sister was right, you know. You *are* going to be fine. You're in the best tropical medicine ward in either Dakota."

"This is a tropical medicine ward?"

"Oh yes. Indeed. One of the finest in the Dakotas."

"Jesus," Ben said, "a tropical medicine ward."

"Top drawer. Up there with the chief in Rapid City."

"What do you have?" Ben asked.

"One saw you though the crack where the panels of my screen are joined. One saw everything. One saw your bum. It *is* smeared, rather. What do *I* have? Lassa fever, old thing. Came down with a touch of it last year. Year it was discovered actually. In Nigeria. Odd that. Well *I* wasn't in Nigeria. I was in Belize, Brit Honduras, with RAF. What I meant was, Lassa *fever* was discovered in Nigeria. Trouble with a clipped rather precise way of talking, articles left out, references left dangling, pronouns understood, is that it's often imprecise actually, rather."

"What was odd?"

"Beg pardon?"

"You said, 'Odd that.' What was odd?"

"Oh. Sorry. Well. That a disease could be said to be *discovered*. Of course all that's usually meant is that they've isolated a particular virus. But I mean, if you *think* about it the virus must have been there all along, mustn't it? And I should have thought that people, well, you know, *natives*, had been coming down with the bloody thing since *ages*. I mean, when Leif Erikson, or whoever, was discovering your States, some poor devil must have had all the symptoms of Lassa fever, even dying from it, too, very probably, without every knowing that that's what was killing him because the disease had never been *named*, you see. Now it has. Officially, I'm only the ninth case—oh yes, I'm in the literature—but I'll bet populations have died of it."

"I don't think I understand what—"

"Well, only that I know where I stand, don't I? Just as you, if you were right about yourself, know where *you* stand. Is that an ad*van*tage? I wonder. Quite honestly I don't know. Yes, and that's strange, too, isn't it, that I know things but don't know what to make of them? Incubation period one week. Very well. Weakness? Check. Myositis? Check. And the fever of course. And ulcerative pharyngitis with oral lesions. Yellow centers and erythemystositic halos. Rather like one of your lovely Mister Softee concoctions rather. Myocarditis, check. Pneumonitis, pleuritis, encephalophitathy, hemorrhagic diathesis? Check. Well, check some, most. What the hell? Check them *all*. Sooner or later they'll come. I mean I *expect* they will. Gibberd's been very straight with me. I think it pleases him how classic my case has been. Yet one can't tell, can one? I mean, what about the sleeplessness? Or the blurred speech? One has somethings but not others. There was the headache and leg rash and even the swollen face, but where was the leg *pain*? And this is the point, I think: What I have is incurable and generally fatal. Generally fatal? *Generally? Fatal?* Will this classic condition kill me or not? Incurable. *A*lways incurable. But only generally fatal. Oh, what a hopeful world it is! Even in hospital. So no more racket, you understand? No more whimpering and whining. Be *hard*, Mister Softee!"

"All right," Ben said.

"Yes, well," his roomate said. "Are you ambulatory? I couldn't really tell. I saw you stand. But I saw Sister help, *Are* you? Am*bu*latory?"

"Yes."

"Oh, good. I wonder if I could trouble you to come back of the screen. One is rather in need of help."

"You want me to come back there?"

"If you would. If it isn't too much bother. Oh, I see. The contagion. Well. There's nothing to fear. Lassa can't be contracted from anyone who's had the disease for more than thirty-two days. One's had it a year and a half."

One could call the nurse, Ben thought. I have been orphaned and I have been blinded. I am Mister Softee here and Chicken from the Colonel there. Godfathers have called me to their deathbeds to change my life and all this has been grist for my character. I am in one of the go-ahead tropical medicine wards in Rapid City, South Dakota, and a Lassa fever pioneer needs my help. Oh well, he thought, and left his bed and proceeded down the long empty ward toward the screen at its rear. He stood by the screened-in sick man.

"Yes?" Ben said.

"What, here so soon? Well, you *are* ambulatory. Good *show*, Mister Softee! I'm Flight Lieutenant Tanner incidentally. Well then, could you come back of the screen, please just?"

"Come back of it."

"Yes. Would you just?"

Flesh went behind the screen. The Englishman was seated beside his bed in a steel wheelchair. Heavy leather straps circled his weakened chest and wrapped his flaccid legs to hold him upright in it. Flesh looked down meekly at the mandala of spokes, then at the Englishman's bare arms along the chair's wide rests. They were smeared with a perspiration of blood. Tiny droplets of blood freckled the man's forehead, discrete reddish bubbles mitigated by sweat and barely deeper in color than blown bubble gum. A sort of bloodfall trickled like tears from the hollow beneath his left eye and out over the cheekbone and down his face.

"Eukopenia, check," the English said.

"My God, you're bleeding all over."

"No. Not actually *bleeding*, old fellow. It's a sort of capillary action. It's complicated rather, but the blood is forced out the pores. It's all explained in the literature. Gibberd told me I might expect it. It was jolly good luck *your* happening to be by. There's a box of Kleenex in that nightstand there. Would you mind? If you'll just tamp at the bloody stuff. Oh, I say, forgive that last, would you just? I should have thought to think that would do me rather nicely."

"Maybe I'd better call the nurse."

"She's *rather* busy, I should expect. There are people who really need help, for whom help is of some help, as it were. As I don't seem to be one of them—incurable, generally *fatal*, I'm taking the darker view just now, old boy— I should think you would have thought we might work this out between ourselves."

"Yeah, between ourselves," Ben said. "Pip." He took the Kleenex and began to dab at the man's skin.

"There's a good fellow. That's got the arm. I think," the Englishman said.

"This never happened before?"

"No no. Absolutely without precedent. I say, do you *realize*?"

"What?"

"That if this disease really *was* discovered in 1970—well, it was, of course, but I mean if it didn't *exist* before 1970—why, then I'm only the ninth person to have experienced this particular symptom. We're breaking freshish ground here, you and I."

Ben, working on the bloodfall at its headwaters just under the Englishman's left eye, started to gag. He brought the bloodied Kleenex up to his lips.

"Be firm, Mister Softee." Ben swallowed and looked at him.

"I think that's it, rather," Ben said quietly.

"Yes, well, it would be, wouldn't it, except that the insides of my thighs seem a bit sticky."

"No no. I mean that's *it*. *Generally* fatal. I'm taking the lighter view. I'm calling the nurse."

"Mister Softee."

"What?"

"We've the same doctor."

The same spring that Ben Flesh lay in the tropical medicine ward of Rapid City General—the prime interest rate was 6¾ percent—a record heat wave hit the northern tier of the central plains states. Extraordinary demands on the energy supplies caused breakdowns and brownouts all over. The hospital had its own auxiliary generator, but the power situation was so precarious that the use of electricity, even there, was severely cut back, if not curtailed entirely. There was no electricity to run the patients' television sets, none for air conditioning in any but the most crowded wards, or in those rooms where the heat posed a threat to the lives of the patients. It was forbidden to burn reading lamps, or to play radios that did not run on batteries. All available electricity was directed toward keeping the lights and equipment in good order in the operating theaters, maintaining the kitchens with their washers and driers, their toasters and refrigeration units (even at that Flesh suspected that much of what he ate was tainted or turning), to chilling those medications that required it, to operating the laundry services (though the sheets were changed now every third or fourth day instead of daily), and to keeping the power-hungry instruments going that analyzed blood and urine samples and evaluated the more complicated chemistries and tests. The X-ray machines, which required massive doses of electricity, were now used only for emergencies and only the dialysis machine and iron lung, top priorities, were unaffected by the brownout. Even electroshock therapy was suspended for all but the most violent cases, and Flesh was kept awake nights by the shrieks and howls of the nearby mad, people so far gone in their terror and delusion that even powerful tranquilizers like Thorazine were helpless to calm them.

"It isn't the heat," the Englishman said, as they both lay awake one night while the screams of crazed patients in an adjacent ward came through their open windows. (The windows had to be opened, of course, to catch whatever breeze might suddenly stir.) "It's the humidity drives them bonkers."

"They were already bonkers," Flesh said irritably.

"That exacerbated it then," the Englishman said just as irritably.

"Shit."

"You know," the Englishman said, "I don't remember heat like this even in Brit Honduras."

"Brit Honduras, Brit Honduras. Why can't you say British Honduras like everybody else?"

"Everyone in RAF called it Brit Honduras."

"And that's another thing—Raf. Can't you say R.A.F. like any normal human being?"

"I'll say what I bloody well please."

"Then be consistent. Say 'Craf.' " (The Englishman had been on detached duty with Canadians at their air base in Brandon, Manitoba, when the first symptoms of his Lassa fever had begun to manifest themselves.)

"Why should one say 'Craf' when it's the Royal *Canadian* Air Force? I should have thought you would have heard of the Royal Canadian Air Force *exer*cises. I'd have to say 'RCAF,' wouldn't I? The whole point of an acronym is to save time. One could, I suppose, say '*R*-caf.' That might be all right, I should think. Yes. '*r*-caf.' That's not bad. It has a ring, just. One *could* say that."

"Don't say anything."

"I say. Are you saying, don't say anything?"

"Don't say bloody anything. Shut bloody up. Go to sleep just. Close your eyes and count your symptoms, check."

"Well, we *are* in a temper. You're bloody cheeky, Yank."

" '*Yank*.' Jesus. Where'd you train, on the playing field of the back lot? Why don't they run my tests? I know what I have anyway. Why don't they read the lumbar puncture thing?"

"Well, they've their priorities, haven't they? The lumbar puncture. *That* was manly. You screaming like a banshee. Louder than our lunatic friends."

"That needle was big as a pencil."

" 'Please stop. *Please!* Oh goddamn it. Oh Jesus. Oh shit. Oh fuck.' Oh me Oh my. Oh dear. Be adamant, Mister Softee. Be infrangible. Be *stiff*, Mister Softee. Be obdurate, be corn, be kibe!"

Flesh shut his eyes against Tanner's taunts and took the darker view. "I'm taking the darker view," he said quietly. "I'm taking the darker view because I'm going to kill him."

In the morning the nurse came for Ben with a wheelchair. It was more than a hundred degrees in the ward.

"Is it my tests? Are my tests back?"

"You have a phone call. You can take it at the nurses' station."

"A phone call? Gibberd?"

"No."

"I can't think who it could be. No one knows I'm here. Is it a woman?"

"A man."

She wheeled Ben to the phone and put the receiver in his left hand.

"Mr. Flesh?"

"Yes?"

"Zifkovic."

He'd forgotten about his manager. "Yes, Zifkovic, what is it?"

"How you feeling, sir?"

"The same. I'm waiting for my test result. Is anything wrong?"

"The stuff's all turned, sir. It's rancid glop. There must be a ton of it. The Mister Softee's all melted and running. We were working with ice for a time but I can't get no more. It's a high tide of ruined vanilla. The fruit flavors are staining everything in sight. I got the girls working on it with pails and mops but they can't keep up. A truck come down from Fargo with a new shipment today. I told him that with this heat wave we couldn't accept, but he just dumped it anyway. It's outside now. A whole lake of the shit. What should I do, Mr. Flesh? Mr. Flesh?"

"It's a plague," Flesh said. "It's a smoting."

"What? Mr. Flesh? What do you want me to do? You wouldn't believe what this stuff smells like."

"I'd believe it."

"You got any suggestions, Mr. Flesh? I didn't want to trouble you. I know you got your own problems, but I don't know what to do. You got any ideas?"

"Be hard, Mister Softee."

"What? I can hardly hear you."

"Nothing. I have no suggestions." He handed the phone back to the nurse. "It's the plague," Flesh said. "A fiery lake of Mister Softee, check."

"There you are, Mr. Flesh," another of the nurses said, coming up to him. "Dr. Gibberd has your test results. He's waiting for you."

Flesh nodded, allowed himself to be returned to the ward.

Gibberd, standing at the Englishman's bedside, waved to him. He indicated to the nurse that she set a screen up around Flesh's bed. He was carrying a manilla folder with the results of Ben Flesh's test. They were all positive. It was M.S. all right, Gibberd told him, but of a sensory rather than a motor strain. The chances of its becoming motor were remote. The fact that he'd been in remission all these years was in his favor. He really wasn't in such bad shape. For the time being there would be no treatment. Later, should if shift to a motor M.S., they could give him Ritalin, give him steroids. How would he know? Well, he'd be falling down in the streets, wouldn't he? There'd be speech impairment, wouldn't there? There'd be weakness and he wouldn't be able to tie his shoes, would he? There'd be nystagmus, don't you know? Nystagmus? A sort of rotation of the eyeballs. Anyway, there was no real reason to keep him in the hospital. They needed the beds. Flesh looked around the empty ward.

"As a matter of fact," Gibberd said, "I wish I were going with you. Where you off to now? Someplace cool?"

"I can drive?"

"Of course you can drive. I've told you, there's no strength loss, no motor impairment at all. It's just sensory. A little discomfort in your hand. So what?"

"But it's America's number-one crippler of young adults."

"M.S. is a basket term. You'll be fine. These symptoms should go away in two to three months. Boy, this heat."

"The heat, check."

"Well. Get dressed, why don't you? I'll write up your discharge papers. Be sure to stop by the cashier on the way out. Really. Don't worry about the M.S."

"Sensory discomfort, check."

"I guess you'll be wanting to get back to your Mister Softee stand before you leave. This *heat*. I could use a Mister Softee myself right now."

"The Mister Softees are all melted. The Lord has beaten the Mister Softees back into yogurt cultures."

"What's that?"

"Plague."

"What's all this about plague?"

"The plague is general throughout Dakota. We're being visited and smited."

"Well. Good luck, Mr. Flesh."

"Doctor?"

"Yes?"

"What about him?" Flesh jerked his thumb in the direction of Tanner's screen. The doctor shook his head.

"He'll be shipped off to Guernsey eventually. The R.A.F. maintains a hospital there for incurables."

The doctor extended his hand. A shiver of electric plague ran up Flesh's hand and arm when Gibberd touched him. He felt he could start the hospital's engines just by touching them, that the energy was in his hands now, in the ruined, demyelinating nerves sputtering like live wires in his fingertips.

Gibberd left and Flesh dressed. He was about his business, heading toward the cashier and the Cadillac. (Probably it wouldn't start; the battery dead, check. Check the oil.) Then suddenly Ben turned back. He stood for a moment in the center aisle, staring in the direction of Tanner's screen. "Tanner," he said, "I don't want you to say a thing. Don't interrupt me. Just listen just."

"Gibberd has given me my walking papers. He has given me my dirty bill of health. It's interesting rather. Here we are, two guys from opposite sides of the world. Yank and Limey. Strangers. Do-be-do-be-doo. Flight Lieutenant Tanner of Eng and Brit Honduras with Nigerian virus in his gut, and me, Ben Flesh, American—don't interrupt, please just—Ben Flesh, American, ranger in Cadillac of Highway this and Interstate that. Yet somehow the both of us ill met in this hotshot trop med ward in Rap Cit S-dak. You know what? Don't, don't answer. You know what? Never mind what, I'll get to what later.

"Well. Strangers. Sickmates on the edge of the Badlands. Both incurable and generally fatal. Oh, I know a lot about *my* disease, too. When Dr. Wolfe first diagnosed my case—you remember, I told you about Dr. Wolfe—I boned up on it in the literature, in *What to Do till the Doctor Comes*. It's progressive, a neurological disorder of the central nervous system, characterized by muscular dysfunction and the formation of sclerotic, or hardening—be hard, Mister Softee—hardening patches in the brain. One's myelin—that's the soft, white fatty substance that encases the axis cylinders of certain nerve fibers: what a piece of work is a man—one's myelin sheath is unraveling like wool. It snags, you see? Like a run in a stocking. I am panty hose, Lieutenant. Vulnerable as.

"Incurable. Generally fatal. Usually slow and often, in its last stages, characterized by an odd euphoria. I was blind once, I tell you that? No family to speak of. I have heart disease and many businesses. Is this clear? No, don't answer. The point is, the lines of the drama of my life are beginning to come together, make a pattern. I mean, for God's sake, Tanner, just consider what I've been through. I've told you enough about myself. Look what stands behind me. Theatrical costumes! Songs! My history given pizzazz and order and the quality of second- and third-act curtains, coordinated color schemes for the dance numbers, the solos and showstoppers, what shows up good in the orchestra and the back of the house, and shines like the full moon in the cheap seats. I got rhythm, dig? Pacing, timing, and convention have gone into making me. Oh, Tanner, the prime rate climbs like fever and we ain't seen nothing yet. Gibberd dooms me. You should have heard him. He makes it official. He dooms me, but very soft sell so I can't even be angry with him. It's getting on, the taxis are gathering, the limos, the cops are up on their horses in the street, and I don't even know my lines—though they're coming together—or begin to understand the character.

"What do you think? Shh, that was rhetorical. What do you think? You think I should kick my preoccupations? The stuff about my godfather and my godcousins? All the wandering Jew shit in my late-model Caddy, going farther than the truckers go, hauling my ass like cargo? Aach.

"Me and my trademarks. I'm the guy they build the access roads for, whose signs rise like stiffened peters—Keep America Beautiful—beyond the hundred-yard limit of the Interstates. A finger in every logotype. Ho-Jo's orange roof and the red star of Texaco. D.Q.'s crimson pout and the Colonel's bucket spinning, spinning. You name it, I'm in it.

"So. Doomed. Why? Shh. Because I am built to recognize it: a lip reader of big print and the scare headline. Because I'm one of those birds who ain't satisfied unless he has a destiny, even though he knows that destiny sucks. How did I get this way? I used to be a kid who ate fruit.

"Anyway. As I was saying. You know what? You know what I think? Shh. Hush. I think you're dead. Don't bother to correct me if you're not. That's what I think. I think you're dead there behind your screen, that you'll never see Guernsey. The dramatic lines demand it. Theatricality's gravitational pull. Who are you to go against something like that? You're too weak. You have to be strapped to your chair, for God's sake. So. It's nice how you can let your hair down with strangers. We were strangers, right? Have we ever met, sir? Do you know me; has there been communication between us in any way, shape, or form; have we gotten together before the show; have promises been made to you? *Thank you very much, sir. Thank you very much, ladies and gentlemen.*

"So it's agreed. We're strangers, locked each into his own symptoms, you into Lassa fever and me into my sensory problems. And somehow, as strangers will, somehow we got to talking, and gradually understood each other. I wiped your blood up. You saw my asshole with its spoor of shit. Well, strangers get close in such situations. Now I have my dirty bill of health and I'm told to move and Dr. Gibberd tells me you're for Guernsey when your orders come through. And here's where I'm supposed to go behind them screens and shake hands. Well, I won't! I won't do it. That ain't going to happen. Because you're dead! Slumped in that queer way death has of disarraying things. So that's it. The destiny man thinks you've been put here on earth to satisfy one more cliche, to be discovered stone cold dead in Rapid City General wheelchair. For what? So one day I'll be able to say in my impaired speech—'There wash thish time in Shouf Dakota, and I wash on the shame woward wi-with thish young chap from the R.A.F. (He called it "Raf.")—And we got pretty close. The two of us. There was a terrible heat wave and neither of us could sleep. We were kept up half the night by the screams of mental patients who couldn't be quieted because the power was out, and even though the hospital had its own auxiliary generator, there wasn't enough power for electric-shock treatments, so we told each other the story of our life, as fellows will in hospital, and got pretty close to each other, and finally I was discharged and I went over to young Tanner's screen to say goodbye and found him dead.'

"Well, fuck *that*, Lieutenant! I like you too much to use you around fireplaces. We'll just skip it because I ain't going behind no screen to make certain, because if you *are* dead, by Christ, I don't think I could take it. I would grab a scissors and cut the lines of my drama. On the other hand, please don't disabuse me of my sense of the fitness of things. Keep still just. So long, dead guy."

He turned and started to the exit, but just as he got there he heard a loud, ripping, and unruly fart. Well, how do you like that? he thought. What was it, the critique of pure reason? Or only the guy's sphincter relaxing in death? Flesh shoved hard against the handle on the fire doors.

RONALD SUKENICK

from Long Talking Bad Conditions Blues

the islands highest mountain was
called Mt. Medwick it was high enough
to have snow in the winter and had a
good steep downhill slope in summer
the main attractions were the waterfall
and the view the view was really a
mutiple of views as you went up and
around the mountain there was no one
place from which you could see the
whole island but you could get a kind of
collage overview of the whole thing
from one viewpoint to the next the
waterfall was spectacularly high so that
the water as it went over the brink and
down its long free fall fell into chunks
and irregular mass of grey of green of
was caught and channeled in its chute at
the distant bottom in a narrow sluice
with amazing speed one day they all
rented a car it was time to get out of the
city to get a little perspective they
brought food and wine and drove up
the mountain for the day starting at
dawn he and Charleen stayed up all
night to do it because they knew they'd
never get up at dawn so did Veronica
and Victor Tony and Drecker were the
only ones used to getting up in the

morning Drecker was driver Tony was the only other person awake as they drove through the countryside toward Mt. Medwick he was able to afford the car because he had taken the job writing reports he had gone to see Bennett the exile Bennett looked like a seal very slick and streamlined and spoke with a very weird accent from having been on the island so long a speech neither island nor native but something new and unearthly like a computer taught to speak by a panel of international cyberneticists let me explain said Bennet you know nothing about maternity good but what is maternity maternity is making something out of nothing now you as a scientist engaged in research are involved in essentially the same kind of activity is it not and furthermore what is a report a report is a bureaucrat's way of making nothing of something now we have a situation here of demographic growth heading toward disastrous overpopulation with at the same time high infant mortality aggravated because the land can no longer support the growing population which moves into the city at a rapid rate where there are no facilities jobs or housing but on the other hand attempts at population control lead to charges of oppression and genocide therefore nothing can be done it is how do you say it a blind alley no way out when there is nothing to be done what you do is write a report and that is why you are writing a report on make something of nothing in order to make nothing of something though undoubtedly at a higher level of information and that is indeed our task as savants to struggle relentlessly to elevate the level of information it changes nothing but it is an end in itself in the end it is our substitute for god if you know of any other end please let me know Drecker was trying to explain to Tony his idea of units you see he said everything has to be measured it doesn't matter how it's measured as long as it's measured measure is the mark of man if you see what I mean said Drecker I'm with you so far said Tony okay said Drecker so my idea of units is a way of applying measure to things we haven't even thought of measuring before like love affairs like history like feelings like all our little every day experiences for example mathematicians have recently found a way to measure irregular catastrophic events do you see what I mean said Drecker I don't see a goddam thing said Tony the windmills the sheep the deserted farmhouses and barns fled by like migrating birds as the car sped down the straight empty two lane highway there was absolutely nothing in the left hand lane the road was smooth as a blackboard they could have been standing still and the scenery moving on millions of tiny wheels what difference thought Drecker with two jets flying 600 mph in the same direction you have the impression neither is moving standing still is a form of movement Drecker told Tony tell that to the boys on the assembly line said Tony but Drecker had his mind on vague blocks of matter emerging diverging converging they were starting to to go up the mountain the road ascending descending coiling back on itself the three in the back seat began to wake up oh shit where are we said Charleen I never know where you're at said Tony that's right cowboy said Charleen go back to sleep Carl said next to her she snuggled up to him she's at her best when she's waking up he thought or going to sleep Victor between Tony and Drecker in the front seat woke up with a jerk said invisible insane went back to sleep Carl lit a cigarette and threw the rest of the pack out the window he was trying to stop smoking as they climbed the mountain he started to think about the upcoming decline the upcoming decline was at the bottom of the new conditions along with the revolution of rising expectations when rising expectations hit the upcoming decline hell was going to break loose it was already starting to break loose the mountain was full of unemployed doctors of philosphy living in the woods and getting into witchcraft and astrology and who were responsible for the growth of the new cult of achronicianity an astrology based religion which rejected the notion of time for that of distance yesterday was not a different time you were in a different place everything was happening at the same time but in different places they did not believe in emotion they believed in location where are you at they would ask ideally you were centered when they asked you about yourself they would say what are your coordinates instead of holy writ they had maps and charts they taught their children not to read or write but to draw and act out reading and writing were considered forms of repression deviations from the oral tradition bulwarks of capitalism the children watched television and made origami everyone was more or less aware of the upcoming decline yet expectations continued to rise causing a loss of direction in high places which resorted increasingly to low methods producing a lapse of confidence provoking a flight of capital hastening decline stimulating official optimism raising expectations increasing contradictions Tony rolled a joint and passed it around

Drecker turned the radio on and got Charlie Mingus doing Eat That Chicken which woke everybody up and got them hungry Veronica started passing around pieces of chicken and Tony opened a bottle of wine the car humming along the joint going around the bottle going around the chicken going around the bread and pate and bananas and oranges getting high chattering laughing good music on the radio the local radio played mostly jazz and rock plus the island songs which were also very good especially to dance to the lyrics were all about revolution but the rhythms went right to the hips and groin they were all right in the car driving up the mountain direction purpose destination the destination wasn't important the important thing was to keep moving he knew stasis waits like a gaping hole at the peak in Medwick Park they peered over a precipice the famous view the tiny city and beyond the engulfing sea peaceful and glistening in the sun but vast out of scale threatening by the pure extent of it appending a note of pathos to their questionable paradise and he saw in his mind the fountain in Ferrell Anderson Place representing the explusion from Eden which had always seemed to him so anachronistic in the perfect afternoons they had eaten all their food in the car but they had several bottles of wine they opened and sat around the wooden table in the thin air the sun warmed them but it was chill in the shadows Victor and Charleen were getting along unusually well Victor was telling her about his latest money making scheme relief maps for blind tourists Charleen was derisive but not insulting almost good humored in fact obviously high Charleen would never have been able to get away with the things she got away with if she weren't so beautiful though she wasn't getting away with so many of them lately people were getting to know here her reputation was catching up with her and she was visibly ageing you could tell that soon it was going to be a long desperate race between cellulite and silicone when he wasn't angry with her these days he was feeling sorry for her except when she was waking up or falling asleep when he still could love her Veronica and Drecker were still high and coasting obviously getting it together again they went for a walk to the woods down below timberline Tony on the other hand was getting grouchy and so was Carl he was getting that soggy feeling from too much bad wine leading to one of those awful same day hangovers the thin air was making it worse lack of oxygen ten steps and he started breathing hard there were still patches of snow on the north side of boulders but the small intense spring flowers were coming up orange azure yellow the sky was luminous blue but he knew clouds could mass quickly over the mountain lowering curtains of heavy snow he felt ill at ease there were few others up here at this season the park was officially closed signs warned of uncertain weather and cautioned about the risks of exposure of losing one's way remember the signs said the mountains don't care they tallied the number of people who had died or disappeared on the various trails this year beware they said of possible abrupt and violent modifications Tony was looking surly and bored he got his transistor radio from the car and tuned in some country music oh christ said Charleen something wrong said Tony we didn't come up here to listen to your cheap gadget said Charleen look this thing set me back

close to nine hundred balls and it comes
with the right to listen to it said Tony
are you always counting your balls she
said I know how many I got he said I
didn't ask how many you have are your
worried about it she said lady I don't
need your shit he said what makes you
think I'm concerned about what you
need she said women like you ought to
be whipped every morning he said
that's always the answer for your
type she said I don't have a type he said
I would say it's rather common she said
you must must have something real
nasty up your ass he said how
boring she said you're mean as a
how boring she said you're mean as a
rabid bat he said does that indicate
you're angry I realize you find articu-
lation difficult perhaps you need a little
help she said I know what you need he
said take a ride cowboy she said I'm
thinking about it he said Victor asked if
anybody wanted to hike Carl went off
with Victor Tony and Charleen still
arguing when they got back the radio
was off Tony and Charleen were very
quiet good he thought soon everybody
will have slept with everybody maybe
then they'd be like a big family maybe
that was the only kind of family possible under the new conditions sisters
and brothers in communal incest on the
other side of jealousy or maybe they
should all just register for mates with
the government bureau of marriages
the marriage bureau was a highly
successful social experiment that
matched men and women on the basis
of computerized genetic calculations
designed to produce successful off-
spring its escalating popularity was the
consequence of claims by satisfied users
that sympathetic genes produced satisfying relationships whose relative longe-
vity was confirmed by statistics that encouraged neodarwinians some said it

was merely a new form of the marriage of property taking progeny as property the fact is in many cases it gave a basis to matrimonial coupling that no other tendency could even begin to claim and provided the data for a school of erotic realists who were proponents of what they called unromantic love which however differed radically from the policies of the bureau of marriages in denying the necessity of matrimony whereas the bureau insisted on the marriage of the matching couple sight unseen claiming the importance of a social matrix while the realists objected that an imposed matrix was meretricious deleterious and an invasion of civil liberties and that furthermore the government's enforced traditionalism based on an absolutely hallmark sensibility including kitsch ceremony shoes rice and elaborate honeymoons only served to sentimentalize and remystify the essentially gut-bucket nature of the relation though as many observers pointed out that was probably the government's motive as an institution since institutions needed their mystiques and mystiques needed their institutions and institutions needed their pet projects to which they could point in order to downgrade the upcoming decline by demonstrating a steady rise in the quality of life meanwhile fat slow flakes of snow were drifting down like little parachutes and Veronica and Drecker had not returned soon the contours of the ground were covered with a smooth white sheet they decided to split into two parties Tony and Victor would wait while Carl and Charleen would look they slid down among the boulders toward tree line it wasn't that he was jealous it was that now she was going to be

dreamy and moony about Tony for
the next several weeks until she got
bored with it he was waiting to hear
about the virtues of the proletariat the
rude strengths of the workingman
maybe she would even go so far as to
get a job that would be nice they would
probably be eating spaghetti every
night what's wrong with you said
Charleen as they skidded among the
boulders nothing he said you look
jealous she said about what he said
you have no right to ask me that she
said I'm not jealous he said yes you are
she said it doesn't compromise you she
said that's just your own cheap reaction she said you're incredibly middle
class she said it's going to become a
factor with Tony that's all he said too
bad the boys won't be able to hang out
together on the street corner anymore
she said I told you I don't care what
you do as long as it doesn't become a
factor he said with you everything
becomes a factor I think you want
factors maybe you want to sleep with
Tony maybe that's a factor boys will be
boys I'm tired of your factors I can
make love with people without it
becoming a factor she said wouldn't it
be pretty to think so he said meanwhile
they had forgotten to look for Veronica
and Drecker it was starting to get dark
the wind was rising the snow was
heavier it was noticeably colder let's
go back I don't see them anywhere he
said okay she said where are you going
he said it's this way he said are you
going to start another argument she said
you know you have no sense of direction
he said I've never known anybody who
was so consistently wrong about everything she said I've never known anybody who was so consistently never
wrong about anything he said it was
getting quite cold they were dressed

Ronald Sukenick

in light clothing they were standing in the middle of a blank white space their footprints were covered over almost as soon as they made them visibility whited out at about ten feet it was like nowhere it was like walking into nothing look this is the reality principle let's be serious he said I miss my children she said

SUSAN SONTAG

Unguided Tour

I took a trip to see the beautiful things. Change of scenery. Change of heart. And do you know?
What?
They're still there.
Ah, but they won't be there for long.
I know. That's why I went. To say goodbye. Whenever I travel, it's always to say goodbye.

Tile roofs, timbered balconies, fish in the bay, the copper clock, shawls drying on the rocks, the delicate odor of olives, sunsets behind the bridge, ochre stone. "Gardens, parks, forests, woods, canals, private lakes, with huts, villas, gates, garden seats, gazebos, alcoves, grottoes, hermitages, triumphal arches, chapels, temples, mosques, banqueting houses, rotundas, observatories, aviaries, greenhouses, icehouses, fountains, bridges, boats, cascades, baths." The Roman amphitheater, the Etruscan sarcophagus. The monument to the 1914-18 war dead in every village square. You don't see the military base. It's out of town, and not on the main road.

Omens. The cloister wall has sprung a long diagonal crack. The water level is rising. The marble saint's nose is no longer aquiline.

This spot. Some piety always brings me back to this spot. I think of all the people who were here. Their names scratched into the bottom of the fresco.

Vandals!
Yes. Their way of being here.
The proudest of human-made things dragged down to the condition of natural things. Last Judgment.
You can't lock up all the things in museums.

"Unguided Tour" is included in Susan Sontag's new collection of short stories I, etcetera, *to be published April 19, 1979, by Victor Gollancz Ltd. at £4.95.*

Aren't there any beautiful things in your own country?
No. Yes. Fewer.
Did you have guidebooks, maps, timetables, stout shoes?
I read the guidebooks when I got home. I wanted to stay with my—
Immediate impressions?
You could call them that.
But you did see the famous places. You didn't perversely neglect them.
I did see them. As conscientiously as I could while protecting my ignorance. I don't want to know more than I know, don't want to get more attached to them than I already am.
How did you know where to go?
By playing my memory like a roulette wheel.
Do you remember what you saw?
Not much.
It's too sad. I can't love the past that's trapped within my memory like a souvenir.
Object lessons. Grecian urns. A pepper-mill Eiffel Tower. Bismarck beer mug. Bay-of-Naples-with-Vesuvius scarf. David-by-Michelangelo cork tray.
No souvenirs, thanks. Let's stay with the real thing.
The past. Well, there's always something ineffable about the past, don't you think?
In all its original glory. The indispensable heritage of a woman of culture.
I agree. Like you, I don't consider devotion to the past a form of snobbery. Just one of the more disastrous forms of unrequited love.
I was being wry. I'm a fickle lover. It's not love that the past needs in order to survive, it's an absence of choices.
And armies of the well-off, immobilized by vanity, greed, fear of scandal, and the inefficiency and discomfort of travel. Women carrying parasols and pearl hand-bags, with mincing steps, long skirts, shy eyes. Mustached men in top hats, lustrous hair parted on the left side, garters holding up their silk socks. Seconded by footmen, cobblers, ragpickers, blacksmiths, buskers, printer's devils, chimney sweeps, lacemakers, midwives, carters, milkmaids, stonemasons, coachmen, turnkeys, and sacristans. As recently as that. All gone The people. And their pomp and circumstance.
Is that what you think I went to see?
Not the people. But their places, their beautiful things. You said they were still there. The hut, the hermitage, the grotto, the park, the castle. An aviary in the Chinese style. His Lordship's estate. A delightful seclusion in the midst of his impenetrable woods.
I wasn't happy there.
What did you feel?
Regret that the trees were being cut down.
So you have a hazy vision of natural things. From too much indulgence in the nervous, metallic pleasures of cities.
Unequal to my passions, I fled the lakes, I fled the woods, I fled the fields pulsing with glowworms, I fled the aromatic mountains.
Provincial blahs. Something less solitary is what you need.

I used to say: Landscapes interest me only in relation to human beings. Ah, loving someone would give life to all this . . . But the emotions that human beings inspire in us also sadly resemble each other. The more that places, customs, the circumstances of adventures are changed, the more we see that we amidst them are unchanging. I know all the reactions I shall have. Know all the words that I am going to utter again.

You should have taken me along instead.

You mean him. Yes, of course I wasn't alone. But we quarreled most of the time. He plodding, I odious.

They say. They say a trip is a good time for repairing a damaged love.

Or else it's the worst. Feelings like shrapnel half worked out of the wound. Opinions. And competition of opinions. Desperate amatory exercises back at the hotel on golden summer afternoons. Room service.

How did you let it get that dreary? You were so hopeful.

Rubbish! Prisons and hospitals are swollen with hope. But not charter flights and luxury hotels.

But you were moved. Sometimes.

Maybe it was exhaustion. Sure I was. I am. The inside of my feelings is damp with tears.

And the outside?

Very dry. Well—as dry as is necessary. You can't imagine how tiring it is. That double-membraned organ of nostalgia, pumping the tears in. Pumping them out.

Qualities of depth and stamina.

And discrimination. When one can summon them.

I'm bushed. They aren't all beautiful, the beautiful things. I've never seen so many squabby Cupids and clumsy Graces.

Here's a cafe. *In the cafe.* The village priest playing the pinball machine. Nineteen-year-old sailors with red pompoms watching. Old gent with amber worry beads. Proprietor's granddaughter doing her homework at a deal table. Two hunters buying picture postcards of stags. He says: You can drink the acidic local wine, become a little less odious, unwind.

Monsieur René says it closes at five.

Each picture. "Each picture had beneath it a motto of some good intention. Seeing that I was looking carefully at these noble images, he said: 'here everything is natural.' The figures were clothed like living men and women, though they were far more beautiful. Much light, much darkness, men and women who are and yet are not."

Worth a detour? Worth a trip! It's a remarkable collection. Still possessed its aura. The things positively importuned.

The baron's zeal in explaining. His courteous manner. He stayed all through the bombardment.

A necessary homogeneity. Or else some stark, specific event.

I want to go back to that antique store.

"The ogival arch of the doorway is Gothic, but the central nave and the flanking wings—"

You're hard to please.

Can't you imagine traveling not to accumulate pleasures but to make them rarer?

Satiety is not my problem. Nor is piety.

There's nothing left but to wait for our meals, like animals.

Are you catching a cold? Drink this.

I'm perfectly all right. I beg you, don't buy the catalogue. Or the postcard-size reproductions. Or the sailor sweater.

Don't be angry, but—did you tip Monsieur René?

Say to yourself fifty times a day: I am not a connoisseur, I am not a romantic wanderer, I am not a pilgrim.

You say it.

"A permanent part of mankind's spiritual goods."

Translate that for me. I forgot my phrase book.

Still, you saw what you came to see.

The old victory of arrangement over accumulation.

But sometimes you were happy. Not just in spite of things.

Barefoot on the mosaic floor of the baptistery. Clambering above the flying buttesses. Irradiated by a Baroque monstrance shimmering indistinctly in the growing dusk of the cathedral. Effulgence of things. Voluminous. Resplendent. Unutterable bliss.

You send postcards on which you write "Bliss." Remember? You sent one to me.

I remember. Don't stop me. I'm flying. I'm prowling. Epiphany. Hot tears. Delirium. Don't stop me. I stroke my delirium like the balls of the comely waiter.

You want to make me jealous.

Don't stop me. His dainty skin, his saucy laughter, his way of whistling, the succulent dampness of his shirt. We went into a shed behind the restaurant. And I said: Enter, sir, this body. This body is your castle, your cabin, your hunting lodge, your villa, your carriage, your luxury liner, your drawing room, your kitchen, your speedboat, your tool shed . . .

Do you often do that sort of thing when he's around?

Him? He was napping at the hotel. A mild attack of heliophobia.

In the hotel. Back at the hotel, I woke him up. He had an erection. I seated myself on his loins. The nub, the hub, the fulcrum. Gravitational lines of force. In a world of perfect daylight. Indeed, a high-noon world, in which objects cast no shadows.

Only the half wise will despise these sensations.

I'm turning. I'm a huge steering wheel, unguided by any human hand. I'm turning . . .

And the other pleasures? The ones you came for.

"In the entire visible world there is hardly a more powerful mood-impression than that experienced within one of the Gothic cathedrals just as the sun is setting."

Pleasures of the eye. It had to be emphasized.

"The eye can see nothing beyond those glimmering figures that hover overhead to the west in stern, solemn rows as the burning evening sun falls across them."

Messengers of temporal and spiritual infinity.

"The sensation of fire permeates all, and the colors sing out, rejoicing and sobbing."

There, in truth, is a different world.

I found a wonderful old Baedeker, with lots of things that aren't in the Michelin. *Let's.* Let's visit the caves. Unless they're closed.

Let's visit the World War I cemetry.

Let's watch the regatta.

This spot. He committed suicide right here, by the lake. With his fiancée. In 1811.

I seduced a waiter in the restaurant by the port two days ago. *He said.* He said his name was Arrigo.

I love you. And my heart is pounding.

So is mine.

What's important is that we're strolling in this arcade together.

That we're strolling. That we're looking. That it's beautiful.

Object lessons. Give me that suitcase, it's heavy.

One must be careful not to wonder if these pleasures are superior to last year's pleasures. They never are.

That must be the seduction of the past again. But just wait until now becomes then. You'll see how happy we were.

I'm not expecting to be happy. *Complaints.* I've already seen it. I'm sure it'll be full. It's too far. You're driving too fast, I can't see anything. Only two showings of the movie, at seven and at nine. There's a strike, I can't telephone. This damned siesta, nothing's open between one and four. If everything came out of this suitcase, I don't understand why I can't cram it all back in.

You'll soon stop fretting over these mingy impediments. You'll realize you're carefree, without obligations. And then the unease will start.

Like those upper-middle-class Protestant folk who experience revelations, become hysterical, suffer breakdowns under the disorienting impact of Mediterranean light and Mediterranean manners. You're still thinking about the waiter.

I said I love you, I trust you, I didn't mind.

You shouldn't. I don't want that kind of revelation. I don't want to satisfy my desire, I want to exasperate it. I want to resist the temptation of melancholy, my dear. If you only knew how much.

Then you must stop this flirtation with the past invented by poets and curators. We can forget about their old things. We can buy their postcards, eat their food, admire their sexual nonchalance. We can march in their workers' festivals and sing the "Internationale," for even we know the words.

I'm feeling perfectly all right.

I think it's safe to. Pick up hitchhikers, drink unbottled water, try to score some hash in the piazza, eat the mussels, leave the camera in the car, hang out in

waterfront bars, trust the hotel concierge to make the reservation, don't you?
Something. Don't you want to do something?
Does every country have a tragic history except ours?
This spot. See? There's a commemorative plaque. Between the windows.
Ruined. Ruined by too many decades of intrepid appreciation. Nature, the whore, cooperates. The crags of the Dolomites made too pink by the sun, the water of a lagoon made too silver by the moon, the blue skies of Greece (or Sicily) made too deep a blue by the arch in a white wall.
Ruins. These are ruins left from the last war.
Antiquarian effrontery: our pretty dwelling.
It was a convent, built according to a plan drawn up by Michelangelo. Turned into a hotel in 1927. Don't expect the natives to take care of the beautiful things.
I don't.
They say. They say they're going to fill in the canal and make it a highway, sell the duchess's rococo chapel to a sheik in Kuwait, build a condominium on that bluff with a stand of pine, open a boutique in the fishing village, put a sound-and-light show in the ghetto. It's going fast. International Committee. Attempting to preserve. Under the patronage of His Excellency and the Honorable. Going fast. You'll have to run.
Will I have to run?
Then let them go. Life is not a race.
Or else it is.
Any more. Isn't it a pity they don't write out the menus in purple ink any more. That you can't put your shoes outside the hotel room at night. *Remember.* Those outsize bills, the kind they had until the devaluation. *Last time.* There weren't as many cars last time, were there?

How could you stand it?
It was easier than it sounds. With an imagination like a pillar of fire. And a heart like a pillar of salt.
And you want to break the tie.
Right.
Lot's wife!
But his lover.
I told you. I told you, you should have taken me along instead.

Lingering. In the basilica. In the garden behind the inn. In the spice market. In bed, in the middle of the golden afternoon.
Because. It's because of the fumes from the petrochemical factories nearby. It's because they don't have enough guards for the museums.
"Two groups of statuary, one depicting virtuous toil, the other unbridled licentiousness."
Do you realize how much prices have gone up? Appalling inflation. I can't conceive how people here manage. With rents almost as high as back home and salaries half.
"On the left of the main road, the Tomb of the Reliefs (the so-called

Tomba Bella) is entered. On the walls round the niches and on the pillars, the favorite objects of the dead and domestic articles are reproduced in painted stucco relief: dogs, helmets, swords, leggings, shields, knapsacks and haversacks, bowls, a jug, a couch, pincers, a saw, knives, kitchen vessels and utensils, coils or rope, etc."

I'm sure. I'm sure she was a prostitute. Did you look at her shoes? I'm sure they're giving a concert in the cathedral tonight. *Plus they said.* Three stars, I'm sure they said it had three stars.

This spot. This is where they shot the scene in that movie.

Quite unspoiled. I'm amazed. I was expecting the worst.

They rent mules.

Of course. Every wage earner in the country gets five weeks' paid vacation.

The women age so quickly.

Nice. It's the second summer for the Ministry of Tourism's "Be Nice" campaign. This country where ruined marvels litter the ground.

It says. It says it's closed for restoration. It says you can't swim there any more.

Pollution.

They said.

I don't care. Come on in. The water's almost as warm as the Caribbean. I want you, I feel you. Lick my neck. Slip off your trunks. Let me...

Let's. Let's go back to the hotel.

"The treatment of space in Mannerist architecture and painting shows this change from the 'closed' Renaissance world order to the 'open,' 'loose,' and deviating motions in the Mannerist universe."

What are you trying to tell me?

"The harmony, intelligibility, and coherence of the Renaissance world view were inherent in the symmetrical courtyards of Italian palaces."

I don't want to flatter my intelligence with evidence.

If you don't want to look at the painting, look at me.

See the sign? You can't take the boat that way. We're getting near the nuclear-submarine base.

Reports. Five cases of cholera have been reported.

This piazza has been called a stage for heroes.

It gets much cooler at night. You have to wear a sweater.

Thanks to the music festival every summer. You should see this place in the winter. It's dead.

The trial is next week, so now they're having demonstrations. Can't you see the banner? And listen to that song.

Let's not. I'm sure it's a clip joint.

They said. Sharks, I think they said.

Not the hydrofoil. I know it's faster, but they make me sick.

"The sun having mounted and the heat elsewhere too extreme for us, we have retired to the tree-shaded court-yard." It's not that I loved him. But in a certain hour of physical fatigue . . .

At the mercy of your moods.

Contented sometimes. Even blissful.
Doesn't sound like it. Sounds like struggling to savor.
Maybe. Loss of judgment in the necropolis.
Reports. There's a civil war raging in the north. The Liberation Front's leader is still in exile. Rumors that the dictator has had a stroke. But everything seems so—
Calm?
I guess . . . calm.

This spot. On this spot they massacred three hundred students.
I'd better go with you. You'll have to bargain.
I'm starting to like the food. You get used to it after a while. Don't you?
In the oldest paintings there is a complete absence of chiaroscuro.
I feel well here. There's not so much to see.
"Below the molding, small leafy trees, from which hang wreaths, ribbons, and various objects, alternate with figures of men dancing. One is lying on the ground, playing the double flute."
Cameras. The women don't like to be photographed.
We may need a guide.
It's a book on the treasures they unearthed. Pictures, bronzes, and lamps.
That's the prison where they torture political suspects. Terror incognita.
Covered with flies. That poor child. Did you see?

Omens. The power failure yesterday. New graffiti on the monument this morning. Tanks grinding along the boulevard at noon. *They say.* They say the radar at the airport has been out for the last seventy-two hours.
They say the dictator has recovered from his heart attack.
No, bottled water. Hardier folk. Quite different vegetation.
And the way they treat women here! Beasts of burden. Hauling those sacks up azure hills on which—
They're building a ski station.
They're phasing out the leprosarium.
Look at his face. He's trying to talk to you.
Of course we could live here, privileged as we are. It isn't our country. I don't even mind being robbed.
"The sun having mounted and heat elsewhere too extreme for us, we have retired to the shade of an oasis."

Sometimes I did love him. Still, in a certain hour of mental fatigue . . .
At the mercy of your moods.
My undaunted caresses. My churlish silences.
You were trying to mend an error.
I was trying to change my plight.
I told you, you should have taken me along instead.
It wouldn't have been different. I went on from there alone. I would have left you, too.

Unguided Tour

Mornings of departure. With everything prepared. Sun rising over the most majestic of bays (Naples, Rio, or Hong Kong).

But you could decide to stay. Make new arrangements. Would that make you feel free? Or would you feel you'd spurned something irreplaceable?

The whole world.

That's because it's later rather than earlier. "In the beginning, all the world was America."

How far from the beginning are we? When did we first start to feel the wound?

This staunchless wound, the great longing for another place. To make this place another.

In a mosque in Damietta stands a column that, if you lick it until you tongue bleeds, will cure you of restlessness. It must bleed.

A curious word, wanderlust, I'm ready to go.

I've already gone. Regretfully, exultantly. A prouder lyricism. It's not Paradise that's lost.

Advice. Move along, let's get cracking, don't hold me down, he travels fastest who travels alone. Let's get the show on the road. Get up, slugabed. I'm clearing out of here. Get your ass in gear. Sleep faster, we need the pillow.

She's racing, he's stalling.

If I go this fast, I won't see anything. If I slow down—

Everything. —then I won't have seen everything before it disappears.

Everywhere. I've been everywhere. I haven't been everywhere, but it's on my list.

Land's end. But there's water, O my heart. And salt on my tongue.

The end of the world. This is not the end of the world.

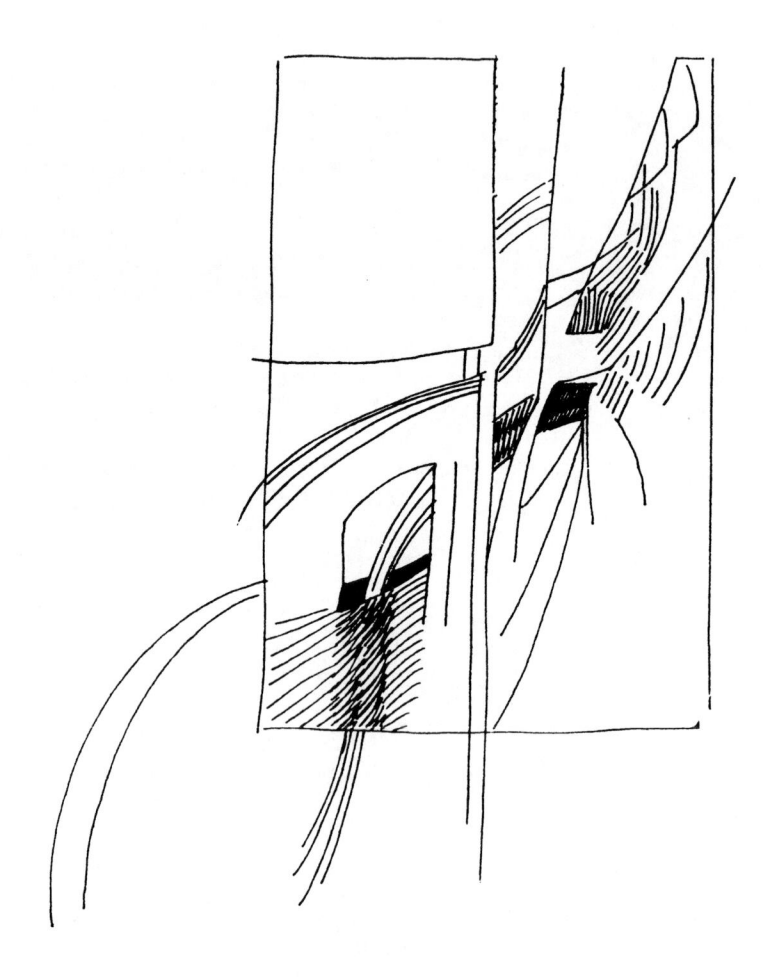

HENRY DAVIS

A Plug for Bukowski

There is an American literature that is anti-intellectual, apolitical, and anti-social. It's not taught in universities (I hope) and cannot be abstracted from the conditions of its production; it is reactionary, in that it opposes the move towards an increasing complexity in linguistic relations and denies the connection between social structure and linguistic structure which justifies that complexity. It is based, beyond language, in the attempt to retrieve reality through the personal struggle of the writer, holding together the sliding surfaces of Self and World through the act of writing itself. It demands total commitment and absolute integrity. Charles Bukowski is its major contemporary exponent.

"WHEN YOU LEAVE YOUR TYPEWRITER YOU LEAVE YOUR MACHINE GUN AND THE RATS COME POURING THROUGH." For Bukowski writing is a last ditch stand: the writer isn't observer or commentator but urban guerilla involved in a war of words:

"... advertizers be damned, he might only be able to write one column but that one column might get a million readers thinking—for a change—and nobody could tell what might happen then." (This written in *Open City*, the alternative to the alternative L.A. *Free Press*.) Bukowski sees a revolution taking place through the very media which control America: he wants to turn upside down a structure where words and images flow from the top down, where the consumer is exploited through a language which replaces the world with the vast fiction of America.

The problems of writing fiction where everything is fiction, and where the fiction of the writing must organize itself around a reality which subverts the the fiction are central to Bukowski's work. He concentrates the desperate energy of his writing into pulling the metaphorical structure of reality apart. His short stories continually employ the device of introducing the miraculous in order to illuminate the unreal: somebody wakes up covered in green and yellow polka-dots, goes out with a shotgun and causes a freeway pile-up before discovering, too late, that his colour is normal white; a losing baseball team is rescued by a boy with wings ("they couldn't hit anything out of our infield and everything in the outfield was a sure out") who has his wings cut off by a betting operator before the last, crucial game of the season; an echantress shrinks her lover down to pocket-size and uses him as a human dildo. Each is a collapsible structure designed to bring down the unspoken and spoken values which it employs. Meaning is a two way process: not just the creation of a language to make sense of the world, but it's periodic destruction in order to recreate the world. And as a writer courageous enough to jeopardize his own integrity for the sake of his writing, Bukowski deserves reading.

ROCK LP's ON STALL
STOCKS of JAZZ
FOLK, BLUES & CLASSICAL LP's

GARON RECORDS
70 king st &
open market
cambridge,
Covered
market
oxford

new & secondhand

Lots Of Deleted Material.

MANY BARGAINS.

OXFORD PLAYHOUSE

**OBSERVER OXFORD
FESTIVAL
OF
THEATRE**

29 april — 12 may

Have you graduated yet?

GRANTA/203

BOSWELL met JOHNSON in a bookshop.

So hang around

heffers:

20 Trinity Street Cambridge

ROBIN WATERFIELD LTD
Antiquarian Booksellers &
Dealers in Literary Property

the latest and largest
second-hand bookshop
in Oxford
50,000 books on 4 floors

open Monday to Saturday
9.00a.m. to 5.30p.m.

BOOKS BOUGHT

36 Park End Street
Tel : Oxford 721809

THE COFFEE MILL

*good english cooking
fully licensed*

*open: 08:15-18:00 mon-sat
09:00-18:00 sun*

lunches served 11:30-14:30

*evening functions done
on request*

100 Regent Street
Cambridge CB2 1DP

Telephone (0223) 58092

FAR EAST
AUSTRALIA

Bangkok 157.00
Singapore 163.00
Tokyo 270.00
Sydney 300.00

FOR GROUP TRAVEL,
CONTACT DAVE NOLAN,
ON 0223-54648

Paris 22.60
Florence 59.55
Rome 63.60
Athens 109.00

Zacharama
+TRANSALPINO
0223-64931

ARTS CINEMA

Market Passage, Cambridge. Tel 0223•52001

Monday to Saturday 16th-21st April
Mon-Fri at 2.30, 6.15, 8.30; Sat at 2.15, 4.30, 6.45, 9.00
MON ONCLE/U/Jacques Tati/France 1958
Sunday 22nd April at 3.00, 6.15, 8.30
LOVE AND DEATH/A/Woody Allen, Diane Keaton/USA
Monday to Saturday 23rd-28th April
Mon-Fri at 2.30, 6.15, 8.30; Sat at 2.15, 4.30, 6.45, 9.00
VIOLETTE NOZIERE/X/Claude Chabrol Stephane Audran Isabelle Huppert/France 1978
Sunday 29th April at 3.00, 6.15, 8.30
PICNIC AT HANGING ROCK/A/Peter Weir Rachel Roberts/Helen Morse/Australia 1975
Monday to Saturday 30th April-5th May
Mon-Fri at 2.30, 6.15, 8.30; Sat at 2.15, 4.30, 6.45, 9.00
NEWSFRONT/A/Philip Noyce/Bill Hunter Australia 1978

LATE NIGHT SHOWS AT 11.00 pm

Wednesday 18th April
PERFORMANCE/X/Nicholas Roeg Mick Jagger GB 1967
Thursday 19th April
WOODSTOCK/X/Jimi Hendrix The Who Arlo Guthrie Joan Baez/USA 1969
Friday 20th April
VALENTINO/X/Ken Russell Rudolf Nureyev Leslie Caron
Tuesday 24th April
REBEL WITHOUT A CAUSE/X/James Dean Nicholas Ray Natalie Wood/USA 1955
Wednesday 25th April
GIANT/James Dean/George Stevens Elizabeth Taylor USA 1956
Thursday 26th April
EAST OF EDEN/A/James Dean/Elia Kazan Julie Harris/USA 1955
Friday 27th April
BADLANDS/X/Malick/Sissy Spacek/USA 1974

EXPRESS EXPORT SERVICES LTD.

Offers Students:

personalised freight service (road/rail/air & sea)
complete packing service
insurance arranged
pick-up from your college

Telephone Ray Brown for quotes
at Royston (95) 46380
Day or night

London Head Office
Arlette House
143 Wardour Street
London W1
Tel: 01—734—8358

New Royston Branch
9 Kipling Road
Royston

We're always in favour of a worthwhile cause.

that's the value of
WOOLWORTH

THE BEST SELECTION OF CHRISTIAN BOOKS IN CAMBRIDGE

PLUS

A wide selection of

RELIGIOUS CARDS AND RELIGIOUS MUSIC

MOWBRAYS BOOKSHOP

14 KING'S PARADE
CAMBRIDGE

Telephone Cambridge 58452

Don't wait this long...

GET YOUR TROUSERS DOWN

BARNEY'S STORES

Up Mill Road!

Always 5000 pairs denims in stock
☆ at half price and under ☆

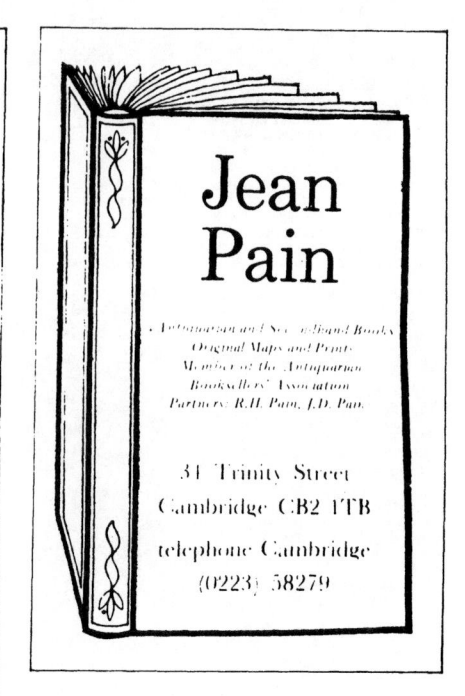

Jean Pain

Antiquarian and Second-hand Books
Original Maps and Prints
Member of the Antiquarian
Booksellers' Association
Partners: R.H. Pain, J.D. Pain.

34 Trinity Street
Cambridge CB2 1TB
telephone Cambridge
(0223) 58279

'CROPPERS'

UNISEX HAIRCUTTERS

13 St Johns Street,
Cambridge
Telephone: 55339

Notes On Contributors

WILLIAM WARNER is a graduate of The University of California at Berkeley, and is now living and writing in New Haven, Connecticut.

JOHN HAWKES has published short stories, plays, and a number of novels, including *The Cannibal*, *The Second Skin*, *The Blood Oranges*, and *Death, Sleep, and The Traveler*. He is a Professor of English at Brown University.

WILLIAM GASS teaches philosophy at Washington University in St. Louis. He has published two novels, *Omensetter's Luck* and *Willie Master's Lonesome Wife*; a collection of short stories; two collections of essays, *Fiction and The Figures of Life* and *The World within the Word*; and a philosophic inquiry, *On Being Blue*. He is presently at work on a new novel, *The Tunnel*.

JOYCE CAROL OATES has published short stories, plays, verse, critical studies, and a number of novels, among them *A Garden of Earthly Delights*, which was given the Rosenthal Foundation Award, and *Them*, which won the National Book Award in 1970. *Night-Side*, her new collection of short stories, has just been published by Victor Gollancz Ltd, who will also publish *Son of the Morning* this summer. Joyce Carol Oates is the Writer-in-Residence at Princeton for this academic year.

TONY TANNER is a Fellow of King's College, Cambridge, and has published a number of articles and books on American fiction including *The Reign of Wonder* and *City of Words, A Study of American Fiction in the Mid-Twentieth Century*.

MARC GRANETZ is a graduate of Harvard and presently studying at Emmanuel College, Cambridge. He has published a number of book reviews and articles and is a regular contributor to the *New Republic*.

NORMAN BRYSON received his Ph.D. from Cambridge University and is presently a Fellow of King's College. He has just completed a book, a structuralist history of eighteenth century French painting.

LEONARD MICHAELS is the author of two highly praised collections of short stories, *Going Places* and *I Would Have Saved Them If I Could*. "The Men's Club" is a part of a novel that he is expected to finish this summer. He is a Professor of English at the University of California at Berkeley.

Notes on Contributors

JAMES PURDY was born in Ohio and now lives and writes in Brooklyn, New York. He has published several collections of stories and poetry, plays, and a number of novels, including *Malcolm*, *The Nephew*, *Cabot Wright Begins*, *Eustace Chisholm and the Works*, *I Am Elijah Thrush*. *Narrow Rooms* and *A Day after the Fair*, a collection of short stories printed by Note of Hand Publishers, are two of his more recent works.

TILLIE OLSEN has published one book of short stories, *Tell Me A Riddle*, which won the O. Henry Award, and one novel, *Yonnondio: From the Thirties*. Her most recent work is *Silences*, which was published last year by Delacorte Press in New York. She lives in Santa Cruz, California.

DONALD BARTHELME's short stories have appeared widely, notably in the *New Yorker*. He has published two novels and several collections of short stories, including *Come Back, Dr. Caligari*; *Unspeakable Practices, Unnatural Acts*; *City Life*; *Sadness*, which won the National Book Award in 1972; and *Amateurs*, which was published in England last year. His latest work, *Great Days*, will be published by Routledge and Kegan Paul. He lives in New York City.

DON DAVID GUTTENPLAN is a graduate of Columbia University and a Kellett Fellow now studying at Clare College, Cambridge.

JONATHAN LEVI is a graduate in comparative literature of Yale University and is presently a Mellon Fellow at Clare College, Cambridge.

JOHN DUGDALE is a research student at Trinity College, Cambridge, and is about to finish his Ph.D. on Thomas Pynchon.

STANLEY ELKIN teaches in The Writing Program at Washington University. He is the author of two collections of stories and four novels. His new novel, *The Living End*, will be published in America this June.

RONALD SUKENICK is the author of three novels, including *98.6*, and one collection *The Death of the Novel and Other Stories*. His new novel, *Long Talking Bad Conditions Blues*, is to be published this autumn by the Fiction Collective. He teaches at the University of Colorado at Boulder.

SUSAN SONTAG has published two novels, *The Benefactor* and *Death Kit*. Her other books include two collections of essays, *Against Interpretation* and *Styles of Radical Will*; *Trip to Hanoi*; *On Photography*, which won the National Book Award; and *Illness as Metaphor*.

HENRY DAVIS is a student of English at King's College, Cambridge.

Graphics by:

BRIDGET STEVENS is a student of King's College, Cambridge, and has done graphics and illustrations for a variety of magazines.